INSTITUTION/

Troubled Identities in a Postmodern World

Edited by

JABER F. GUBRIUM
University of Florida

JAMES A. HOLSTEIN
Marquette University

New York • Oxford
OXFORD UNIVERSITY PRESS
2001

Oxford University Press

Oxford   New York
Athens   Auckland   Bangkok   Bogotá   Buenos Aires   Calcutta
Cape Town   Chennai   Dar es Salaam   Delhi   Florence   Hong Kong   Istanbul
Karachi   Kuala Lumpur   Madrid   Melbourne   Mexico City   Mumbai
Nairobi   Paris   São Paulo   Singapore   Taipei   Tokyo   Toronto   Warsaw

and associated companies in
Berlin   Ibadan

Published by Oxford University Press, Inc.,
198 Madison Avenue, New York, New York, 10016
http://www.oup-usa.org

Oxford is a registered trademark of Oxford University Press

Library of Congress Cataloging-in-Publication Data

Gubrium, Jaber F.
    Institutional selves : troubled identities in a postmodern world /
Jaber F. Gubrium, James A. Holstein.
        p.   cm.
    Includes bibliographical references and index.
    ISBN 0–19–512928–8 (pb. : alk. paper). —ISBN 0–19–512927–X (cl.
: alk. paper)
    1. Human services—Psychological aspects.   2. Social service—
Psychological aspects.   3. Self.   4. Self—Social aspects.
5. Identity (Psychology)—Social aspects.   I. Holstein, James A.
II. Title.
HV40.G83   2000
361.1—dc21   99–38032
                                                  CIP

Printing (last digit): 9 8 7 6 5 4 3 2 1

Printed in the United States of America
on acid-free paper

Contents

Self-Change and Resistance in Prison *176*
Kathryn J. Fox

peer

Preface

For at least a century, the self has been viewed as the ordinary center of experience. Notions of a personal self as opposed to a social self have competed for the spotlight as Americans contemplated the shape and sources of individual identity. Most recently, commentators have railed against the increasing institutional intrusions into the province of the self. Sometimes it seems as if organizations and institutions of all sorts—schools, clinics, counseling centers, self-help groups, and so forth—are contending among themselves for who will play the central role in defining who and what we are, and will be.

In a companion volume, *The Self We Live By: Narrative Identity in a Postmodern World* (Oxford University Press), we present this important story in detail. Its point of departure is the classic formulation of a transcendental self, one that Descartes and other philosophers like him pictured as standing over and above everyday life. But the real action starts when early American pragmatists— William James, Charles Horton Cooley, and George Herbert Mead, along with others—turned away from the transcendental self of philosophical reflection, supplanting it with a radically mundane self. This placed the self squarely in the midst of individuals' ordinary lives, where it was shaped and developed in relation to all manner of social influences.

Over the years, the story took what many commentators viewed as some very disturbing turns. According to some, post–World War II pressures toward conformity gave rise to "organization men" and "other directed characters" who seemed to sacrifice their individuality to the demands of social participation. Other commentators presented individuals falling in with the wrong crowd; their resulting selves became "deviant"—"outsiders." And today, according to some postmodern voices, the self doesn't amount to much at all anymore; the story of the self has come to an end. The self is a mere shadow of what it once was. Now evanescent, ungrounded, ephemeral, and experientially decentered, the self we once lived by has disappeared from the spotlight.

In *The Self We Live By*, we offered a different ending to the story of the self. Rather than allowing the self to recede from its central location in experience, or leaving it insignificantly dangling in our lives, we relocated it in a vast landscape of self-construction processes and potential identities. This turn in the self's narrative allowed us to conceive of countless opportunities for meaningful self-presentation and moral direction.

Still, while these opportunities are now greater than ever, not just anything goes. As abundant as the chances are for establishing our identities, self-construction is disciplined by the practical conditions under which it unfolds. These conditions include the operating discourses of subjectivity that comprise the institutional panorama in which we live our everyday lives. More and more, we find that these organizations are explicitly in the business of constructing the selves they need to do their work; they create the selves we live by in the process.

That is the principal theme of *Institutional Selves*. We have assembled nine distinctive chapters that collectively address the institutional construction of troubled selves. From the victims and villains of television talk shows, to battered women in support groups, to the violent selves of prison inmates, the chapters show how personal identity is structured in response to the pragmatic demands of participating in settings where personal and interpersonal troubles are under consideration. The theme is relatively straightforward, and each chapter vividly illustrates the institutional practices entailed in these activities.

Significantly, the authors of these chapters teach us that the process is never as simple as it might appear at first. This is no "cookie-cutter" matter of stamping out institutional personas. The articulation of available identities with the biographical particulars of the lives in question involves considerable "identity work." Ignoring this risks creating a picture of self-construction that is overly determined by institutional preferences. It risks losing sight of how deft and creative the social construction of selves is in practice. Furthermore, it blinds us to the continuing resistances of both old and new constructions that always come with the territory. And it makes it difficult to detect the inventive formulations that may emerge in the process. This is the message we've gleaned from the contributing authors of this book.

As a group, they have been unflinchingly cooperative and professional in helping us to develop these themes. In their respective ways, they also have reminded us to maintain a flexible analytic focus on the *interplay* between the circumstantial conditioning and the everyday inventiveness of self-construction. Their chapters highlight the variability and nuance of the process, even as they reveal how institutional factors now endlessly mediate the production and reproduction of our identities. We are deeply grateful to each of the authors for their support.

Notes on Contributors

ABOUT THE EDITORS

JABER F. GUBRIUM is Professor of Sociology at the University of Florida. His research focuses on the descriptive organization of personal identity, family, the life course, aging, and adaptations to illness. He is the editor of the *Journal of Aging Studies*, and the author or editor of 20 books, including *Living and Dying at Murray Manor, Oldtimers and Alzheimer's, Out of Control,* and *Speaking of Life.*

JAMES A. HOLSTEIN is Professor of Sociology at Marquette University. He has studied diverse people processing and social control settings, including courts, schools, and mental health agencies. He has published numerous books, including *Court-Ordered Insanity, Dispute Domains and Welfare Claims, Reconsidering Social Constructionism,* and *Social Problems in Everyday Life.* He is also coeditor of the research annual *Perspectives on Social Problems.*

Collaborating for over a decade, Gubrium and Holstein have developed their distinctive constructionist approach to qualitative inquiry in a variety of projects, including *What Is Family?, Constructing the Life Course, The Active Interview,* and *The New Language of Qualitative Method.* Their work explores the theoretical and methodological implications of interpretive practice as it unfolds at the intersection of narrative, culture, and social interaction. Their most recent book, *The Self We Live By: Narrative Identity in a Postmodern World,* is the companion volume to this one; it reconsiders the construction of selves in a postmodern context of increasingly varied situational demands and institutional identities.

ABOUT THE AUTHORS

SUSAN E. CHASE is Associate Professor of Sociology and cofounder of the Women's Studies Program at the University of Tulsa. She is the author of *Ambiguous Empowerment: The Work Narratives of Women School Superintendents.* Currently, she and Mary Rogers are writing *Mothers and Children: Feminist Analyses and Personal Narratives.*

KATHRYN J. FOX is Assistant Professor of Sociology at the University of Vermont. Her areas of special interest are social constructionism, qualitative methods (ethnography), and deviance/social control. She is a coauthor of *Ethnography Unbound* with Michael Burawoy, et al. Her previous research projects include a study of punks and an AIDS-prevention project for injection drug users. She is continuing her research on the discursive dimensions of prison rehabilitation.

JOSEPH HOPPER is Harper Fellow and Instructor in the College and Department of Sociology, University of Chicago. He is also a Faculty Research Associate at the Population Research Center and the Center on Aging at NORC and the University of Chicago.

DONILEEN R. LOSEKE is Associate Professor and Chair of the Department of Sociology, University of South Florida. She is the author of *The Battered Woman and Shelters: The Social Construction of Wife Abuse* (1992), which won the Charles Horton Cooley Award from the Society for the Study of Symbolic Interaction. She is also the author of *Thinking About Social Problems: An Introduction to Constructionist Perspectives* (1999), which examines the process of constructing social problems as well as how images of social problems inform social services and sense making in daily life.

KATHLEEN S. LOWNEY is Professor of Sociology at Valdosta State University. Her research blends an interest in religion with her concern for the cultural construction of personal problems and their meaning. She is the author of *Passport to Heaven: Gender Roles in the Unification Church* (1992). Her chapter in this volume grows out of her work on television talk shows that is also published in *Baring Our Souls: TV Talk Shows and the Religion of Recovery* (1999).

GALE MILLER is Professor of Sociology in the Department of Social and Cultural Sciences at Marquette University. He has published more than 20 books and numerous journal articles. Much of his research has focused on social problems theory and how social policies are implemented within contemporary human service institutions. Recently, Miller has examined the social and discursive organization of brief therapy and related constructivist approaches to human troubles and social problems. He is currently working on cross-cultural studies of brief therapy practice and therapy talk across a variety of institutional settings.

MELVIN POLLNER is Professor in the Department of Sociology at UCLA. His teaching and research interests include self and society, mental illness, and sociological theory.

J. WILLIAM (JACK) SPENCER is Associate Professor of Sociology at Purdue University. His research interests center around the discursive constructions of social problems. His work includes analyses of face-to-face encounters between human service agents and their clients and, more recently, analyses of media images of the homeless and youth violence.

JILL STEIN is a lecturer in the Department of Sociology and the Executive Director of the LeRoy Neiman Center for the Study of American Society and Culture at UCLA. Her research and teaching interests include social psychology, mass media, and higher education.

DARIN WEINBERG is Assistant Professor of Sociology at the University of Florida. His current research focuses on how notions of mental disorder and addiction are used in various historical and contemporary contexts. In particular, he is interested in the ways these uses exemplify how boundaries are formulated between the social and natural forces that govern human action. His work has appeared in *Social Problems*, *Sociological Theory*, and *Symbolic Interaction*. He is currently compiling a reader in qualitative research methods to be published by Blackwell.

Introduction

Trying Times, Troubled Selves

These are trying times for the personal self. We are constantly besieged by questions of who and what we are as we move through the myriad settings of everyday life. Our identities often seem uncertain or unstable. The selves we share with others can shift rapidly in response to the changing demands of being the "right" person at the right place and moment. We are buffeted about the identity landscape, as possibilities are paraded before us in ordinary interaction, in the mass media, and even in our imagination. Contemporary life poses apparently boundless options for what we could be.

At the same time, when everything appears to be in flux, we are sustained by the conviction that, deep down, a singular authentic self resides within us. We maintain an inner sanctum for the self that insulates it against the moral ravages of today's world and the related pushes and pulls of daily living. While social life may shape who we are, permanently blemish our identities, or lead us astray, the popular belief is that a "true self" resides somewhere inside, in some privileged space. As besieged or hidden as it may be, the personal self is nonetheless available as a resolute beacon to guide us. We take for granted that in our most private recesses, we don't need to divide ourselves between countless identities. Deep inside, it is possible to get in touch, and be at one, with our real selves.

In our culture, we place great stock in this notion of an inner beacon, in a self that stands fundamentally apart from the social world. While it may be socially influenced, we presume that the self ultimately exists separately from—outside of—our everyday social transactions. It's immersed in social affairs, to be sure, but it's figured to be an autonomous social agent in those affairs. We also believe that, in its inner cloister, this self speaks to itself more authentically than it speaks to anyone else. It is a self virtually owned by the individual, independent and distinct from the social marketplaces in which individuals gain purchase on identity. Categorically distinguished from social life, this personal self is repeatedly conjured up in familiar phrases such as "the individual versus society," "the core, true self," and "who I really am" (as opposed to who I merely give the impression of being).

Without reflection, we harbor this belief from early childhood, as significant others—parents, teachers, and even our peers—tout the value of being true to oneself. It lurks behind admonitions to be "self-reliant" or to build "self-esteem," qualities that we assume are influenced by social life, but which also somehow stand above it (Hewitt 1998). External influences aside, members of our culture believe that the personal self has a life of its own, residing deep within. We cherish its autonomy and authenticity.

Trials and tribulations have beset this personal self as an ever-expanding panoply of organizations and communications media have penetrated its privileged space. Today, identity no longer emanates from within, but penetrates us from every angle. From self-change groups and 12-step programs, to welfare agencies and psychiatric clinics, to self-help books and television talk shows, who and what we are in practice has been dislodged from our inner spaces, to be relocated in the self-defining activities of varied institutions. These "going concerns," as Everett Hughes (1984) liked to call social institutions, are explicitly in the business of structuring and reconfiguring personal identity. Contrary to the popular image of the inner self, we are now seeing how even the deepest enclaves of the self are infiltrated by outside interests which threaten the very foundations of personal privacy. The personal self, we might argue, is increasingly *deprivatized* (Gubrium and Holstein 1995; Holstein and Gubrium 2000). Our most private essence is now being constructed and interpreted under the auspices of decidedly *public* going concerns.

Nevertheless, the belief in the self as a discrete, private entity endures. Our commonplace experiences and everyday folk psychologies tell us that the personal self hasn't disappeared from our culture (see Cahill 1998). It remains one of the leading experiential themes of our lives, continuing to inform our own and others' moral attention as we seek to develop beyond what we are, reform ourselves, or return to former identities. In the face of the institutional onslaught, our commitment to the personal self can leave us clinging to, even yearning for, a deep authenticity. At the same time, we continually confront the practical contingencies of occupying an institutional terrain that places more and more identity-shaping demands on all of us.

This book takes a serious look at the self in relation to today's challenging social landscape. It shows how, in a variety of organizational settings, the personal self is discerned in public space and produced in social interaction. It examines how our modern notion of an individually controlled, private space for the personal self relates to a postmodern panorama of public sites of self-construction, whose venues diversely produce and manage personal identity. The book tours the almost dizzying array of institutions comprising this postmodern environment, a world where selves are regularly decentered from their inner recesses and recentered in institutional life. As we will see, the postmodern self is continually assembled from the complex definitional handiwork of these going concerns even as participants cling to the belief in its personal, private recesses.

The Personal Self

As a point of departure for the tour, let's consider some recent commentary on the state of the personal self. This deserves our attention from the outset because, even though the chapters of this book focus on the institutional construction of selves, the belief in the personal self perseveres underneath it all. Indeed, as the commentary shows, this belief sustains an image of a social world persistently at odds with the personal self.

Kenneth Gergen's (1991) book *The Saturated Self* presents one of the most personally poignant stories of the plight of the self. Gergen marshals a compelling argument that the self is desperately seeking relief from the hubbub of contemporary life, which has left it overwhelmed, virtually saturated with social demands. As Gergen notes, this fast-paced and multidimensional—postmodern—world is so full of meanings and messages that it routinely floods the self, leaving the self with no life of its own. Filled to overflowing, the self dilutes and squanders any sense of a true identity. The real self, according to Gergen, should have a life held in abeyance from the plethora of social influences that bear upon it. It is a self that can only breathe a sigh when it gets away from these relationships; it feels most at home separated from the madding crowd. Somewhere in the sequestered niches of experience, Gergen hopes, the self can come into its own, unencumbered by society. This is the only way we can maintain at least partial ownership of who and what we are.

The first chapter of the book, entitled "The Self Under Siege," is telling. It's apparent that it is the author himself who is inundated, whose self-ownership is at risk. Gergen feels pulled in myriad directions at once. He wants to maintain mastery over his affairs, but this eludes him. His life seems to spin out of control at every turn. He begins this opening chapter by recounting what awaits him as he settles into his college office after a brief trip out of town:

> An urgent fax from Spain lay on the desk, asking about a paper I was months late in contributing to a conference in Barcelona. Before I could think about answering, the office hours I had postponed began. One of my favorite students arrived and began to quiz me about the ethnic biases in my course syllabus. My secretary came in holding a sheaf of telephone messages, and some accumulated mail . . . My conversations with my students were later interrupted by phone calls from a London publisher, a colleague in Connecticut on her way to Oslo for the weekend, and an old California friend wondering if we might meet during his summer travels to Holland. By the morning's end I was drained. The hours had been wholly consumed by the process of relating—face to face, electronically, and by letter. The relations were scattered across Europe and America, and scattered points in my personal past. And so keen was the competition for "relational time" that virtually none of the interchanges seemed effective in the ways I wished. (P. 1)

Honorific as this seems, something is missing, something that, if it were in place, could signify a sense of being at one with oneself. Gergen soon tells us what that is: "I turned my attention optimistically to the afternoon. Perhaps here I would find moments of *seclusion, restoration,* and *recentering*"—three characteristics of a distinctly modern view of the private, autonomous self. From the start, Gergen conveys the personal contours of the self he desires, which he is apparently losing to the frenzied pace and diverse spaces of postmodern life. This is a self that gains the measure of who it genuinely is by getting away from the daily rat race. While there is no doubt that such a self is at home in social experience, ironically, it is most likely to be who it truly is when it is separated from that. In seclusion, it can take stock of its real identity and restore itself.

This self needs to be periodically recentered, that is, placed at the heart of one's personal life as opposed to being bandied about by diverse and competing social influences. Gergen cringes from the exponential growth of these influences, which are "producing a profound change in our ways of understanding the self" (p. 6). According to Gergen, we are no longer coherently thinking or deeply feeling entities; we increasingly incorporate into ourselves a "multiplicity of incoherent and unrelated languages of the self" (p. 6). He decries a variety of negative consequences as the self is fragmented and the "authentic self" is displaced to a thousand locations on the social scene.

> For everything we "know to be true" about ourselves, other voices within respond with doubt and even derision. This fragmentation of self-conceptions corresponds to a multiplicity of incoherent and disconnected relationships. These relationships pull us in myriad directions, inviting us to play such a variety of roles that the very concept of an "authentic self" with knowable characteristics recedes from view. The fully saturated self becomes no self at all. (Pp. 6–7)

There is a clear experiential geography to this saturated self. It is battered and bullied by a world *external* to itself. Its source of strength is its *interiority*. This vision is extended by metaphors of *volume* and, especially, *depth*. The self might be fragmented by the diverse demands of social life, but it remains a substantial repository with an impressive inner capacity and an ability to hold out against the social storm outside. At its greatest depth, the self is secure from the vicissitudes of daily living. The deeply authentic self, while socially nurtured and informed, is capable of fending off the social influences that can spoil who it truly is. In a sense, the very conditions of interaction and communication that supposedly nurture the self—social relationships—become its adversaries.

In her book *The Managed Heart*, Arlie Russell Hochschild (1983) makes extensive use of such metaphors to present a sensitive account of how the personal self can stave off an increasingly commercialized sociability. Focusing on the commercialization of feelings in the airline industry, Hochschild introduces her reader to the "emotion work" of flight attendants. Their job is to keep customers happy. Hochschild describes how they try to preserve their true selves in the face of the nagging demands of selflessly, cheerfully serving others.

Hochschild's is a narrative of resistance, not a lament over the state of the personal self in contemporary life, as Gergen's is. Rather than expressing a desire for repose and restoration, Hochschild provides a strategy for combating the saturated and commercialized self, a way of preserving the authentic "me" we feel in our heart of hearts. To be sure, flight attendants are a very special category of "emotion worker," yet they epitomize the way people can respond to a world where feelings are commodified and emotion management is rife. In such a world, Hochschild explains, the true self is overrun by false selves that have been mobilized to ward off these demands of social life. As outside, especially commercial, interests inundate the self, it retreats inward, leaving only uncomfortable false personas directed toward others. This is the way the personal self preserves itself.

Hochschild explains that the "false self" is a "disbelieved, unclaimed self, a part of the individual that is not 'really me.'"

> [T]he false self embodies our acceptance of early parental requirements that we act so as to please others, at the expense of our own needs and desires. This sociocentric, other-directed self comes to live a separate existence from the self we claim. In the extreme case, the false self may set itself up as the real self, which remains completely hidden. More commonly, the false self allows the real self a life of its own, which emerges when there is little danger of its being used by others. (P. 194)

In Hochschild's view, false selves perform an important, self-preserving function. They can be set up in service to others, leaving the authentic, core self protected. This is a way of accommodating the demands of social life; it serves as a buffer between external demands and an internal core that may be at odds with such demands. In today's world, according to Hochschild, false selves are necessary for preserving the true self while living civilly among others with so many ancillary interests in tow.

Emotions are the beacons of our true selves, in Hochschild's view. Every emotion serves a "signal function," Hochschild argues (p. 29), explaining that "it is from feelings that we learn the *self*-relevance of what we see, remember, or imagine" (p. 196). Emotions put us in touch with the personal "me," providing us with an inner perspective for interpreting and responding to experience. Social life becomes problematic, however, in that it often demands that we harness our feelings. This emotion management, Hochschild notes, intervenes in the signal function of feelings (p. 130), diluting or confusing a person's sense of self. With the commercialization of emotion management, we are asked to manipulate feelings and, by implication, our selves, for purely instrumental ends. As this happens, our feelings come to belong "more to the organization and less to the self" (p. 198). The result, according to Hochschild, is "burnout" and "estrangement."

The emotion work of the flight attendants illustrates the costs. Flight attendants, Hochschild explains, are not only asked to smile as they serve their customers, but are instructed to feel and project a warmth and sincerity that conveys the smile as genuine. But with emotion management and the distinction between real and projected selves in view, Hochschild asks,

> What happens to the way a person relates to her feelings or her face? When worked-up warmth becomes an instrument of service work, what can a person learn about herself from her feelings? And when a worker abandons her work smile, what kind of tie remains between her smile and her self? (Pp. 89–90)

The answer is clear: flight attendants and, by implication, the rest of us in our own ways, become estranged from themselves.

Still, people know that "social engineering" affects their behavior and feelings. From time to time we are all asked to present images and emotions that don't emanate from our inner, authentic selves. We give impressions and convey emotions that are dictated by social circumstances, organizational policies, and the like. We do emotion work as much to shield our true selves and deep feelings as we do it to manage social situations. It's a way of resisting social intrusions, a technique for counteracting the demands placed on who we really are or should be.

At the same time, in Hochschild's view, this resistance serves to further isolate and insulate the true self: "We make up an idea of our 'real self,' an inner jewel that remains our unique possession no matter whose billboard is on our back or whose smile is on our face. We push the 'real self' further inside, making it more inaccessible" (p. 34). If our relationships threaten the true self, it's our defenses against social life that can ultimately be the self's undoing. As we cloister our personal self, pushing it increasingly inward, we virtually lose sight of who we are. Trying times indeed!

The Social Self

No doubt, these commentaries ring familiar. We regularly speak in these terms when the pace of life increases and demands on our time overwhelm us. Such talk all but admits that the complex and varied circumstances of everyday live are at odds with personal identity and integrity. As we lament trying times, we cast social life as the personal self's ordeal, if not its looming adversary, pitting the personal and private against the public and social.

But is social life truly at loggerheads with the personal self? Must social interaction always involve some sort of "holding action" against the ostensibly divisive encroachments of the outside world? What is absent from this scenario is an equally compelling view centered on the *social* self. This view holds that the self is a thoroughly social structure. From the start and throughout its life, the self unfolds within society, never in some private space separate from it. From this perspective, if there is a personal self, it is not a private entity so much as it is a shared articulation of traits, roles, standpoints, and behaviors that individuals acquire through social interaction. It's not so much the essential core of our being as it is an important operating principle that we use to morally anchor our thoughts and feelings about who and what we are. In talk and interaction, the personal self becomes the central narrative theme around which we convey our identity. It is, in other words, our primary subjectivity, the entity we construct, and comprehend ourselves to be, as we go about our everyday lives.

If the self is social, it's immersed in communication. When we interact with others, we openly refer to ourselves and, in giving voice to our identities, convey a sense of who we are, how we feel about ourselves, and what we will do about it. Ordinary statements—often beginning with "I" and ending in "me"—describe the self to others in revealing detail. "*I'm* the kind of guy who'd give my life and everything I own for those I love. That's *me*." "*I'm* a good person. My momma raised me to believe in God and I'm goin' to heaven. He's got a place up there for *me*." "*I've* always been one tough SOB. Nobody's gonna take advantage of *me*." "*I* thought I knew myself, but when she said those things about *me*, it really opened my eyes!"

Such references to "I" and "me" apply equally to our inner conversations with ourselves. As we think things through, "I" and "me" are very much like two separate, yet related, entities. It's as if we can stand outside of ourselves, look back, and identify who we are. We take stock of our identities, evaluate what we see, formulate who we are, and proceed as if we are the kind of person we've been considering. The "I" makes statements about the other, as if that other—"me"— were someone to be singled out, critiqued, and evaluated. The "me" takes on a distinct life of its own, as an object that we might love, hate, or not understand. What we describe, what we feel, and what we do about that "me" can be as rich, varied, and consequential as if the "me" were actually someone else.

It's striking how much the inner relationship between "I" and "me" parallels social relations between two different people interacting with one another. Individuals can think and feel deeply about each other, leading them to come together, avoid each other, cherish or detest the very ground they walk on, or silently pass right by each other, with no sign of recognition. It's the same with ourselves; we can think, feel, and do nearly everything that we can do in relation to others. We can be comfortably at one with ourselves, or remain distant and detached; we can admire or despise who we are, or not think or feel much at all about ourselves at any particular moment.

The past and future, too, are full of such references. We look back on what we've done and assume that it led us to become what we are today. We take stock of who we are and figure on where that will take us in the coming years. Who we have been and who we are becoming are guideposts for what we think, do, and say. Decisions we make about ourselves and others, or feelings that we have in relation to them, are enveloped in our sense of our own identities. From cradle to grave, we communicate who and what we are, how and why we've come to be that way, and what we expect to be in the future. We hear our mind's voice silently speak about ourselves, with glee, dismay, or indifference, just as we might hear somebody else offering the commentary. Even when we're alone, our selves are never socially isolated because this voice is always with us. Our silent self-conversations echo the myriad ordinary, daily conversations we have with others.

Interaction and communication are clearly the basis for the social self. As we converse with ourselves and others, we learn and tell about who and what we are. We "talk our selves into being" in social interaction, so to speak. But not just anything goes, either in social exchanges with others or in our inner conversations with ourselves. Social identities are not tokens in a pinball machine, ricocheting and rebounding, totally without design or restraint. What we say about and to ourselves is always spoken in terms of—and through—our social relationships. We speak of ourselves in ways that are recognizable and meaningful within the various social contexts in which we communicate. When we refer to ourselves, we do so with respect to the identities in question, in terms that others will recognize. Identities don't develop from within us as much as they emerge from the circumstances of self-construction. The same applies when we communicate within ourselves; we communicate as if we were conversing with others—with the same social restraints—even if this is an "inner conversation."

Decades ago, George Herbert Mead (1934) drew our attention to the origins of this social self and to the related inner conversations between "I" and "me." At the same time, he cogently apprised us that the self was as "ordinary" as the everyday social relations that organize our lives. Mead argued that the self was a malleable social structure, one that was constantly unfolding in interaction. Moreover, it was as varied as the relationships that mediated its construction. This was a quite radical position—especially in relation to the cultural belief in the personal self—because it meant that it was impossible to conceive of a pure "I"—an entirely private, personal self. For Mead, a socially untainted state of being was experiential fiction, a philosophical mirage that somehow escaped the influence of everyday life. Arguing to the contrary, Mead held that our sense of who and what we are, were, or will be, couldn't exist separately from our communicative relations with ourselves and others.

At about the same time, Charles Horton Cooley (1902) was also contemplating a social self. To capture its essence, he coined the phrase "looking-glass self." This was a captivating vision, using an easily grasped metaphor to convey how the self reflected social input. We see ourselves, wrote Cooley, through the eyes of others, as if we were looking in a social mirror. We then retransmit that self in light of what others have been telling us. Mead, however, had a more complex version of the social self in mind. He envisaged a self that was more behavioral, less imagined, than the one Cooley presented. It was a self that actually was engaged with the everyday world, one whose social encounters formulated its recognizable contours. For Mead, the self was actively involved in producing its own shape and substance in order to cope with the ongoing practical demands of daily living. In place of a mere social reflection, Mead's vision suggested that the social self was something that we constructed to live by (Holstein and Gubrium 2000).

Writing at midcentury in his book *The Presentation of Self in Everyday Life,* Erving Goffman (1959) underscored this practical character, showing just how deeply and actively implicated self can be in defining and managing social situations. Displays of self, Goffman argued, reveal and control information about who we are, what we are likely to do, and what others can otherwise expect from us. Self-presentation, as Goffman called it, amounts to the way "the individual in ordinary work situations presents himself and his activity to others, the ways in which he guides and controls the impression they form of him, and the kinds of things he may or may not do while sustaining his performance before them" (p. xi). Clearly, Goffman figured that the self shaped interaction as much as it was shaped by it. Individuals, he argued, present selves to accomplish particular moral ends. And, while they are modeled as personal selves, the image of the personal self is itself a presentation that is publicly and pragmatically accomplished (see Cahill 1998).

Of course, this self we live by is not conjured up out of thin air. While the self is communicatively shaped, we can't make just any claim about who or what we are. The self is always crafted in light of the social conditions and biographical particulars of one's life. Images of self are accountable to features of our lives that others can see and interpret. They reflect the circumstances under which self-interpretation takes place. What's more, the self is constructed and projected using culturally recognizable images and culturally-endorsed formats. Our identities must resonate with our community's understandings of who and what individuals might possibly be, or else we have some explaining to do. Broadly speaking, the self emanates from the *interplay* between circumstantial demands, restraints, and resources, on one hand, and self-constituting social actions on the other.

Troubled Identities

Conceiving of the self as a *social* structure leads us to reassess the meaning of trying times and troubled selves. In one respect, postmodern times pose a distinctly turbulent environment for self-construction. Sometimes it seems that everything is "up for grabs." Troubles for the self lurk around every social corner, as Gergen and Hochschild seem to suggest. In another respect, however, the postmodern landscape is increasingly populated by institutions devoted to identifying and fixing personal troubles; the renovation of selves is socially ubiquitous.

Since earlier in the 20th century, social relationships have come under the purview of countless institutions—schools, correctional facilities, clinics, family courts, support groups, and self-improvement programs, among others—that function increasingly to assemble, alter, and reformulate our identities. From Alcoholics Anonymous to Weight Watchers, these institutions immerse the communicative contours of the self in a complex and variegated world of troubles. In this context, these are trying times for the self not because the self is personally afflicted by a saturating social environment, but because the personal self itself is constructed out of a burgeoning supply of troubled identities. We might say that times are tough for the self because they are riddled with available models of troubles (Rose 1988, 1990, 1996).

Troubled identities come in many forms. Taken together, cultural and institutional images set the "conditions of possibility" (Foucault 1979) for who and what we might be—or are likely not to become, as the case might be. These identities establish general parameters for how the troubled self might recognizably and accountably be constructed, including even the core self. In some quarters, troubles are officially constructed in terms of "too much" or "too little" of virtually every conceivable combination of thought, feeling, and action. This can range from too much restlessness, talkativeness, and grandiosity, which are among the diagnostic criteria of manic episodes, to too little passion about life or "not caring anymore," which are notable features of depression.

One of the most commonly used guides to troubled identities—the *Diagnostic and Statistical Manual* of the American Psychiatric Association—organizes its categorization precisely along these lines. New troubles are added periodically as problematic features of everyday life are distinguished and their excesses or shortcomings indicated, debated, and configured into diagnostic criteria. Of course, the process of official troubles designation is not nearly as automatic as the mere specification of excesses and shortcomings. It usually entails considerable public debate over the accuracy, utility, and necessity of categories; this may lead to heated political controversy concerning competing cultural images of who and what we are or should be (Kirk and Kutchins 1992; Spector and Kitsuse 1987).

Needless to say, not all troubled identities are medicalized or become the targets of psychotherapeutic efforts. Today's array of troubles extends across the wide variety of human service institutions and beyond, from the pastoral care and spiritual fellowships offered by churches to behavioral rehabilitation programs imposed on violent offenders in prison. Some troubled identities are viewed in decidedly nonmedical and antipsychotherapeutic terms. Alcoholics Anonymous (AA), for example, construes uncontrollable drinking as a spiritual and moral failure, not just a mental and physical disease. Mainly, it is a refusal to recognize that one's actions are not self-governed. Troubled persons in AA embark on the path to recovery only when they accept this and begin to take "the steps" in the right direction. Guidance comes from those who have "been there," as voices of experience speak louder and with more impact than those of the experts or professionals. Self-help is the key, participants drawing upon the common and collective support of those similarly troubled.

The ubiquity and variety of troubled identities suggest an important point linking the personal and the social self. At the heart of this book, the point is this: in a postmodern world, the traditional relationship between the personal self and society is reversed. In a *modern* context, while the personal self is viewed as socially influenced, it also is believed to have its own private location separate from society, a space centered in personal experience. In this context, social life may be considered as important for growth and development, but, in excess, it can be portrayed as besieging, saturating, and commodifying the self. This view persists in our cultural belief system, as we have seen. The personal self experiences trying times because it is being slowly eroded, if not engrossed, by the heartless intrusions of public life. Social commentators like Gergen and Hochschild, as well as prominent voices such as David Riesman (1950), William H. Whyte (1956), Richard Sennett (1974), and Christopher Lasch (1977, 1979) paint this disturbing picture.

In a world understood in *postmodern* terms, however, the relationship between the personal self and society dramatically changes. The social self moves to the foreground, as the personal self is decentered from itself and recentered into myriad going concerns. As we've noted, many of these concerns are literally in the business of constructing or reconstructing personal selves; many are explicitly devoted to identifying and managing troubles. The identities they provide are the sources of the "institutional selves" that are examined in this book.

The personal self, however, doesn't vanish from the postmodern world. It remains in the form of the belief from which we construct subjectivity. The personal self persists in the tenet that there is an individual agent or subject inside or behind the surface appearances of our actions. Most significantly, in a postmodern context, personal selves are being constructed in more settings than ever (Gubrium and Holstein 2000). Each of the institutions considered in this book constructs personal selves according to the identities that the institutions formulate and promote. In some settings, participants become "recovering alcoholics," in others they are "battered women." In still others, they are "normal" or "competent" individuals just momentarily mired in life's myriad travails. From this tableau, one thing is clear: postmodern life provides an abundance of troubled identities for self-construction. That is the upshot of deprivatization for the troubled self.

By the same token, there are more "untroubled" selves than ever before. Just because the self-construction industry tends to focus on troubles doesn't mean that the untroubled are not equally diversified. The untroubled know their "normality" in contrast to what it is like to be "troubled." Troubled identities such as being "alcoholic," a "battered woman," or "mentally ill" not only specify troubled selves, but they also inform the untroubled, in turn, that they are not alcoholic, not battered, nor mentally ill, as the case might be. Thus, at a time that there are more troubled selves than at any previous time, there also are more ways to be untroubled than ever. The growing deprivatization of experience assures this, too.

Identity Work

Institutional identities are locally salient images, models, or templates for self-construction; they serve as resources for structuring selves. But as ubiquitous, prominent, and varied as troubled identities have become, the process of assembling them into institutional selves is anything but a matter of simply picking and choosing. Making connections between the personal self and a troubled identity involves a great deal of interpretive activity, work that is conditioned by the setting in which it is conducted. In her chapter in this book, Donileen Loseke refers to this as "identity work." Elsewhere, we have used the term "biographical work" to describe the similar effort entailed in the construction of the life course (Gubrium and Holstein 1995). Holstein and Gale Miller (1993) and J. William (Jack) Spencer (1994) use the terms "social problems work" and "client work," respectively, to highlight the person-building activity entailed in the everyday construction of social problems such as mental illness and unemployment. In each case, the terminology used conveys the sense in which the often chaotic or even contradictory facts of lived experience are concertedly sorted out in talk and interaction to construct particular selves (see Cahill 1998 for a related discussion of self-construction and the "sociology of the person").

Recognizable identities, such as those of "the" alcoholic or "your" classic battered woman, are used reflexively to make sense of the lives, circumstances, and personal travails that led to troubles. Some researchers view this as a matter of typification, involving the work of categorizing a particular person as a member of an identifiable group or classification (Schutz 1967). In the process, an individual may come to be seen as the typical homeless person, the typical child abuser, or the typical serial killer, as the case might be. Whatever the eventual typification, the lesson is that the connection between personal selves and troubled identities always needs to be constructed.

Because the connection isn't automatic, the individuals in question may not necessarily experience themselves as distinctively troubled. This means that in the context of a going concern focused on troubles, such as a support group for abused women, identity work entails framing lived experiences in terms of being troubled. As Loseke shows in her chapter, some ostensibly "battered" women come to support groups with only vague senses that it is *they* who have been abused, beaten, and abandoned. Some don't readily acknowledge that they have been victimized. They arrive in the groups with physical bruises perhaps, and they may be in emotional turmoil, but they are still unsure of their identities. At times, it's evident from what these women say that they are uncertain about whether they have any significant problems to speak of. Some view themselves instead as, say, merely experiencing the ups and downs of domestic life. Some don't see their husbands or partners as perpetrators, but rather take them to be the sort of men who are difficult to live with at times, who may have had good reasons to respond to them as they did. Similarly, the divorce attorneys that Joseph Hopper discusses in his chapter don't necessarily encounter clients who think of themselves as legal actors in civil litigation. They don't identify themselves in legalistic terms *as* divorce clients, in other words. Rather, they see themselves in moral terms, as having serious domestic "beefs," as victims of heartless domestic betrayal. As Hopper shows, these are legally useless identities in the courtroom; divorce proceedings require selves structured in legally relevant, not exclusively moral, terms.

Not all of our social relationships are professional. Identity work is not necessarily a bureaucratic or credentialed activity; often it's quite ordinary. Family members, friends, and significant others frequently spearhead the project, as spouses, partners, and parents, for example, attempt to figure the troubles that ail us. They come armed with a variegated stock of knowledge about such matters, which may overlap considerably with professional knowledge. The individual in question may herself take up the same question, as she asks herself, "Is something the matter with me?" She may wonder what it is that is "making [her life] miserable," "taking such a toll on [her] emotions," "causing [her] to feel lonely, be in despair, and drinking excessively," among other spoken references to a troubled self. Even distant relationships such as those presented on TV talk shows, which ply us daily with every conceivable troubled identity we could imagine, are part of the picture. As Kathleen Lowney and James Holstein tell us in their chapter, the diverse linkages that might be drawn between selves and troubled identities also resound more remotely from stage and screen.

A Panorama of Discursive Environments

Which of these social relationships will foster the identity work that constructs who and what we are? Where are we most likely to find out just who we might be? Will our selves be constructed primarily in relation to significant others, or in the give-and-take of organizational life? Will identity be processed through the ritualistic meetings and mantras of going concerns like Alcoholics Anonymous, which reveal who their participants are in no uncertain terms? Or will our selves be constructed informally, by those who know us "best"? Or by those who "know the ropes"? Or by professionals who claim to be experts in such matters?

In practice, none of the identities offered in this broad range of relationships are necessarily privileged over the other, even while differences of opinion about this can be part of the rhetoric of identity work. Even though we often feel that professionals and their advice are paramount in discerning troubled selves, a plethora of other relationships—from self-help groups to the personally experienced—can vie for the same status. Indeed, some groups are established specifically to compete with, if not to combat, the advice of professionals, who, according to these sources, "view things in very narrow terms," are "only out to make a buck," or "haven't been through it themselves, so how could they know?" The voice of experience can speak volumes where identity is concerned. So do the voices of loved ones, figures of authority such as the police and employers, even those to whom one regularly turns for advice simply because they seem to "make a lot of sense."

The postmodern world presents us with a striking panorama of *discursive environments* for identity work. These distinctive milieus for self-construction comprise institutional discourses that characterize particular settings (see Miller 1994), but they also encompass the practical contingencies of interaction as well as the material features of the environments, as they are interpretively brought to bear on self-construction. Their interpretive demands and varied discourses of identity present multiple options for constructing troubled selves.

As ubiquitous and varied as they might be, however, these environments are unequally distributed across the social landscape. Not everyone has access, or is subjected, to the same field of possibilities. For those who are disturbed, addicted, impoverished, or otherwise destitute, such as the individuals who present themselves at the agencies Jack Spencer and Darin Weinberg describe in their chapters, the selves these individuals become are soon lodged in one of the few relationships they can afford, to which they turn for their very survival. For those more privileged, such as the university students whose sexual identities Susan Chase describes in her chapter, the varied campus dialogs concerning diversity and acceptability differentiate those who will feel at ease in "being out" and comfortable with their sexual selves from those who retreat to the "closet" to shelter what might be taken as an ignominious self.

Michel Foucault (1979) reminds us that discursive environments set the conditions of possibility for the construction of troubled (and untroubled) selves. We must present ourselves in terms of reasonably familiar identities or we risk being seen as eccentric, if not outrageous. If we don't work with recognizable identities, our claims to selfhood will be treated as nonsense. To say, for example, "I'm a bloody warclub"—implying "that's me"—doesn't usually make much sense in our society. It isn't a readily recognizable identity. But its meaning may be perfectly clear in a society whose vocabulary of identity makes frequent reference to a shunned fraternity of unruly warriors plagued by dreams of bloody sacrifice. In fact, it might even make sense in our own society if we found ourselves among members of a survivalist group who share a premonition of enduring a battle with a world rent with evil. The point here is that the possibilities for who we might be as troubled persons are not set in stone, but vary across time and social circumstance.

Today's range of discursive environments for self-construction was unheard of a century ago. Our forebears were likely to have constructed themselves in relation to spiritual, familial, or communal identities. They simply didn't encounter the profusion of institutional offerings and demands that confront us today. Their lives weren't spread across the dozens of sites and situations that now call for distinctive kinds of self-presentation. Indeed, today's panoply of identities has strangely reconfigured some of the standard parameters of self-construction. If we are convinced by Hochschild's (1997) engaging book, *The Time Bind*, the traditional experiential relationship between work and home has even been reversed with respect to where we seek our identities.

Today, the vast majority of American adults are employed outside the home, participating daily in the institutional life of organizations large and small. This is a major departure from the adult life of, say, 100 years ago. According to Hochschild, work rather than home has sometimes become a preferred location for the personal self, a place where one finds him- or herself to be most centered and whole. Now, more than ever, we seek the respite and authenticities of the workplace in discerning who and what we are. The discursive environment of the workplace may even be formally sensitive to the need to repair the troubled self for everyday functioning.

The family friendly company called "Amerco," where Hochschild conducted her study, is a case in point. Amerco has instituted a Total Quality (TQ) management system, replacing the traditional top-down, scientific framework. It is a discursive environment that ostensibly empowers workers to make decisions on their own. Amerco's TQ principles not only offer a nurturing environment for workers on company grounds, but seek to heal the troubled selves that employees often work by. The self, itself, is firmly recognized as critical to company policy and subject to redesign, as the following description indicates.

> At Amerco, employees are invited to feel relaxed while on the job. Frequent recognition events reward work but also provide the context for a kind of play. Amerco's management has, in fact, put thought and effort into blurring the distinction between work and play (just as the distinction is so often blurred at home) . . . there are even free Cokes, just as at home, stashed in refrigerators placed near coffee machines on every floor.
>
> Amerco has also made a calculated attempt to take on the role of helpful relative in relation to employee problems at work and at home, implicating the social selves in question. The Education and Training Division offers employees free courses (on company time) in "Dealing with Anger," "How to Give and Accept Criticism," "How to Cope with Difficult People," "Stress Management," "Taking Control of Your Work Day," and "Using the Myers-Briggs Personality Test to Improve Team Effectiveness." . . . Amerco is also one of about a hundred companies that enrolls its top executives in classes at the Corporate Learning Institute. . . . One can, at company expense, attend a course on "Self-Awareness and Being: The Importance of Self in the Influence Process." (Hochschild 1997, pp. 205–6)

But Hochschild sees an unanticipated consequence of TQ's cognitive and emotional involvement in workers' personal lives: it inadvertently turns the workplace into another home—or place for recentering—encouraging a particular kind of self-surveillance. A premium is placed on the expression of feelings, the sharing of emotional labor, and a cooperative spirit of family like corporate responsibility. This, in effect, puts TQ in the business of reconstructing its participants' personal selves, purportedly for the greater good of all concerned.

The result is a corporate workplace that competes with the home for addressing identity issues, even matters extending to the core self. According to Hochschild, the demand and enticement to put in long hours at work—called the "time bind"—upsets the traditional work-family balance. A "third shift" has emerged for these workers that entails keeping the time-pressured and increasingly rationalized household at bay so that workers can devote themselves—their selves—to the evidently attractive emotional allures of work. For many of Amerco's employees, the workplace is more of an experiential haven than they find at home; Amerco offers emotional relief and interpersonal sustenance away from the rush and turmoil of the domestic front. This, ironically, transposes the preferred cultural geography of privacy, making the workplace more of a self-sustaining sanctuary than the home.

Amerco may be at the forefront of the movement to make the workplace more inviting, but it is also part of a massive vanguard of institutions that are intimately involved in self-construction and the repair of troubled selves. People are more and more likely to turn to human service professionals and agencies to interpret, define, and respond to personal quandaries, vague dilemmas, and wrenching heartaches. These agencies offer help and advice at every turn. Schools, day care centers, and churches socialize the young, while recovery programs and support groups see us through midlife and the later years. These are but a fraction of the discursive environments that construct who and what we are. On any Sunday, for example, one can read the local newspaper and find literally dozens of self-help groups listed for parents of the troubled or gifted, alcoholics, codependents of substance abusers, cancer sufferers, survivors of cancer, Gulf War veterans, victims of sexual assault, perpetrators of domestic violence, AIDS patients, the friends and significant others of Alzheimer's disease sufferers, and transvestites and their spouses, among myriad others. We are seeking help in defining our selves in countless ways, so much so that Robert Wuthnow (1994) estimates that 40 percent of the U.S. population now participates in such groups.

Add to this the human interest programming we encounter on television, in movies, and in print, and it's clear that troubled identities are on display nearly everywhere. Ordinary life has become a supermarket of options for self-construction. Images of sullied selves come alive and are acted out before our very eyes on TV talk shows, facilitated if not encouraged by the likes of Oprah Winfrey, Jenny Jones, Ricki Lake, and Jerry Springer. We witness living models of every conceivable troubled identity we could become, from the deeply anxious children of ax-murderers to the dysfunctional families of cocaine addicts and road ragers. Virtually every personal self is implicated and potentially spoiled.

Institutional Ethnographies

If we are to understand the self and identity in a postmodern world, we can't limit our attention to personal life; we must turn directly to the environments in which selves are constructed. Carefully attending to the social interaction and discourse of these settings reveals both the variety of identities we could, or could not, be, as well as the practices by which identities are attached to the selves in question. We learn in the context of AA, for example, that our deepest inner turmoils need to conform to the linear contours of recovering, but never fully recovered, alcoholics; the Twelve Steps move us along at their own pace, with the ostensible help of others and a higher power. We learn in ecosystemic family therapy, in contrast, that personal troubles are never completely our own but are part of the ecology of sick families; the entire family system of social relationships provides a web of attachments that shapes what we become. Reading Miller's and Weinberg's chapters, we are instructed that different therapeutic settings can have sharply contrasting preferences for working identities, leading to the construction of different sorts of selves for ostensibly "similar" individuals.

The contributions in this book are *institutional ethnographies*, the aim of which is to document the way the social and discursive environments of particular going concerns provide for the construction of troubled selves (also see Gubrium and Holstein 1997; Miller 1994; Smith 1987). In varying measure, these studies combine an ethnographic eye for the scenic influences of institutional life with a discourse-analytic ear for situated talk and interaction. Each chapter shows how locally salient identities are articulated with personal selves through the identity work of the settings' participants. Procedurally, this requires attending both to *what* is locally available by way of identity resources in these discursive environments and to *how* the complex process of self-construction unfolds in relation to these resources. The former task highlights the descriptive contours of available identities, while the latter underscores the work of self-construction.

None of the authors examine one component to the exclusion of the other. While, in some sense, the institutions studied here "speak" and present distinct troubled identities to, and for, their participants, these discursive resources must nonetheless be put into practice. Each chapter attends to prevailing identity discourses, even as they focus on the identity work that constructs troubled selves. Taken together, the chapters elucidate the interplay between these institutional *whats* and *hows* that constitutes institutional self-construction.

Still, each chapter takes either the *whats* or the *hows* of institutional self-construction as its point of departure or principal emphasis, and we have organized the book accordingly. The chapters of part 1—"Institutional Identities"—focus on their institutional settings' discursive environments, accentuating the *whats* of identity work. Here, analysis works from the top down, so to speak, considering the discourses of troubled identity that are brought to bear in self-construction. These chapters show how discourse-in-practice constructs the troubled selves the respective institutions need to do their work.

Kathleen Lowney and James Holstein's chapter, "Victims, Villains, and Talk Show Selves," examines the formulaic, almost ritualistic, production of troubled selves on TV talk shows. Looking at the on-screen action of talk shows like *The Jerry Springer Show,* the authors describe how talk shows use well-established thematic conventions and production devices for designing selves to establish the outrageous characters that entertain their audiences. Production techniques virtually embody the "victim" and "villain" personas upon which the shows rely for their emotional appeal.

Melvin Pollner and Jill Stein turn us to a different set of rituals of self-construction in "Doubled Over in Laughter: Humor and the Construction of Selves in Alcoholics Anonymous." They present the ways in which humor is used in AA meetings to display the alcoholic selves that are subject to rehabilitation by way of AA's Twelve Steps. Humor, the authors argue, provides an effective vehicle for introducing participants to institutionally sanctioned identities.

Gale Miller's chapter "Changing the Subject: Self-Construction in Brief Therapy," is an account of a shift in institutional discourse that led to an altered way of conceptualizing selves. Miller discusses how the practice of "brief therapy" at a prominent clinical facility changed from an ecosystemic to a solution-focused approach. With the change in discourse came a new vision of clients' selves. Where clients once were envisioned as parts of systemic problems, they came to be seen as active agents involved in, and capable of, providing their own solutions.

In his chapter entitled "Self-Empowerment in Two Therapeutic Communities," Darin Weinberg pursues a similar theme. He compares the institutional discourses of two therapeutic programs for individuals dually diagnosed as mentally ill and substance abusers. Whereas Miller shows how discursive environments may change over time, offering up divergent identities for self-construction, Weinberg describes how two purportedly identical programs formulated dissimilar selves to accommodate different residential circumstances. Variations between inpatient and outpatient facilities, argues Weinberg, mediate therapeutic practice and self-construction; the resulting discursive environments of the two programs comprise vastly different vocabularies of treatment.

The chapters of part 2, which appear under the heading "Constructing Institutional Selves," highlight the *hows* of institutional identity work. Analysis here tends to begin from the lived experiences of those concerned and traces the complexities of articulating them with institutionally preferred identities. The lesson of part 2 is that identity is not formed within the self, nor is it automatically imposed by social institutions. Rather, as the authors cogently demonstrate, troubled selves are crafted out of the "messy" details of actual lives through talk and interaction.

Donileen Loseke sets the tone by showing how the apparently chaotic complexity of lived reality may contrast with institutionally formulaic identities. Her chapter, "Lived Realities and Formula Stories of 'Battered Women,' " points to the tensions that infuse identity work in support groups for these women. Loseke argues that while support groups promulgate the identity of "the battered woman" as a way for participants to understand themselves, the biographical particulars of women's domestic lives are often at odds with the battered woman formula story. The consequent disjunctures make institutional self-construction more problematic than we might expect.

Joseph Hopper elaborates on the disjunctures in self-construction in his chapter on "Contested Selves in Divorce Proceedings." He contrasts the divorcing individuals who typically conceive of their domestic trials and tribulations in terms of "moral selves," with divorce professionals who work to establish the "legal selves" best suited for civil litigation. While legal selves are certainly most compatible with the formal machinery of divorce proceedings, they often prove unsatisfactory to divorcing persons who feel the need to see themselves in moral and relational terms.

Susan Chase takes us into more diffuse contexts of self-construction in her chapter "Universities As Discursive Environments for Sexual Identity Construction." The chapter compares the alternate conditions of possibility for sexual identity on two college campuses, where quite different discourses of diversity and sexual orientation are in place. Chase illustrates through personal narratives how the contrasting discursive environments promote divergent climates for understanding and appreciating sexual selves, even as they fail to dictate the selves that individuals are willing to present.

Jack Spencer resurrects the theme of identity work in his chapter "Self-Presentation and Organizational Processing in a Human Service Agency." Focusing on an organization devoted to assisting the homeless, Spencer examines how clients' self-presentations are engaged by the competing discourses of service-worthiness that mediate staff-client interactions. In institutional circumstances where staff members hold all the organizational cards, so to speak, we see how the staff's preferred discourse of "rules and resources" is used to counter clients' appeal for services on "moral" grounds. In the process, staff members construct troubled selves in strictly institutional terms.

Finally, Kathryn Fox takes us to the most coercive institutional setting in this volume, a program of cognitive self-change for imprisoned violent offenders. The chapter, entitled "Self-Change and Resistance in Prison," presents the program's seemingly coercive discourse of violent criminal selves. But, as oppressive as the setting is, identity work is required to produce the selves needed for successful change, or at least a reduced sentenced based on an ostensible shift in identity. Significantly, Fox shows us how inmates' own identity work resists the straightforward construction of institutional selves.

Taken together, these chapters describe a diverse array of self-constructing institutions, even if they represent only a small part of the landscape of troubled identities. Their focus on the everyday lived realities and social construction of troubled selves teaches us that who and what we are is refracted through institutional practices and articulated by many voices, across increasingly varied discursive environments. They instruct us, too, that the personal self, with or without troubles, is something we use and apply to experience as much as it is something we experience as central to our lives.

There is considerable variation in moral tone between the different chapters with respect to these messages. Several of the chapters imply that institutional self-construction may be unduly coercive; they suggest an "iron cagelike" environment of discursive options for the self. Cast like this, institutions may appear to tyrannically impose limited conditions of possibility for self-construction. This vision provokes us to evaluate critically the complex conditions that a self-constructing postmodern world forms in relation to questions of who and what we are, and can be.

Other chapters, in contrast, show us the myriad sites and methods that are currently available for constructing selves that comfortably accommodate the biographical particulars of our lives. They also point out the artfulness that self-construction demands, even under the strictest of institutional conditions. This optimistically orients us to the moral potential of a postmodern world. It reminds us that while circumstances of self-construction play a pivotal role in how we view ourselves, they do not dictate identities nor construct selves outright. To the extent that we inhabit a world of multiple institutional affiliations, we encounter abundant opportunities for discerning even our core identities, for constructing our deepest senses of who and what we are.

Social life is fully penetrating and engrossing. We can't escape the social because it's built into our beings, into the very ways we view ourselves. Following Gergen, we can read this as an indictment of the self-saturating diversification of the postmodern world. Equally compelling, and certainly more hopeful, are the possibilities for self-construction offered by an unprecedented and expanding horizon of identities. Our ability to chose between options—to use some options in order to resist others, or to construct new ones—can be as liberating as it is overwhelming and debilitating.

REFERENCES

Cahill, Spencer E. 1998. "Toward a Sociology of the Person." *Sociological Theory* 16: 131–48.
Cooley, Charles Horton. 1902. *Human Nature and the Social Order*. New York: Scribners.
Foucault, Michel. 1979. *Discipline and Punish*. New York: Vintage Books.
Gergen, Kenneth J. 1991. *The Saturated Self*. New York: Basic Books.
Goffman, Erving. 1959. *The Presentation of Self in Everyday Life*. Garden City, N.Y.: Anchor.
Gubrium, Jaber F., and James A. Holstein. 1995. "Life Course Malleability: Biographical Work and Deprivatization." *Sociological Inquiry* 65: 207–23.
———. 1997. *The New Language of Qualitative Method*. New York: Oxford University Press.
———. 2000. "The Self in a World of Going Concerns." *Symbolic Interaction* 23:111–27.
Hewitt, John P. 1998. *The Myth of Self-Esteem*. New York: St. Martin's Press.
Hochschild, Arlie Russell. 1983. *The Managed Heart*. Berkeley: University of California Press.
———. 1997. *The Time Bind: When Work Becomes Home and Home Becomes Work*. New York: Henry Holt and Co.
Holstein, James A., and Jaber F. Gubrium. 2000. *The Self We Live By: Narrative Identity in a Postmodern World*. New York: Oxford University Press.
Holstein, James A., and Gale Miller. 1993. "Social Constructionism and Social Problems Work." In *Reconsidering Social Constructionism: Debates in Social Problems Theory*, ed. J. Holstein and G. Miller, 151–72. Hawthorne, N.Y.: Aldine de Gruyter.
Hughes, Everett C. 1984. *The Sociological Eye*. New Brunswick, N.J.: Transaction Books.
Kirk, Stuart A., and Herb Kutchins. 1992. *The Selling of DSM: The Rhetoric of Science in Psychiatry*. Hawthorne, N.Y.: Aldine de Gruyter.
Lasch, Christopher. 1977. *Haven in a Heartless World*. New York: Basic.
———. 1979. *The Culture of Narcissism*. New York: Norton.
Mead, George Herbert. 1934. *Mind, Self, and Society*. Chicago: University of Chicago Press.

Miller, Gale. 1994. "Toward Ethnographies of Institutional Discourse: Proposal and Suggestions." *Journal of Contemporary Ethnography* 23: 280–306.

Riesman, David. 1950. *The Lonely Crowd*. New Haven, Conn.: Yale University Press.

Rose, Nikolas. 1988. "Calculable Minds and Manageable Individuals." *History of the Human Sciences* 1: 179–200.

———. 1990. *Governing the Soul: The Shaping of the Private Self*. London: Routledge.

———. 1996. *Inventing Our Selves: Psychology, Power, and Personhood*. Cambridge: Cambridge University Press.

Schutz, Alfred. 1967. *The Phenomenology of the Social World*. Evanston, Ill.: Northwestern University Press.

Sennett, Richard. 1974. *The Fall of Public Man*. New York: Vintage.

Smith, Dorothy. 1987. *The Everyday World as Problematic*. Boston: Northeastern University Press.

Spector, Malcolm, and John I. Kitsuse. 1987. *Constructing Social Problems*. Hawthorne, N.Y.: Aldine de Gruyter.

Spencer, J. William. 1994. "Homeless in River City: Client Work in Human Service Encounters." In *Perspectives on Social Problems*, vol. 6, ed. James A. Holstein and Gale Miller, 29–46. Greenwich, Conn.: JAI Press.

Whyte, William H. 1956. *The Organization Man*. Garden City, N.Y.: Doubleday.

Wuthnow, Robert. 1994. *Sharing the Journey: Support Groups and America's New Quest for Community*. New York: Free Press.

PART 1

Institutional Identities

KATHLEEN S. LOWNEY AND JAMES A. HOLSTEIN

Victims, Villains, and Talk Show Selves

Just when you think it can't get any worse, switch channels and you'll find the latest episode of "I'm African American and I Hate Black People!" or "Dad Wants to Be a Woman!" Perhaps you'll channel surf across "Back Off, Boys! I'm a Lesbian and You'll Never Have Me." Jerry, Ricki, Sally, and Jenny. Misfits, perverts, lowlifes. Flailing, biting, scratching. Fear, conflict, pain, exploitation. Cultural and psychic casualties. Drivel. Trash.

Some say that daytime television talk shows have become the traveling circus—the carnival sideshow—of the late 20th century (see Gamson 1998; Lowney 1999; Twitchell 1992). But, reviled as they may be (see Abt and Seesholtz 1994; Heaton and Wilson 1995), talk shows are an exploding (and explosive) entertainment genre that offers viewers an important "window on the world"—or at least some very outrageous corners of that world.

Talk shows, like all TV programming, rely upon a reliable stock-in-trade to garner viewers and support high ratings. Indeed, the production conventions of *The Oprah Winfrey Show* or *The Jerry Springer Show* are becoming as familiar to viewers as those of the nightly news or *The Tonight Show*. While myriad production techniques contribute to their success—their "personality" hosts, topical subject matter, "colorful" or "intriguing" guests, just to name a few—a staple of the daytime talk show is the interpersonal carnival that serves up the selves of "outrageous" guest subjects for public scrutiny, inquisition, approbation, and/or condemnation. As Everett Hughes (1984) might have put it, the on-camera pageant of captivating, scandalous, even contemptible, characters is a principal "going concern" of the TV talk show. More and more, the spectacle of human torment, degradation, and depravity has become the driving impulse behind talk show programming.

This chapter examines the ways in which TV talk shows—especially the new, more confrontational shows that dominate programming at the turn of the century—convene and assemble troubled identities for their guests in order to produce the contentious scenarios their audiences crave. Of course the individuals who populate talk shows bring with them their own biographical particulars, their own lived experiences. Guests are diligently selected for the personal attributes, attitudes, and actions that make them popular with viewers (Gamson 1998; Lowney 1999). Nevertheless, production conventions, combined with the interactional manipulation of identities—"good, bad, and ugly" personas, so to speak—produce selves to fill all three rings of the postmodern talk show circus.

Constructing talk show selves, as we shall see, is deliberate and artful. Hosts and producers adroitly manage guests so as to present shocking characters and sensational stories. While these selves are virtual works of art, they are by no means "originals." Whereas each guest is presented as a unique package of traits and troubles, taken together, talk show participants represent a rather limited range of standard—even classic—cultural images. Show after show formulaically—almost ritualistically—conjures up types of persons who are effectively guaranteed to arouse viewers' passions (see Pollner and Stein in this volume for a parallel discussion of the ritual production of selves in Alcoholics Anonymous).

If talk shows draw upon familiar archetypes as identity templates for their guests, the general personas of "victims" and "villains" are the most commonly invoked. They repeatedly employ familiar self-construction formats to provide uniquely embodied, yet recognizable, "stock" characters that generate the emotion and excitement upon which their audiences thrive. While individual selves are deftly constructed, with considerable situational nuance, these are also ritualized *re*-productions of sympathetic and despised cultural icons. As we compare numerous episodes of different talk shows, it's evident that the selves produced are both formulaic and inventively crafted at the same time.

Thematic Conventions

Talk show programming has transmuted, if not evolved, since its popular explosion in the 1980s. Initially daytime versions of nighttime "variety" shows with well-known guests who both performed and chatted with hosts, talk shows also began exploring controversial social and moral issues. This development required shows to produce the characters—with extravagant selves and memorable identities—necessary to titillate, provoke, and entertain, if not appall, curious audiences.

During the 1980s and early 1990s, talk shows were typically organized around three major conventions, each of which still exists today, although in changing measure (see Lowney 1999). First, there is the *informational* convention. These shows usually involve topics relating to health, medicine, psychiatry/psychology, science, or social policy and politics. In this convention, shows teach audience members about how to cope with medical, personal, or social problems in order to improve their lives. Their titles signal the informational themes: "Shortened Hospital Stays Are Dangerous to Newborns," "Obsessive-Compulsive Behavior in Children and Adults," and "Memory Loss and Other Mental Deficiencies."

The second traditional convention is pure *entertainment*, involving popular culture or "show business" themes. Such shows are also easy to identify: "Celebrity News: Star Predictions for the Coming Year," "Oprah and Viewers in Hollywood," and "Inside the Life of a Celebrity." Some of these shows include well-known Hollywood insiders or movie critics, whose expertise provides clues about what is going to be popular, and why. Other shows feature entertainment "personalities" themselves, promoting their latest books or movies while viewers peer into the "private" selves of these "public" figures.

A third convention is *salvational*. These shows attempt to rescue people from destructive, sick, or "deviant" lifestyles, habits, or relationships. In many respects, shows of this ilk resemble the carnival-revival of centuries past (Snow 1983). They provide both entertainment and titillation, offering some of the spontaneity, rowdiness, and even chaos of the carnival, while also serving up the almost sacred rhetoric of revivalism's "conversion" testimonials. These shows typically revolve around guests who have fallen prey to their own weaknesses or foibles, or have been ensnared by others with pernicious intent. The guests typically have their psychic or social afflictions graphically exposed, but, eventually, they are set on the road to recovery or redemption (see Lowney 1994, 1999). *Salvation* shows thus require subjects who are first degraded, but who can subsequently be resurrected. Identity construction, while often far from subtle, is nonetheless artful in that it must conjure up spoiled selves that retain the potential for change or deliverance.

Through the 1980s into the mid-1990s, the salvational convention dominated talk show programming. In 1996, for example, approximately 70 percent of all "mainstream" shows aimed at salvation in one way or another (Lowney 1999). But by the late 1990s, a close relative of the salvation theme has come to dominate many of TV's daytime talk shows. While many themes were adumbrated, if not fully exploited, in salvational programming, the appearance of shows like *The Ricki Lake Show, The Jerry Springer Show,* and *The Jenny Jones Show* transformed the carnival-revival into a "real-life" hybrid of the circus side show and "Big Time Wrestling"—with clear vestiges of the spectacle and carnage of ancient Romans throwing Christians to the lions in the Coliseum. In place of crowds yelling "kill, kill, kill," *Jerry Springer* viewers chant "Jer-ry, Jer-ry, Jer-ry" (see Gamson 1998, p. 8).

This new convention is broadly based on *confrontation*. It is conflict TV, plain and simple, built on virtual showdowns between persons, beliefs, and lifestyles. By comparison, shows from the other conventions seem tame, short on energy and excitement. Even ostensibly "responsible" mainstream hosts have dipped deeper into this new convention (for example, Sally Jessy Raphael), while other traditional stalwarts like Phil Donahue have retired from the scene. More and more, talk shows present guests with something merely outrageous and provocative to say, and who are likely to say it loudly—even if it has little intrinsic informational or entertainment value. These are characters hell-bent on conflict, whose appeal lies in their "shock value." As Joshua Gamson (1998, p. 75) tells us, these new talk shows "need heat, and the easiest thing to do is to find people to espouse readily recognizable conflict packages."

The subjects required for *confrontation* shows have to be "up front" and "out there." Guests are expected to interact passionately with one another, to trade insults and condemnations. If they actually assault one another, so much the better. Interpersonal conflict, relational strife, social rebellion, and other antisocial attitudes and behaviors are acted out broadly, coarsely, and violently; physical encounters are the pièce de résistance. Onstage "street fights" and "school yard brawls" have now been added to the parade of relational "freaks" comprising the talk show *circus maximus*. There's no holding back in the presentation of these selves, no place for self-consciousness or reserve.

While physical confrontation is now almost formulaic on *The Jerry Springer Show* (with guests sometimes assaulting one another even before words are exchanged), it's not a necessary ingredient for all shows of this genre. Bizarre personas, cultural misfits, guests who flagrantly and outrageously confront, deny, and flaunt societal norms or mores, or interpersonal renegades who profess not the slightest regard for social conventions, manners, or niceties can propel a show without physical confrontations—although this is becoming increasingly rare. Even if guests don't actually brawl with one another, a character spewing "I don't give a rat's ass about what anybody thinks or feels" is bound to disgust and offend most viewers, and arouse *some* emotion in virtually everyone. Confrontation—physical or not—emanates from the audacious, even bodacious, selves that clash with conformity and convention, if not with one another.

The titles of confrontation shows trumpet the convention: "Outrageous Confessions," "You're Gay. How Dare You Raise a Child," "Listen Family, I'm Gay. It's Not a Phase. Get Over It," "Girly to Burly: Women Who Become Men," "You're Not the Man I Married," "Teen Boys Tell Their Moms, 'I Want to Be a Woman,'" "Family Secrets: Straight Women, Gay Husbands," "My Boyfriend Turned Out to Be a Girl." What could be more quintessentially confrontational than "Watch Me! Today I'm Going to Break Up My Ex and His New Chick"? (See Gamson pp. 254–59.)

Close cousins, salvation and confrontation themes are not totally distinct from one another. Rather they exist on a continuum from those emphasizing redemption to those merely promoting violent spectacle. Even Jerry Springer, who hosts shows where physical aggression is clearly the raison d'être (indeed, shows where violent combat is so predictable that it has lost its element of surprise), delivers a brief "sermonette" at the close of each show, admonishing viewers to repudiate the "bad examples" he has just aired.

This chapter concentrates on talk shows drawn from the confrontation and salvation conventions. Based on the examination of dozens of transcripts of talk shows from the past decade, we analyze how the shows draw upon troubled social identities to construct the selves that such shows require. First, we consider the production devices, then the formulas, that are used to produce the talk show personas that will captivate—even outrage—viewers. We discuss some of the ritualistic institutional practices and schemes that produce the selves upon which such shows rely. Then, we turn to some of the nuances of interactional identity work that constitute talk show selves.

Identity-Promoting Devices

Talk shows are relatively brief, typically an hour long. To ensure that the desired characters emerge within that hour, which may be divided among several guests, talk shows must expeditiously promote conspicuous, intrepid, loathsome, or sympathetic identities for their central participants. They need brazen on-screen personas to fulfill the dramatic or spectacular promise of their conventions, and they need them fast in order to set the frenzied pace audiences have come to expect.

Booking the "right" guests, of course, is crucial. Talk show producers go to great lengths to line up the sorts of characters their shows demand (see Gamson 1998; Lowney 1999). But simply recruiting captivating guests and opening up controversial discussions doesn't guarantee the desired effect. Merely introducing teenage prostitutes, transvestites, or satanists doesn't make "good" talk show TV.

Addressing this problem, talk shows employ a broad spectrum of identity-promoting devices to cultivate the characters that populate their stages. Depending upon the preferred outcome, the raw material—the biographical particulars—of the recruited guest must be framed, managed, and profiled so as to achieve the shows' implicit salvational or confrontational goals. Clearly, the sympathetic, even pathetic "loser" is a prime candidate to be "saved" on *Geraldo*, and the more outrageous and combative the character, the better for Jerry Springer and company. But even the less flamboyant *Phil Donahue Show*, for example, routinely attempted to portray "outcast" guests—those with stigmatizing features or stigmatized lifestyles—as being "just like you or me," at least to some extent. Phil would regularly present ordinary-appearing, rational-sounding guests who would reveal their "secret" deviance with reserve and dignity (Gamson 1998). The objective was to "normalize" the "abnormal," to literally redeem the guest in the eyes of the audience. This is a far cry from how Ricki Lake or Jenny Jones today might shape the persona of a guest from one of these very same groups whom they hope to thoroughly glamorize or demonize.

Achieving the desired personas requires skillfully deployed implements of self-design, including techniques such as *framing* and *staging*. Talk shows use these standard production devices to ensure that guests become the on-air personalities that programming conventions demand.

Framing

Talk shows depend heavily upon affective framing to establish the desired appreciation of guests and their situations. The outrageous personality, the social pariah, and the casualty of interpersonal or cultural turmoil all depend upon a certain emotional "shock value" to achieve maximum viewer appeal. Aiming for emotional arousal, talk shows unveil persons to be pitied, blamed, mocked, or saved from "monsters" or appalling social circumstances that inspire viewer disgust, aversion, and contempt. The task is often to make sure one guest is viewed as sympathetic, while another is seen as despicable, worthy only of disdain.

A variety of framing devices are central to this interpretive process. Titles and opening statements or introductions, for example, announce to the audience the types of persons that are about to appear. They serve as prefaces (see Holstein and Gubrium 2000) or schemes of interpretation (Schutz 1970) that pave the way for subsequent narratives of self and experience. Visual and audio production devices (for example, graphics, montages, camera angles) augment and accent aspects of the persons and circumstances to underscore salient plot lines and identity features. Geraldo Rivera, for instance, often modulates his voice when introducing a topic in the salvational convention, beginning his opening introductions in a loud voice and slowly lowering it, until he is barely whispering as he describes the pitiful plight of an unfortunate victim. He sounds almost confessional by the time he suggests the gravity of the issues he is about to explore.

Verbal framing often personalizes the issues at stake in order to make it absolutely clear how the audience is to feel about the guests. Manifestly, the host introduces topics and guests, but, in doing so, he or she also cues the audience into the "actual" selves behind, or deep inside, the persons, in the process instructing viewers as to how they should relate emotionally to these characters. Consider the following introductory segment from *Geraldo* (11/17/97):

> You've seen the images of the young ladies of the night. They're out there in their impossibly sexy or provocative outfits, their very, very short skirts, their—their spiked heels. You know that they're hookers. You know that they're very, very young. You wonder at times what brought those ladies to that place in their life, why they're working the streets. Why are they putting themselves at such tremendous risks? Why, at that tender age, are they doing, perhaps, the most dangerous profession they could possibly be following? Take a look, ladies and gentlemen, at the young ladies on our panel today. They are all, each of them, teenagers. They are also moms. They are all also prostitutes. Some of them began at the age of just 13 years old. They are teens turning tricks, they tell us, for their toddlers. On a good night, Stephanie—hi, Stephanie . . . brings home a grand, $1000. . . . She says she does it for her two-year-old son. His father—the kid's father is in jail. The father of the baby used to be Stephanie's pimp. Now she has a new boyfriend. She . . . also is expecting her second child. And you're just a baby, really, Stephanie. Are you really doing it for your—for your kids, or are you doing it because you choose it as your calling? . . . How'd this guy get you into it?

Clearly, the subjects of this show could reasonably be seen as despicable characters: sluts, whores, incorrigible children, and indiscreet parents. But Geraldo adroitly crafts from contrasting depictions both of what these teenagers could (wrongly) be taken to be, and what they "actually" are. Portrayed as "young ladies," "teenagers," and "moms" of a "tender age," Geraldo casts them as immature, innocent victims of circumstance and exploitative and uncaring adults. While their actions are suspect, their motivations, Geraldo implicitly assures us, are honorable (that is, they are "turning tricks," but doing it to support their kids), undermining the moral condemnation usually reserved for members of their "profession." The selves behind or underneath the appearances are virtuous, even if they have fallen prey to circumstance.

As Geraldo personalizes his introduction, he speaks directly to the girls, but his monologue simultaneously teaches viewers how to understand the identities of these guests, casting them in a sympathetic light, preparing the audience to accept them as victims of difficult lives. The introductory framing is a virtual discourse of guilelessness and sympathy-worthiness. While Geraldo temporarily withholds explicit judgment, he skillfully adumbrates the pain, grief, abuse, and bad choices that will soon be splashed across the screen. Again, it's not what the girls have done, but who they "actually" are, that Geraldo seeks to portray.

Typically, the opening gambit of a talk show segment designates how the characters should be interpreted, at least initially. While subsequent presentations of alternate selves or "startling revelations" may alter audience opinions, the initial framing provides a predisposition—a paradigm for understanding (Kuhn 1962)—for how viewers should interpret and react to the "facts" and characters of these little dramas.

Staging

While talk shows foster the appearance of being unrehearsed, on-screen actions are typically staged to achieve the desired outcomes. This doesn't mean the shows are literally scripted or "fake," but it does involve manipulating what the audience will see and how, concretely, it will be presented. In a sense, identity staging involves the "material mediation" of self-disclosure (see Holstein and Gubrium 2000). This means that unfolding self-presentations (Goffman 1959) may entail the use of strategic physical "props" as well as concerted "teamwork" to pull off the desired effects.

Some staging is merely practical (see Abt and Mustazza 1997; Gamson 1998). For instance, shows have rules about what is considered appropriate on-air attire. Guests (and, for that matter, even audience members) are frequently told what to wear. Audience members are instructed to remove (if possible) all clothes that suggest seasons or holidays, since shows are often rerun. Guests and audience members are also told not to wear beige or white, for these colors "fade out" too much against background sets.

On many occasions, however, clothing and other aspects of superficial appearance become integral to establishing the guests' identities. It's not just about the "look" of the guest, but also about constructing the character behind the appearance—the innocence, evil, or helplessness of those concerned. When Nazi youth are featured, they appear as tattooed "skinheads." "Big hair" and profuse makeup are de rigueur in establishing some outlandish feminine identities, while leather and chains underscores other "deviant" personas, both masculine and feminine. Viewers are implicitly told that embedded in these material trappings are the selves whose features are being conveyed.

While material staging may seem "matter of fact," it can also be the dramatic centerpiece of a talk show segment. For example, in an episode of the *Sally Jessy Raphael Show* (2/14/96), two teenage girls talk with Sally about their mothers, whom they claim are the town "sluts." They accuse the mothers of acting and dressing like "hookers," calling them, among other things, "spandex queens." According to the girls, their mothers go braless, wear "short shorts," "wear things that you can see their butts . . . navels . . . cleavage . . . breasts." One of the girls, Tammy, is upset because her mother, Linda, "will go to the grocery store, and she will wear a tight black dress, two sizes too small, mini—and when she bends over, she has no underwear." Tammy is concerned that many people think that she behaves just like her mother, something Tammy vehemently denies.

Later, Sally greets the mothers, but they don't simply appear on camera. Instead, they sashay on stage, as if on a fashion show "runway," "spandex queens" literally on parade. As advertised by their daughters, they are revealingly clad, looking much like the "sluts and hookers" the daughters described. While the daughters' dialogue framed the mothers from the girls' point of view—predisposing viewers to see the bad side of the mothers—the mothers' full-blown material presence provides a thoroughly visceral understanding of the girls' disgust with their mothers' appearance and a deep appreciation for the mothers as the culprits of this scenario. Their physical, material comportment assures us that they *are* the despicable selves their daughters have portrayed them to be. While Sally goes on to try to "save" these women from their wanton ways, their sheer corporeal appearance etches their contemptible identities into viewers' hearts, minds, and *eyes*. They *are* women who disrespect themselves and their families by putting it all "out on the street."

In many such instances—where salvation and "makeovers" are the ultimate design—ignoble guests enter dramatically from offstage, allowing the audience ample opportunity to scrutinize their offending selves. This is quite different from the typical presentation of "innocent" accusers, who typically are onstage from the beginning, sitting demurely as they recount their stories. "Miscreants," in contrast, quite literally march in review in front of the audience, like circus performers, fashion models, or sideshow freaks. Material staging draws moral boundaries between and around the audience, the "good" guests, the hosts, and those with troubled selves. On the sets of the more "chaotic" shows like *The Jerry Springer Show*, the hovering presence of "bouncers" posing as stagehands provides further material evidence of the types of characters that are likely to appear. Production conventions and devices thus ensure that identity types are visibly embodied by "in-the-flesh" guests.

Constructing Victims and Villains

If staging and framing are standard self-construction tools, then character archetypes are the "blueprints" for talk show selves. To varying degrees, both salvation and confrontation shows thrive on clashes between "good" and "evil" to produce either the basis for redemption or fuel for conflict. One of the primary means of setting up (and setting off) emotional shock waves is to cast guests in the starkly personal terms of virtue versus depravity. Passion often boils over when the contrast personifies veritable *victims* and *villains*. While the means of developing these character types may vary, the desired outcome is the clear authorization of one party as the innocent "prey," "dupe," or "casualty" of the heinous victimizer. Indeed, establishing a victim typically requires the simultaneous manufacture of the villain (Holstein and Miller 1990). Accordingly, talk shows conscientiously develop obvious victims and villains, or victimizers, as the case may be. By ritualistically reproducing these identity icons, the shows supply ready-made conflict packages rife with confrontation.

Producing Victims

One way of envisioning "victimization" is to think of it as the process whereby someone is interpretively constituted as a person unjustly harmed or damaged by forces beyond his or her control (Holstein and Miller 1990). This involves dividing the world into oppositional categories: good and bad, hero and scoundrel, innocent and guilty, victim and villain. The categories provide good reasons to despise, punish, or rehabilitate the perpetrator and sympathize with and heal the victim. The categories help us appropriately formulate our emotions.

Clearly, victimization generates much of talk shows' emotional energy. Unjust pain and suffering propel their narrative themes and emotional momentum. Their discursive and affective environments center on the harm that one party gratuitously inflicts upon another. Indeed, victims are typically talk shows' central characters, "co-starring," of course, with their victimizers. They are often introduced first and allowed to tell their stories relatively uninterrupted. This predisposes viewers to their point of view, and promotes an initial sympathy for the character. (Villains, however, may also appear first for a similar reason—to develop instant and initial antipathy. See Lowney 1999.)

Talk shows serve up many forms of victimization, from criminal exploitation, physical harm, and sexual assault, to emotional betrayal and infidelity. The point is to establish at least one (temporarily) sympathy-worthy self, whether it is to set him or her up for salvation, to establish the victimizer as worthy of punishment or rehabilitation, or to simply generate conflict and audience antagonism toward the guests onstage. By cultivating stereotypic images of their guests, talks shows almost ritualistically reproduce emotionally charged, culturally familiar characters.

Sometimes there's no question about who is being portrayed as the victim and who is cast as the villain. This can be achieved by simply allowing a sympathy-worthy guest to tell his or her story in extended, graphic detail. On one episode of *The Montel Williams Show* (11/27/95), for example, the topic for the day was "box-cutter assaults." In order to establish the hideous nature of this new "trend" in crime, and to indelibly imprint upon the audience just how serious the injuries were, Montel sympathetically invited Peaches, a 17-year-old female, to recount her horrifying experience.

Her narrative is several minutes long, a virtually uninterrupted tale of how Peaches's best friend, Aires, had suddenly and inexplicably attacked Peaches with a box cutter during lunch hour at school. The story is graphically dramatic. The audience shares Peaches's horror and confusion when a typical school day results in a trip to the hospital and scars for life—both physical and emotional—as Peaches is literally shredded with a box cutting knife. The shock and gore are revolting; blood flows narratively as Peaches stands by helplessly, not even trying to defend herself.

Over the course of her account, Peaches did far more than describe the action, however. Just as importantly, her self-presentation established that she was a "victim" on different levels. As she tells the story, she narrates her own essential innocence as well as the horrible transmutation of character that somehow motivates Aires's assault. Viewers learn that the girls were "really close," "best friends" who shared the intimacies of adolescence. Peaches makes it clear that both girls cared for and trusted one another deeply. Right to the end, Peaches is baffled by Aires's attack. Simultaneously, she outlines a dark transformation in Aires, one that Peaches could only sense, but could not explain. In its entirety, Peaches's account is, figuratively (but almost literally), the story of an innocent lamb being led to slaughter.

Presented this way, it's "obvious" that Peaches is the victim of an unprovoked assault; her narrative leaves no doubt about who is the casualty and who is the cause. The moral certainty conveyed in the presentation guarantees sympathy for Peaches and animosity toward her victimizer. The deep pathos attending the incident results as much from the identities that are presented as from the attack itself. This helps fulfill the institutional expectation—even demand—that the show produce victims clearly worthy of viewers' sympathy and villains who will raise viewers' ire.

Frequently, talk show hosts are active in interactionally promoting the "victimization" of their guests. In the previous example, Montel merely provided the space and incitement for Peaches to tell her tale, but in the following instance, we see Sally Jessy Raphael actively working during the on-screen interview (see Holstein and Gubrium 1995) to ensure that her guest was thoroughly identified as the victim. There was considerable challenge to this, since the topic at hand was "I'm Ready to Divorce My Children" (2/15/96), an act that only an ostensibly "heartless" mother might consider. In this case, Penny was attempting to rid herself of her 12- and 13-year-old daughters. This, of course, contradicts our cultural predisposition to adore children and to mandate parental responsibility to offspring. The challenge confronts Sally as she sets out to "victimize" Penny—that is, to interpretively make a victim out of her.

SALLY:	Please meet Penny. Penny is in bad shape, aren't you Penny? Penny says that she has two daughters, 12-year-old Ashlee and 13-year-old Amanda, and they are the demons from hell. She says that the 12-year-old started sleeping with boys when she was 11 and since then she has slept with four boys. We are assuming not using protection of any kind.
PENNY:	No, none.
SALLY:	She says that her 13-year-old has a violent temper. Will throw food and ashtrays at you?
PENNY:	Yes.
SALLY:	At your head.
PENNY:	Yes, anything she can get her hands on at the time.
SALLY:	Now, Penny says that it is impossible to control the 12- and 13-year-olds. Tell me what each one is doing. What's—why so violent?
PENNY:	Ashlee—
SALLY:	I mean they are 12 and 13.
PENNY:	Right. Ashlee is the 12-year-old, she's having sex, she's drinking, she's smoking. She chases men, not boys. Because she says she's "hot."
SALLY:	She's hot? And she's 12.
PENNY:	And she's 12.
SALLY:	Someone told me that she steals more than any of the other girls that we've ever met.

PENNY: She is a good thief. . . . She steals pocketbooks, nighties. . . . Yes, she can sit and talk to you, look you straight in the face and at the same time have her hand in your purse taking all your money. . . . She's—she's taken money from my friends. She's not allowed to go to a neighbor's house now, because she did steal from her, steal her money. She's taken—

SALLY: Penny, what's—what's the problem here? I mean, what—do you have any ideas—

PENNY: I've tried everything. I tried to be the best mother I can. I worked until two years ago when I got sick. I took care of them, I gave them anything and everything. She has no reason to steal. She has no reason to, you know, everything that she has asked for, I've tried to provide for them and everything that they need.

SALLY: How does this make you feel? Having these kids. I mean, why come to see me?

PENNY: Well, I was mad. I've been mad for a long, long time. But now it hurts, because I feel like I am doing wrong. And I've tried everything. I've taken them to counseling. I've kept her on house arrest. I body search her every time we go somewhere, tried to embarrass her. I've embarrassed her in front of her friends. I've busted her behind, it does no good. She doesn't care.

SALLY: People in town think you are a bad mother?

PENNY: Yes, my—I had her in the store one day, and she calls me a bitch and a whore and a slut and told me that because I wouldn't buy her what she wanted, you know, she'd get it: "I'll get it." . . .

SALLY: Okay, you're Amanda. Amanda, let's start with you. You have heard how upset your mother is about your behavior. Do you care about your mother's feelings?

AMANDA: No, I don't.

Here, at least part of Sally's objective is to present Penny as the victim of disrespectful daughters. Prefacing the segment with "Penny is in bad shape," she allows Penny to tell her side of the story before the "demons from hell" (the daughters) are introduced. Along the way, Sally prompts elaborations with calculated, pointed questions at key junctures. She asks about the girls' violent tempers, elicits a graphic response, then probes for elaboration. Several times, she inquires into other grave transgressions, prompting Penny to embellish her account. Sally also anticipates questions that skeptical viewers might harbor about Penny's competence as a mother, and Penny's strategies for dealing with the girls. In doing so, Sally affords Penny the opportunity to defend herself against unstated accusations and to show the wide range of remedies she has tried. This helps create a sympathetic vision of Penny as a mother who has tried to do right by her "out-of-control" children. Ultimately, Sally ventures "inside" Penny's emotions, asking her how she feels about the situation. This, of course, reveals the extent to which Penny's inner self is an emotional casualty of this domestic turmoil, further warranting her desire to "divorce" herself from her kids.

Building victims' sympathy worthiness is key to talk show construction of selves. (Compare this to Spencer's discussion in this volume of the construction of sympathy worthiness among clients of a human service agency.) It's artful identity work, but it's done using familiar cultural resources. In addition, it may involve the creation of a compassionate emotional climate as much as presenting the "facts" of a guest's circumstance. This is the objective in the following example, where Sally Jessy Raphael gently but diligently produces an atmosphere that is conducive to understanding deep "betrayal" on a show titled "We Just Said 'I Do,' Now We're Through" (3/23/99).

Sally introduces this segment by reminding viewers that Tamica, a young African American woman, had appeared on the show several weeks ago, revealing at the time that she had been unfaithful to her husband, Duane, on the fourth night of their marriage. At that time, Tamica and Duane agreed to reconcile, to try to make the marriage work. It's now four weeks later and Duane, also an African American, has telephoned Sally to report on recent developments. Sally invites him to appear on the show once more.

SALLY: Okay, last week you called us. What's wrong?

DUANE: Well, Tamica is back to her same ways again.

SALLY: What's she doing?

DUANE: She's staying out. She's not coming home. I believe she's cheating on me again.

SALLY: Why are you so desperate to save this marriage?

DUANE: Because a marriage is something that you take pride in, something that you treasure. Not something you throw away just like that. I mean, I love my wife and I made a vow to her to be with her, no matter what . . .

SALLY: How do you live like this, not being sure?

DUANE: I don't sleep at night. I take long walks at night. I think about it. I ask myself is it the right thing to do. . . . Or am I just being a fool?

At this juncture, Tamica makes her entrance from backstage, greets Duane, and sits down in the chair next to him. Her demeanor is cordial, if slightly cool.

SALLY: [To Tamica] So, what's the "*qué pasa*"?

TAMICA: I am not cheating on Duane. I'm not. He is only telling you one side of the story. . . . He goes out, he don't tell me where he goes. He's not affectionate to me. He calls me names because I've gained weight. . . . I thought I loved him.

SALLY: [Breaking in] Do you love him?

TAMICA: I care about him because he's the father of my child, but I do not love him. . . . I want to be with Darrell [the ex-boyfriend with whom she had previously cheated]. I'm sorry. . . .

SALLY: Tamica, you are being very honest. I appreciate your honesty. Are you in love with anyone else?

TAMICA: I care about Darrell. I really do. . . . Yes, I am in love with him [Darrell]. [At this point an extended, heated argument breaks out between Duane and Tamica concerning what it takes to be married.]

SALLY: Duane, are you in love with her?

DUANE: Very much. Because she's my wife. . . . Yes I am.

[Sally responds very sympathetically at length.]

TAMICA: He [Darrell] is a good man. I'm not doggin' Duane, but I deserve a good man and I don't think that I have that from him. And I want to tell you, that I'm here to tell you, I really want to get a divorce.

At this point, the video cuts abruptly to a shot of the audience, where a young African American woman rises to comment. "Hi Duane," she coos. "You are one good lookin' brother. I just want to say that I'm available, baby." And on that note, the segment ends.

Sally's interviewing technique is clearly instrumental in establishing Duane's sympathy worthiness, in making him out to be the victim in this case. She elicits his side of the story, then draws him into a verbal commitment to the sanctity of marriage in principle, and to his marriage to Tamica, specifically. While treating Tamica gently, too, Sally undermines Tamica's moral position from the start. She listens to some of Tamica's depiction of marital discord, but is clearly not interested in its elaboration. Indeed, she even avoids pursuing the issue of weight gain, which is well known to be one of Sally's favorites. At the first opportunity, Sally interrupts Tamica to bring the issue of Tamica's love and commitment to the fore. Playing off her earlier discussion with Duane, Sally gets Tamica to deny that she loves Duane, then immediately provokes Tamica to declare her love for Darrell.

The conversational production and juxtaposition of Duane's and Tamica's stances on love and marriage are clear byproducts of Sally's introduction and questioning. The lead-in divulges Tamica's "fourth-day indiscretion" and Duane is allowed to establish his willingness to stick with the marriage, despite the hurt he has suffered. When Tamica appears, Duane "obviously" comes off as the victim, an artifact of both what Sally has incited, and what she has chosen to ignore. Despite her denials of further sexual betrayal, Tamica is coaxed into admitting that her heart belongs to another, and, finally, to wanting a divorce—even though she is the one who is the marital transgressor. Finally, as if to underline Duane's sympathy worthiness, the show's editors attach the audience member's reaction, which literally embraces Duane as the object of solace and affection. It's clear that Sally and her producers have used cultural models of relational fidelity and betrayal to craft the victim and victimizer, respectively, creating both the conflict necessary to sustain viewer interest, and an emotionally satisfying resolution. Duane's upstanding character is rewarded by an audience member's advances, while Tamica is left sitting alone.

Producing Villains

Constructing victims allows the host, the audience, and perhaps even the victims themselves, to understand in an emotional, visceral way how sullied they have become, how conflict may have damaged them, and how they deserve sympathy, if not salvation. Following this thematic path, the construction of the "victim's" self almost always implicates a "victimizer." Interpretively speaking, one needs the other. Consequently, as talk shows set about designating victims, they simultaneously produce the villains that are necessary to sustain the salvational or confrontation themes of the shows. We can return to the *Sally Jessy Raphael Show* about "divorcing children" to illustrate aspects of this process.

In the segment we previously discussed, not only does Sally help construct the motivation for the audience to compassionately embrace Penny, but she subsequently helps "expose" just how bad the children really are. In order to justify Penny's desire for a "divorce," the daughters must come off as thoroughly odious. If Penny is to be a sympathy-worthy victim, her daughters need to be totally vile, completely unsympathetic. Sally is aggressively complicit in producing this outcome.

After completing her generally sympathetic interview with Penny, Sally brings the daughters, 12-year-old Ashlee and 13-year-old Amanda, onstage. They are instantly rude to Sally, to audience members, and of course, to their mother. Rather than offering the "kid gloves" treatment typically afforded children (Lowney 1999), Sally pointedly interrogates the girls, following up on Penny's accusations, underscoring Penny's indictments. She asks the girls if they steal and if they call their mother obscene names. The daughters belligerently answer yes. Sally then inquires about the allegations of sexual promiscuity. Merely questioning a 13-year-old about having unprotected sexual intercourse is symbolically degrading; eliciting a defiant answer ("Everybody has got to die sometime") solidly confirms the daughters' depravity. For a salvation episode, Sally needs to establish the segment's principal characters in order to designate who will be "saved," who will be rehabilitated. In this instance she not only depicts Penny as the sympathy-worthy victim, but simultaneously constructs the daughters as reprehensible children, the true villains of the scenario.

Confrontation shows also need their victims and villains, most obviously to spark the onstage combat that has become their stock-in-trade. Jerry Springer is masterful at "springing" a surprise revelation on an ostensibly unsuspecting guest in order to set off a combustible confrontation. And he can turn up the emotional heat of audience indignation if it can be made clear just who the "real" villain is. Consider, for example, how Jerry engineers the delivery of a relational "bombshell" in the following segment (3/15/99), where he invites a tall, attractive African American "woman" to the stage. "Diamond" has a secret to tell Ed, her boyfriend of several months. With Diamond alone onstage, Jerry begins:

JERRY: What is your secret you want to reveal?

DIAMOND: I'm really a man!

[Audience gasps, then commences to chant "Jer-ry, Jer-ry, Jer-ry."]

JERRY: And you're going to reveal this to your boyfriend? He doesn't know you're a guy?

DIAMOND: Well look at me Jerry. [Diamond is very attractive, if atypically tall for a woman. Initially she appears totally feminine.]

JERRY:	How long have you been going with him?
DIAMOND:	Three months.
JERRY:	For three months. So, you've been going out with him for three months and, uh, have you kissed him?
DIAMOND:	. . . We've kissed. We've, like, had oral sex.

[Audience gasps, boos, and chants "Jer-ry, Jer-ry."]

JERRY:	Okay. Do you love him?
DIAMOND:	I care for him. . . . I've met his family. We did stuff together on the holidays. [She continues, providing details of a family get-together.]
JERRY:	The holidays . . . and it never came up over the turkey that maybe you should tell him?
DIAMOND:	No, no . . .
JERRY:	All right, well let's see what he says.

Jerry now invites Ed to join Diamond onstage. Ed is an attractive, masculine-looking African American male. He walks confidently up to Diamond, kisses her affectionately, then takes a seat in the chair next to her. Jerry, standing in the audience, reiterates some of the history of their relationship, then turns to direct a question to Ed:

JERRY:	How long have you been together?
ED:	Three months.
JERRY:	And the relationship is good?
ED:	Yeah, fine. [Ed elaborates on the nature of the relationship.]
JERRY:	[To Diamond] Now you have something you want to tell him.
DIAMOND:	[Pause] Well, I'm really not a woman. I'm a man.

At this point, Ed rises from his seat, anger spreading across his face. He charges Diamond, they struggle hand-to-hand. Ed shoves Diamond to the floor. As stagehands intervene and the scuffle continues, Diamond distances herself from Ed, then taunts him:

DIAMOND:	You forget that under all this makeup and nails, I'm still a man.
ED:	You coulda told me that.
DIAMOND:	You didn't ask me!

Ed goes after Diamond again, more scuffling ensues, and they are separated. All the while the audience chants "Jer-ry, Jer-ry, Jer-ry." The dialogue is now virtually unintelligible with every other word a "bleeped out" obscenity. The two exchange what are plainly sexual insults regarding penis size. The crowd cheers. The guests end up vehemently calling each other "Faggot!" Throughout the exchange, Ed is indignant, Diamond defiant. Finally, Jerry gains control of the conversation, and addresses Diamond:

Look, you are what you are, and God bless you, but you have to know that you're playing with people's lives and their feelings and their hearts when you deceive them. [The segment ends as the show goes to commercial.]

Diamond is clearly the villain in this confrontation, but Jerry's stage management primes the audience's reception. While the disclosure of being a man might, in itself, provide sufficient shock to set off the desired confrontation, Jerry also gets Diamond to admit that 1) she has known Ed for quite some time, 2) they have been sexually intimate, 3) she cares for Ed, and 4) she has participated in family gatherings generally reserved for trusted intimates. In light of all this, her "secret" is even more deceitful, more treacherous. Jerry then gets Ed to confirm some of Diamond's description, and sets the stage for betrayal, humiliation, and confrontation by having Ed publicly confirm that he feels that the relationship is going well—"Yeah, fine." Ed, of course, is set up as the dupe extraordinare. Jerry has seen to that. But, not fully satisfied, Jerry, by way of conclusion, sanctimoniously reaffirms where the fault lies in this whole mess, reminding Diamond that she is, in fact, responsible for the deception. While seemingly gratuitous, Jerry's comment underscores the identities that were at stake and the self-destruction that has occurred.

Victim Contests

While conflict between victims and villains provides both grounds for salvation and fuel for confrontation, talk shows turn up the emotional heat by actively involving the host and audience in on-screen identity contents. One recurring format designed for this purpose explicitly creates a victim contest in which observers act as de facto arbiters in deciding who is the victim and who is the victimizer or villain. Sometimes the host seizes this responsibility, simply (but authoritatively and sanctimoniously) pronouncing that one guest is the "bad guy" while another has been wronged. Whether the audience agrees or disagrees, the strong opinion raises the emotional pitch and often instigates even more conflict and confrontation.

Other programming formats build character judgment explicitly into the planned action. Some shows, for example, establish the pretense that the host or audience will "impartially" or "objectively" mediate disputes between guests. For instance, a *Sally Jessy Raphael Show* (2/15/96) titled "Prove That You're Not Cheating" featured three couples in which the female partner suspected the male of infidelity. But rather than stage confrontations in the typical "accusation and rejoinder" fashion, Sally arranged for the men to take polygraph tests to ascertain the truth of the matter. What could be more objective and evenhanded?

Of course, Sally doesn't sit idly by and let the process unfold on its own. Rather, she's solicitous and supportive as the women tell their stories, often reassuring them that contrary to what the men were saying, they (the women) "were not crazy" for being suspicious. Repeatedly referring to the men as "cheaters," Sally demands that the men be truthful to their partners and skeptically—

sometimes sarcastically—parries with the men as they tell their stories. Fueling these domestic controversies with her own suspicions, Sally fans audience members' passions, building a confrontational tension that is intensified by the knowledge that *somebody* is going to be revealed as being either "crazy" or a liar. In effect, Sally uses cultural typologies to clarify the identities at stake and to set up the episode's emotional climax. The test results are withheld until the final eight minutes of the show, and they all reveal the men to be the cheating cads that their partners, Sally, and the audience "always" believed them to be.

While the polygraph is a popular tool for deciding victim contests on some talk shows, the on-screen paternity test is even more exciting, since the suspense entailed adds to a contest's dramatic realization. Another growing favorite embroils the audience in elections over victimhood. Jenny Jones regularly allows viewers to vote for who is right and wrong, good or bad, guilty or innocent. As she put it at the beginning of one show (4/15/99), "I'll be judge Jenny and you can be my jury."

This episode, titled "I Want My Stuff Back," is a classic confrontation show in that the explicit aim is to create and adjudicate discord and, in the process, to decide who is the villain and who is the victim. Family members or close friends comprise the guest pairings. In each segment, one party claims that the other has inappropriately or unfairly expropriated his or her property and won't give it back. One side tells a story, then the other responds. For example, a pair of female former roommates wrangle over possession of household items after they've moved into separate apartments. One claims that the other has kept her stereo, TV, VCR, and some clothes for over a year and won't let her take them back. In another segment, a daughter insists that her parents won't let her claim her rightful personal possessions—a new TV, kitchenware, and the like—after the parents "threw [her] out of the house." The parents counter with tales of the daughter borrowing money to buy the stuff, signing loan agreements with them, then failing to repay any of the money.

The format of this show resembles many of the mock courtroom shows so popular on daytime TV (for example, *People's Court, Judge Judy*), but without the legal trappings. Jenny attempts some mediation but, in the end, she allows the audience to decide who should get to keep "the stuff" in each case. Audience members are outfitted with prepared signs that they hold up to indicate their votes. Each segment concludes with the vote and comments from the audience as to why the vote was justified. The sorts of disputes adjudicated in this fashion range from property claims and legal rights to highly personal opinions (for example, "You May Be Proud of What You've Got, But a Model You Are Not!").

The significant feature of such shows in relation to guests' identities is that self-construction becomes a formally institutionalized part of the programming format. It's neither accidental nor incidental; the express objective of such shows is to endorse locally embodied identities. Such shows quite deliberately constitute the selves they need to entertain; indeed, the self-construction process becomes part of the entertainment itself.

Confounding the Distinction

Whereas salvational shows may require victims to be saved and confrontational shows thrive on the clash of good and evil, both have considerable latitude with respect to how characters might be developed to suit their needs. While victims and villains are integral components, they need not be diametrically opposed to achieve the desired effect. Indeed, on some shows it appears that as long as a plethora of character flaws and aberrant behavior emerges, it doesn't matter much who is at fault or who reaps the most harm. Many shows of this type literally commingle victimhood and villainy in the same characters, denying any pure distinction, but building confrontational and salvational possibilities along the way. Consider the following excerpt, again from *The Jerry Springer Show* (3/15/99).

The second segment of this show involves a couple—Heather and Rick—who had been together for seven years. Heather is introduced first—a young, attractive, white female, dressed casually and provocatively, braless with bare midriff. She enters confidently, even defiantly, resembling Rocky Balboa dancing into a boxing ring. Jerry's introduction indicates that Heather doesn't consider Rick to be her partner any longer. He's now her "ex," Heather claims, and he will not leave Heather and her new boyfriend alone. The implication is that Rick is somehow stalking or harassing them.

The audience initially gasps and groans in sympathy as Heather urges them on, claiming that Rick demands that she choose between him and her family, a choice she alleges Rick originally forced upon her when Heather was only 15 years old. She chose Rick, and he then moved Heather to some far-off places where she felt isolated from all other aspects of her former life. Heather then recounts a recent incident when Rick told Heather that if she (Heather) didn't "have sex with another woman" (apparently Rick wanted to watch), he would abandon Heather. Despite her bravado, Heather is obviously staking claim to being the victim of Rick's domestic domination, if not his sexual perversion.

Now Jerry invites Rick on stage, and Rick appears with a bouquet of flowers. He is a young, slightly built white male, not very imposing in stature or demeanor. The image is not one of the domestic dictator that Heather implied; instead, Rick projects the figure of a sincere, gentle suitor—an almost classic romantic archetype. As he approaches Heather with the flowers, they exchange words:

HEATHER: Don't come by me. [She curses him vehemently at length, berating him about his "girlfriend," and complaining that Rick is harassing Heather and her new boyfriend, Billy.]

RICK: I'm not up here to fight with you. I'm up here to tell you that I love you. . . .

HEATHER: Are you gonna tell your girlfriend that you love me?

RICK: Yeah, I'm gonna tell her. I love *you*. . . . I know that I want a relationship, that I want my family back. You got my kids. [This is the first mention of children as part of the relationship.]

HEATHER: [Goes on to say that Rick is no father to the kids and that they now

> call her new boyfriend "Daddy."] . . . I'm not going to let you see the kids as long as you have a girlfriend.

RICK: . . . You should not keep those kids from their father. . . . I won't have them calling no other guy Daddy.

At this point, Heather launches an extended complaint about how Rick has mistreated her over the years. She recounts an incident when she was eight months pregnant and Rick took the money that she had been saving for a baby crib and used it to play poker. Rick denies this. On another occasion when one of the children was sick, Heather claims, she had to call Rick five times to get him to take the child to the hospital.

When Jerry finally takes command of the conversation, he turns to Rick: "Rick, you say you want to be back with her but you have a girlfriend." "Yeah," Rick replies, " I got a girlfriend." At this point Jerry invites Michele, Rick's girlfriend, onstage, and she immediately assaults Heather. They scuffle and are separated by stagehands, invectives and obscenities flying freely. The audience chants "Jer-ry, Jer-ry." Rick stands by helplessly, shaking his head, finally taking a seat between the two women, who continue to curse each other. Michele is trying to tell Jerry that Rick has made repeated attempts to see the kids, each time to be thwarted by Heather, but soon the two women are fighting again. As stagehands separate them, Michele sternly challenges Heather: "Come on, bitch, come and get it."

Jerry now summons Heather's new boyfriend, Billy. No sooner is he onstage than Rick charges at him and a brawl ensues. The crowd cheers and chants "Jer-ry." The onstage dialogue now consists almost entirely of "bleeped-out" obscenities. The women continue to scream at one another. Eventually, we hear Michele ask Heather how she supports the kids, to which Heather replies that she has a job.

MICHELE: What kind of a job, bitch?

HEATHER: I'm a dancer.

MICHELE: So, you spread your legs for everyone.

Amid the confusion and confrontation, the segment ends as the show goes to commercial.

During this interaction, Heather and Rick repeatedly swapped "victim" and "villain" identities. The initial trajectory of the segment cast Heather as the victim of Rick's domineering ways, but Rick's meek presence, attempts at reconciliation, and professions of love and devotion to Heather and their children turn the tables on Heather. Now she's the "bad" one who curtly rejects the father of her children. Introducing Michele and Billy provides the confrontational icing on this dysfunctional family cake. Their presence physically embodies the complications to what started out as a seemingly simple story of domestic tyranny (also see Loseke, this volume).

The ethos of the confrontation show calls for conflicting personas, but sets no demands on moral purity or self-constructional consistency. Assuredly, villains and victims are fuel for incendiary interpersonal relations, but roles and identities needn't be firmly affixed. Indeed, there appears to be a perverse appeal to situations in which sin and virtue shift back and forth in the give-and-take of accusations and condemnations. Enduring moral certainty takes a back seat to immediate, flagrant transgression. Salvation only requires that someone, at some juncture, be amenable to rehabilitation or redemption. Confrontation demands someone to "dish it out" and someone to "take it," but there's no fundamental need to establish a permanent hierarchy of sympathy or blame. Pure conflict, not its explanation or resolution, is the objective; confounding the victim and villain identities may heighten, not undermine, the explosiveness of the outrageous interpersonal showdowns that talk shows cultivate.

Talk show hosts eagerly play upon the thirst for confrontation. Whereas we saw earlier how Sally Jessy Raphael, on occasion, works hard to clearly establish victims and villains, on other occasions, hosts simply promote conflict, letting the identity chips fall where they may. There's an almost perverse delight in exposing one party, then the other, as the cad of the moment. On one episode of *The Jerry Springer Show* (4/12/99), for instance, the theme of "Scandalous Confessions" would seemingly capitalize on one partner admitting something scandalous, while the other suffered its indignity. It's a surefire recipe in the villain/victim paradigm. Jerry, however, has some tricks up his sleeve.

After the initial revelation is played out at the start of each segment, open conflict predictably erupts. Through the cursing and fighting, the transgressor and the victim clearly emerge. Then Jerry introduces a new twist. Addressing the momentarily prevailing "victim," he coyly asks, "And now what surprise do you have to tell [your partner]?" In each instance, the second revelation is more startling and egregious than the first.

In one segment, for example, Eric makes his scandalous confession, telling his steady girlfriend, Kiki, that he has been sleeping with her sister, Shannon. After a few moments of Eric's futile explanations and Kiki's indignant outrage, Kiki spits back that she (Kiki) has been sleeping with Eric's sister, who now rushes onstage and into Kiki's arms. Homosexuality trumps infidelity as the confrontational grounds shift and the mantles of victim and villain transmute before our very eyes. Partners scuffle with partners, siblings pummel siblings. The women grope each other shamelessly in an open display of sexual passion while their brother/lover looks on.

The original designations of victim and villain are lost in the confusion. To be sure, transgressors and human casualties abound, but the distinction between their embodiments blurs as different individuals occupy the roles. Victim and villain personas remain crucial, but a prevalent moral agnosticism makes it unnecessary to affix them permanently. As elements of sheer confrontation, their inconstancy provides renewable resources for outrage, a seemingly inexhaustible supply of surprises, and targets of indignation.

"Take Care of Yourself"

Perhaps there's no good reason to watch daytime TV talk shows. But millions still do. Part of the reason may lie in the identity formulas we see enacted day after day, so predictably that we know, before we actually see the particulars, that two guests on *The Jerry Springer Show* are going to end up fighting. The selves that talk shows construct for their guests provide outrageous entertainment, to be sure, but they also serve as constant exemplars that may very well serve a self-identifying function.

Jerry Springer and his ilk offer characters who captivate our interests, in part, simply by displaying unforgivable transgressions, despicable selves, and brute passions. Viewers' responses are largely visceral, unthinking reactions to the graphic and energetic staging of acts and persons so contemptible, so atrocious, that they nearly defy belief—even among viewers whose everyday lives desensitize them to the rude, crude, violent, and bizarre. We watch for the same reasons freak shows and automobile accidents attract attention; we're inexplicably drawn to the hideous, to the outlandish selves talk shows construct for our viewing pleasure. The victim/villain contrast adds to our intrigue.

At the same time, these selves provide viewers with points of reference against which viewers must assuredly compare favorably. The extremes of relational insensitivity, defiance of social convention, and disdain for civility probably outpace even our most unseemly behaviors, on even our worst days. They're negative identity exemplars of a sort, living embodiments of *what we are not*. As Emile Durkheim (1964) told us long ago, we need the visible presence of the "pathological" to assure us of what is "normal." Talk shows may help us sense the boundaries of the acceptable; by negative example, they show us the normative contours of self and society (Erikson 1964).

At least that's what Jerry Springer might want us to think. Indeed, his shows routinely point this out to us, as they did on the "Scandalous Confessions" episode we discussed earlier. The final segment of the show involved two sisters who learned on the show that they had both been sleeping with the same man. The revelation was accompanied with the chaos, physical attacks, recriminations, and vulgar denunciations that typify Jerry's shows. But even though he'd betrayed both women, the sisters were still fighting over the man. In the show's final segment, Jerry usually allows audience members to take the microphone and ask questions of the guests—although the questions often turn into vile indictments. In this particular instance, a young woman of approximately the same age as the female guests took the microphone. Addressing the two combative women, and referring to the insults and recriminations that they had previously exchanged, the audience member asked a question and made her point:

> You said he [the man sleeping with the two sisters] had a little (pause) a little weenie. Well tell me, why was you up there fightin' with your sister over a guy with a little weenie? You never catch me doin' somethin' like that.

The point is clear. Talk shows demonstrate things that we should never do; they construct selves that we should never be. "You never catch me doin' somethin' like that." Durkheim couldn't have said it better himself. But, of course, Jerry tries.

In the epilogue to the show, he serves up his daily sermonette. All the guests are now onstage, over a dozen in all. They're packed in, disheveled from the combat, a veritable sideshow of the morally depraved. Ripped clothing dangles from necks and shoulders. Hairpieces are missing. Two men stand naked from the waist up, their shirts completely destroyed, their bodies scratched and bleeding. Jerry is poised alongside this motley crew, on the set, not in the audience. He turns to the guests, thanks them for appearing on the show, then continues:

> I hope you are able, if not to repair your relationships, at least, ah, your family relationships. I hope you're able to work that out. Good luck to you. [Turning to face the camera.] You know, in case you're wondering, this is not how most people live. Most of us don't sleep with our boyfriend's or girlfriend's sister. We don't grab the lover of a cousin. We don't screw our best friend's mate. Most of us aren't like that. I don't know, the moral fiber seems nonexistent here, and the only thing more lacking than good sense is respect. There's no respect for family, for bedmates, for even the most basic customs and traditions of society. It's little more than "I'll sleep with who I want, when I want, the hell with all of you." I know how often we have heard on these shows, "Hey it just happened," or "We'd been drinking." Well, that, of course, is no excuse. Look, a good rule of thumb to remember here is that, as you are heading for the bedroom or the backseat of the car, if (pause) the face you're with is one you've seen around the Thanksgiving dinner table, or other family functions, then just say no. 'Til next time, take care of yourself and each other.

The message is clear. Jerry has used these characters to teach us all a valuable lesson in social relations. He constructs these selves so we may learn from them. But mark his words well, talk show guests. Guard your selves, because Jerry will surely appropriate them to his own purposes. Take care of your selves, or Jerry will take care of them for you.

REFERENCES

Abt, Vicki, and Leonard Mustazza. 1997. *Coming After Oprah: Cultural Fallout in the Age of the TV Talk Show.* Bowling Green, Ohio: Bowling Green State University.

Abt, Vicki, and Mel Seesholtz. 1994. "The Shameless World of Phil, Sally, and Oprah: Television Talk Shows and the Deconstructing of Society." *Journal of Popular Culture.* 28:171–91.

Durkheim, Emile. 1964. *The Rules of Sociological Method.* New York: Free Press.

Erikson, Kai. 1964. "Notes on the Sociology of Deviance." In *The Other Side,* ed. Howard S. Becker, 9–21. New York: Free Press.

Gamson, Joshua. 1998. *Freaks Talk Back.* Chicago: University of Chicago Press.

Goffman, Erving. 1959. *The Presentation of Self in Everyday Life.* New York: Anchor.

Heaton, Jeanne Albronda, and Nona Leigh Wilson. 1995. *Tuning in Trouble: Talk TV's Destructive Impact on Mental Health.* San Francisco: Jossey-Bass.

Holstein, James A., and Jaber F. Gubrium. 1995. *The Active Interview.* Thousand Oaks, Calif.: Sage.

———. 2000. *The Self We Live By: Narrative Identity in a Postmodern World.* New York: Oxford University Press.

Holstein, James A., and Gale Miller. 1990. "Rethinking Victimization: An Interactional Approach to Victimology." *Symbolic Interaction* 13:103–22.

Hughes, Everett C. 1984. *The Sociological Eye.* New Brunswick, N.J.: Transaction Books.

Kuhn, Thomas. 1962. *The Structure of Scientific Revolution.* Chicago: University of Chicago Press.

Lowney, Kathleen S. 1994. "Speak of the Devil: Talk Shows and the Social Construction of Satanism." In *Perspectives on Social Problems,* vol. 6, ed. James A. Holstein and Gale Miller, 99–128. Greenwich, Conn.: JAI Press.

———. 1999. *Baring Our Souls: TV Talk Shows and the Religion of Recovery.* Hawthorne, N.Y.: Aldine de Gruyter.

Schutz, Alfred. 1970. *On Phenomenology and Social Relations.* Chicago: University of Chicago Press.

Snow, Robert P. 1983. *Creating Media Culture.* Beverly Hills: Sage.

Twitchell, J. B. 1992. *Carnival Culture: The Trashing of Taste in America.* New York: Columbia University Press.

MELVIN POLLNER AND JILL STEIN

Doubled Over in Laughter
Humor and the Construction of Selves in Alcoholics Anonymous

Intellectual currents ranging from the classical sociological tradition to recent postmodern thinking have eroded the status of the self as a natural feature of lived experience. The "shape and form" (Gubrium and Holstein 1994, p. 699) of the self and, indeed, its very availability as a category of experience are increasingly appreciated as a sociohistorically shaped, institutionally mediated, and interactionally realized construction. The academic recognition of the contingency of the self is enmeshed with developments in the culture at large. The multiplicity and diversity of discourses circulating in everyday life regarding the self contributes to a popular sense of the self's fluidity and malleability. Some have suggested that the panoply of incommensurable definitions and demands "saturates" (Gergen 1991) the conventional self, producing a "multiphrenia" that subverts the desirability or possibility of a unified "I."

Yet the developments that contribute to the postmodern tide of definitions of selfhood on the one hand provide safe harbors on the other. To be sure, an ever-increasing number of organizations, professions, and professionals proffer versions and visions of one or another aspect of subjectivity—soul, self, or psyche. The discourses and programs of the "psy complex" (Rose 1998), New Age and traditional religious organizations, and the Twelve-Step and recovery movements, are important expressions of the "deprivatization of experience" (Gubrium and Holstein 1995). These and kindred self-processing agents and agencies stipulate the substance and dynamics of subjectivity and provide programs through which the imputed qualities and capacities of the self are formed and reformed. Although an encounter with these varied versions of the self might induce the vertigo envisioned by postmodernists (themselves promoting a discourse specifying yet another shape of the self—albeit amorphous and multiphrenic), anchorage in a particular version offers a grounding in the putative swirl of the postmodern condition.

"Doubling" in Alcoholics Anonymous

A concern with the dynamics through which versions of subjectivity are disseminated and appropriated necessarily turns to one of the most rapidly growing of all self-processing organizations—Alcoholics Anonymous (AA). By its own account, Alcoholics Anonymous is a self-help program for persons who want to stop drinking. The AA program depicts alcoholism as a disease, an "allergy of the body and an obsession of the mind" (Alcoholics Anonymous 1976). The disease is three-fold: "spiritual, mental and physical," and intimately linked to the self. In the words of the most important AA text, known as the "Big Book":

> Selfishness—self-centeredness! That, we think, is the root of our troubles. Driven by a hundred forms of fear, self-delusion, self-seeking, and self-pity, we step on the toes of our fellows and they retaliate . . . our troubles, we think, are basically of our own making. They arise out of ourselves, and the alcoholic is an extreme example of self-will run riot, though he usually doesn't think so. (Alcoholics Anonymous 1976, p. 62)

Sobriety is achieved and maintained by abstinence, following or "working" the Twelve Steps and attending meetings. The steps themselves include acknowledging that one's life had become unmanageable and turning one's will and life over to "a higher power." The rest of the steps call upon members to take a moral inventory of their character defects, make amends to those harmed, continue to take personal inventory, practice prayer and meditation, and carry the message to other alcoholics. Because one is unalterably an alcoholic—"Once an alcoholic, always an alcoholic" (Alcoholics Anonymous 1976, p. 33)—recovery is a ceaseless process. Thus, members are encouraged to take "one day at a time" and to "keep coming back." Speaker meetings, one of several kinds of AA meeting formats, are open to friends, family, and interested outsiders. They feature one or more individuals "telling their story" in accord with the AA suggestion to speak about "what we used to be like, what happened, and what we are like now" (Alcoholics Anonymous 1976). Newcomers are encouraged to attend many meetings in a short period of time and assured that they will eventually hear a story that is similar to theirs. AA groups exist in 141 countries and include an estimated two million members (Makela et al. 1996). As many as one out of 10 adults in the United States may have attended at least one meeting. AA has served as the prototype for 12-step programs for other problems including narcotics, gambling, overeating, and sex.

In many self-processing organizations, the self (or one of its aspects) is defined as inferior, superficial, or pathological and juxtaposed to a superior (actual or attainable), authentic, or healthy self (cf. James 1961). Self-processing organizations introduce and amplify these distinctions, frequently in the context of expert or experienced others, and provide procedures that facilitate "transformation" or "growth" toward the ideal self. In AA, participants are encouraged to understand themselves as "alcoholics" whose lives, thoughts, and actions are dominated by desires, impulses, and "defects of character" over which they have no control. In thus defining themselves, however, another source of thought and action—the "recovering self"—is discursively constituted. In uttering the well known phrase "I am an alcoholic" and thus acknowledging an uncontrolled inner force, the rudiments of the recovering self are given voice: the recovering self is other than, and aware of, the alcoholic self as a potent and insidious source of trouble. In this sense, the alcoholic and recovering selves are twin born.

Doubling of the self is encouraged in a variety of AA practices but perhaps no more so than through opportunities to talk about oneself. In telling "what we used to be like, what happened, and what we are like now," one must necessarily "double back on himself, reflect on himself, hear himself talk and locate himself within a structure of experience in which he is both object and subject to himself" (Denzin 1993, p.345). These narratives are often marbled with humor. Indeed, despite the seriousness of problem drinking and the austerity of AA's public image, AA literature identifies humor as a significant part of the program and members extol the pivotal importance of humor in their recovery. Norman Denzin (1993, pp. 324–25) suggests that until the speaker can inject humor into his or her AA talk, he will not have learned the full meaning of being an AA speaker and that a member's standing partly reflects his humorous distancing from his past. The occurrence of laughter, members say, marks or enables a significant change in self-understanding. Nate, a well-known speaker, describes how laughter allowed a new understanding of himself.

> You see I discovered through the laughter of the program I could clear out the wreckage of my past. Through the laughter I discovered a way to take a thousand pounds of guilt off my back and I laid it down. And through that laughter I discovered that I could truly make a transition. That I no longer had to be that taker, that hustler. I can be a giver, and by being a giver, I will have the world.

The alcoholic self is a recurrent target of humor in AA. When members tell their stories before an audience of other members, their narratives frequently include humorous commentary on wayward or shameful actions: a priest, for example, tells "how he got so pie-eyed at the Eucharist the congregation were lucky they got the wafer in their mouth, because generally they got it in the ear or even the eye" (Bennett 1995, p. 110). The butt of such self-deprecation is the self when it is dominated by alcohol and, more generally, by the pattern of thinking that AA believes accompanies alcoholism. Because the qualities of body, mind, and character comprising the alcoholic self can insidiously emerge even when the individual is not drinking, self-deprecation extends to episodes when individuals are well into "recovery" and find they are still—and always will be—susceptible to the thrall of the alcoholic self.

Humor and laughter are potent resources in doubling the self and more generally in disseminating and appropriating the interpretive procedures for respecifying the self. An essential component of humor is incongruity, typically between two incompatible or conflicting matrices of meaning (Koestler 1964; Oring 1992). The incongruity of humor invites and requires a cognitive doubling in which a situation viewed from one perspective is suddenly viewed from another. Relatedly, humor frequently involves an element of "superiority" in which an individual or group is denigrated while another is implicitly elevated (Gruner 1997). The recovering self adumbrated in AA doctrine is the privileged perspective from which the inferiority or absurdity of the alcoholic self is constituted as humorous. Further, humor involves the release of emotional energy that literally convulses the body. Indeed, laughter might be heard as the embodied explosion simultaneously creating and heralding the discursive rift that will subsequently distinguish alcoholic and recovering selves. Finally, the social context of humor and laughter means that the explosive effects are mutually audible and visible. In laughing with others at the absurdities and profanities of the alcoholic self, one is immersed in a powerful display of consensual affirmation of the appropriateness of the distinction. In effect, laughter divides the self as it displays the unity of the group.

The contribution of self-deprecating humor to articulating the substance and shaping the form of doubled selves in AA is our central focus in this chapter. First, we illustrate how humor is aimed at the alcoholic self. In effect, virtually every aspect of the alcoholic self—behavior, orientation, character, and thought—is the target of mockery and denigration. Second, we consider how these humorous tales of ineptitude, impropriety, and disorientation serve as resources for constructing both individual and collective identity. We suggest that humor and laughter display and induce the bifurcation into recovering and alcoholic selves, specify the alcoholic self as a "trickster" (Apte 1985), provide an opportunity for collective "attunement" (Trix 1993) and affirmation, and serve as a source of attraction by simulating the effects of alcohol.

Our analysis uses transcribed audiotapes of narratives (talks or "pitches") delivered at a variety of AA meetings. We purchased these tapes from organizations producing and distributing materials pertaining to AA and the "recovery movement." The speakers are not a representative sample of AA members, talks, or contexts. They include a disproportionate number of better-known members, often with long-term sobriety, invited to speak at larger meetings and regional conventions. One of the reasons that such members are invited to speak is that they are especially engaging and frequently humorous. These recordings were supplemented with observation of meetings in the Los Angeles area open to outsiders. These field observations suggest that the forms and functions of humor we identify are common in the narratives of more experienced members regardless of setting.

Features and Targets of Self-Deprecating Humor

As a prelude to focusing on the specific targets of self-deprecating humor, it is useful to consider several general features of humor in AA narratives. First, the narratives vary in the incidence and use of humor. In some, humor is a spontaneous and minor aspect of a narrative otherwise constructed in a serious register. Other narratives, however, are humorous throughout and may include anecdotes and observations that have likely been honed before other AA audiences. When the humorous mode (Mulkay 1988) is prominent, it often emerges at the outset, typically through teasing about an aspect of the meeting or the members.

For example, as she was about to speak, Penny chided the chair of a regional meeting in California who asked members for their city or place of origin but neglected to mention Los Angeles, "that little hamlet down the road"; Ginny offered a jocular insult in her very introduction: "My name is Ginny and I am an alcoholic and please don't call me Jeannie, Jennie, Jannie, Joanie, or Judy as some asshole called me the other day." Richard scatters a barrage of jocular barbs that skewer the preceding speaker, the person who gave him directions to the meeting and the state from which she came, the site of the meeting, and all members who live in the area.

RICHARD: Hello everybody, my name is Richard and I'm an alcoholic.

AUDIENCE: Hi, Richard!

RICHARD: Hang on, I want to try something here. This is Sherry's cup. I want to make sure it don't screw up my speech like it did hers. [Audience laughs.] Uh, I'm a little upset that Bobby's not here. I wanted to personally tell her about her directions that she gave me to get to this place. [Audience laughs.] Matter of fact, she'll get a collect call when she gets back to Texas. Anybody that spends any time in Texas oughta be chastised a little bit anyway. Where I'm from in Oklahoma, we refer to that part of the country as Baja Oklahoma. [Audience laughs.] I remember stopping here quite a bit. My father was in the oil fields and we used to spend a lot of time down here. A lovely place in the summertime. It's almost as nice as Bakersfield. [Audience laughs.] By the way, well I mean hell, I used to be from Bakersfield, but I got smart for Christ sakes. [Audience laughs.]

Humorous or not, the typical personal narrative is a tale of redemption or salvation: a self in unmanageable and destructive turmoil is transcended and reconstituted through the fellowship of AA, God or a higher power, and the 12 steps. Even the most jocular of narratives—perhaps especially those—conclude with a solemn tribute to how AA has restored the speaker's dignity, self-respect, and sanity.

Second, the humor is embedded in the rich oral and textual culture of AA. Appreciation of more subtle or ironic references requires the ear of experience (Pollner and Stein 1996), that is, a hearing informed by the background knowledge accumulated through membership and participation in the program. Consider, for example, a speaker's comment that the personal story he was about to relate is "the same thing you hear from everybody else, only mine's greater," which was greeted by laughter. The humor compacted within this "throwaway line" is constructed and appreciated by reference to the knowledge that alcoholics have pride as a character defect and that the idea that all alcoholics' stories are similar is encouraged in AA. Thus, in effect, the speaker asserts a commitment to the program phrased in the manner that the program intends to overcome. Absent the familiarity with the local cultural understandings of the similarity of alcoholics' stories and their endemic boastfulness, however, the humorous impact is akin to the sound of a tree falling in the forest with no one to hear it. The inaccessibility of some AA humor to newcomers is itself an object of commentary: old-timers, for example, may recount their perplexity at the first meetings they attended when seemingly innocuous or inappropriate remarks received gales of laughter.

Third, there is considerable acumen in making laughter happen. In his paper "Funny Mirrors and the Social Construction of Humor," Jack Katz (1996) described persons observing themselves in a funhouse hall of distorting mirrors. His analysis shows how laughter at the grotesque images reflected back to individuals and their companions involves a subtle communicative accomplishment. Peering into the mirror and observing the distorted reflection alone is not sufficient to elicit laughter from oneself or others: the distortion must be mutually appreciated by the individual and (what might fittingly be termed) his peer group. Self-debasement in AA is a metaphorical inspection of distorted reflections in narrative mirrors. Speakers narratively develop images that show them to have been (and to be) incompetent, immoral, disoriented, or indifferent regarding conventional roles and responsibilities.

"It is often not realized that considerable laughter," writes Joyce Hertzler (1970, p. 86–87), "whether of individuals or collectivities, occurs when role performance upsets expectations. We laugh when persons in some way depart from the standard behavior set for them as friends, parents, children, husbands and wives . . . or in almost any other activity characteristic of or essential to a social system." If divergence from the conventional and normative are raw resources of humor (cf. Davis 1993), then problem drinkers are unusually blessed in the experiences that they can mine. Yet, as in the funhouse, communicative coordination must occur if laughter rather than, say, tears are to emerge (as they sometimes do). Indeed, the stuff of self-deprecating humor in AA is equally serviceable as a source of disgust and despair. A variety of comic techniques are mobilized to establish that the reflection is offered humorously and as something other than the speaker's current self. Thus, as we shall shortly see, episodes as extraordinarily painful as a mother sewing her finger to a moccasin at a Cub Scout gathering are alchemically transformed into humorous stories eliciting much laughter.

We turn then to illustrate the spectrum of behaviors, orientations, and qualities of mind and character that are frequent targets of self-deprecating humor. In AA, these tales of deviance and disorientation proclaim the ways of the alcoholic self as they denounce them.

Misbehavior

A catalogue of incongruities emerges from the incapacity to appropriately comport or control oneself. In the following excerpt, Ginny describes how her drinking prevented her from performing her role as a parent. She was so incapacitated that she learned what she had fed her children the previous night by the food stains on their clothing and cheered for the wrong team at her son's Little League baseball games. These artfully told incidents build to Ginny's recounting of an excruciatingly painful episode of incompetence that receives much laughter.

> GINNY: The worst part of it was being a housewife and trying to be what society says you're supposed to be. And "let's go to PTA meetings." I was always drunk or was hung over. And I would volunteer for all these things, you know, headed the Valentine committee and they'd call me up and they'd say [mimics voice], "you're not here, you're supposed to be here making hearts," you know. [Audience laughs.] Now I never could get to those things. [Audience laughs.] Or I'd go to the Little League

game and root for the wrong damn team. [Audience laughs.] Little bottle in my skirt. [Audience laughs.] And we made moccasins once in Cub Scouts, and I remember sewing it, honest to God I can still feel it, onto my finger. [Audience laughs.] Well you might laugh, but I finally had to give up all that fun stuff, all that degradation, all the self-hatred, all the guilt, all the anger, all the shame, all those wonderful things.

If alcohol impairs competent action, it also lifts conventional inhibitions, thus permitting or inducing actions that might otherwise have been held in check. Lou, for example, describes how he would become belligerent when stopped for drunken driving. As is common in AA humor, misbehaviors are ironically described as having their own logic or aesthetic and requiring a measure of skill to bring them off in an effectively self-destructive manner. Thus, Lou describes his technique of becoming progressively more insulting and obscene in his encounters with the police, thereby increasing the likelihood that he will be treated harshly.

LOU: You see, they did me a favor. And I used to take a lot of badge numbers. Any of you drunks ever take a badge number? [Audience laughs.] Boy, if that won't get the shit beat out of you nothing will. [Audience laughs.] You know they'd arrest me, some old boy about eight feet tall and nine feet wide. [Audience laughs.] And I'd look at them and I'd say, "Hey you mother. [Audience laughs.] I want your badge number. [Audience laughs.] I'm a taxpayer in Kern County; you're harassing me." [Audience laughs.] Never paid taxes in my goddamn life. [Audience laughs.] But I wouldn't stop there. [Audience laughs.] I'd wait until I'd get in a crowd of deputy sheriffs. [Audience laughs.] And then you tell them about their mother. [Audience laughs.] Now, if that don't get 'em, then tell them, say, "Yeah and you son of a bitch [audience laughs], I was out with your sister last night." [Audience laughs.] Now that'll get you slapped clean into next week. [Audience laughs.] You see? That's the kind of dumb crap I would pull.

Finally, behaviors directly related to drinking, such as vomiting or incontinence, provide a source of earthy humor redolent of Mikhail Bakhtin's "grotesque body" (1984). Using a variant of the ironic aesthetic of degradation, Penny describes her early failures and subsequent expertise in vomiting.

PENNY: A lot of people come to Alcoholics Anonymous and they have wonderful stories behind them, you know, they had 47 arrests by the time they were 20. Some people have got 86 times in the mental hospital, you know, and I didn't have any of that. The best I can say about me is you are probably looking at the best puker [audience laughs] that has ever come to Alcoholics Anonymous. [Audience laughs.] I am the champ. [Audience laughs.] But it took some training. It took some years to know to lay on the bathroom floor on the cold tile. I didn't know that at 14. I didn't know you were supposed to put your arms lovingly around the toilet bowl. [Audience laughs.] How do I know that at 14? I didn't know you were supposed to get your face very close so nothing splashes. [Audience laughs.] I didn't know that at 14. I was a novice, you understand?

Disorientation

Another source of self-deprecatory humor is the alcoholic's loss of contact with reality. The alcoholic misperceives, misinterprets, misappraises, denies, or is oblivious to what others would regard as obvious, objective, and appropriate. The alcoholic self is enmeshed in a web of distorted, confused, or limited versions of both himself and the world. One form of disorientation that can be turned to humorous advantage is loss of consciousness. Earl, for example, identifies himself as a blackout drinker who would return to consciousness in the midst of circumstances he didn't immediately understand. Speaking on behalf of himself and others who have done this "hundreds of times," he describes the artful strategy of waiting to find out what he had done.

EARL: Blackouts were the normal fare for me. I've "come to" in lots of very weird situations. Come to on Speedway in Venice, talking to four policemen. I have no idea what we're talking about. Just one of those times when you just go, "bing!" [Audience laughs.] You know. [Audience laughs.] Feels like real late at night, and there's four policemen, and they seem very upset. [Audience laughs.] Hmmm. And you know what to do. You've done it 100 times. You just keep your hands where they can see them, and you just nod to whichever one is talking to you, and eventually you're going to find out what's going on. It wouldn't be any use to say, "Excuse me officers, I just got here. [Audience laughs.] It's just a little trick I do where I'm here, I'm not here, I'm here, I'm not here." [Audience laughs.] Ugh. [Audience laughs.]

Other forms of disorientation involve misinterpretation. Charlie, for example, portrays his erroneous interpretation of the judge's ruling regarding alimony payments in his second divorce:

CHARLIE: In 1950, I was standing in front of the judge again because, uh, I had gotten married again to a young gal and, um, she had a baby and then she left me because I was a drunk. And, uh, the judge is looking down, then he says, "I'm gonna give your wife $100 a month for the next 21 years." And I thought, "well that's pretty nice of you your honor, I'll try to give her a couple a bucks myself." [Audience laughs.]

Charlie further develops his odyssey of disorientation by illustrating his impoverished appraisal of what might be recognized by the judge as an acceptable explanation of what he was doing at the time he was arrested.

CHARLIE: In 1950, they threw me in the West Los Angeles jail for drunken driving. In 1951, in the Wilshire Station jail for drunk and malicious mischief. In 1952, I'm standing in front of the Malibu judge and he says,

"What were you doing out there on the Pacific Coast Highway, walking along in the rain and the mud at 3:00 in the morning?" And I said "Well, your honor, I'm a salesman, and I was planning to make a house call." Well, he didn't buy that. He said, "What did you have in your hand?" I said, "It was my briefcase your honor." He says, "No, it says here you were dragging a barstool along." [Audience laughs.]

Disorientation occurs not only with regard to outer reality but with regard to subjective reality. In a variety of ways, alcoholics are represented as disoriented about themselves, their emotions, and their difficulties. Their acrobatic efforts to avoid acknowledging the inner and outer turmoil—and to stay in "denial"—can be the stuff of humorous self-deprecation. Mike recites the rationalizations that helped him avoid recognizing that he was an alcoholic.

MIKE: I wasn't looking forward to this. I resisted this program right down to the bitter end. And I think most alcoholics did. Hell, the day before I came into the program, I wasn't even an alcoholic. No, I was a heavy drinker and a victim of unusual circumstances, rotten drivers, and bad whisky, [Audience laughs.] but I ain't no alcoholic. [Audience laughs.]

The first AA meeting is frequently the occasion of discordant perceptions and judgments. At this point, the alcoholic encounters members who have already begun the process of recovery. From the limited and distorted point of view of an alcoholic entering the program, the very congeniality of members is threatening and suspect. Earl relates his experience as a newcomer.

EARL: Every meeting has got that guy with 90 days sober that just caught fire with Alcoholics Anonymous, [Audience laughs.] gonna give it away tonight. [Audience laughs.] You know who it was gentleman sitting right over there, we go way back. Yeah, Vegas spotted me, and all he saw was a newcomer. I was throwing him every signal I could—you come near me and we're going for it. And it wasn't working. Inside I was just going, "Oh my God, ha-ha, man look at this guy" [Audience laughs.] His, like, hair is all combed and he's neat and he's tidy, and he's got on this big smile. You can't trust a person that smiles like that. [Audience laughs.] And he's coming at me with his hand out like this. And he comes up and he says, "Hi my name is Vegas and I'm an alcoholic." And I said, "So what [audience laughs], me too man, and it ain't exactly the highlight of my life. [Audience laughs.] I don't know what you're so happy about. [Audience laughs.] Get away from me." [Audience laughs.] And he looked at me, and he gave me that very knowing thing. [Audience laughs.] He looked at me and he said, "Keep coming back." [Audience laughs.] Now I'm sitting there thinking, great, "keep coming back," what the hell does that mean? You know a couple of other guys were standing over there and went, oh yeah, you know he did the "keep coming back" thing. [Audience laughs.] Like this was of some deep spiritual significance. [Audience laughs.]

Defects of Character and Thought

The culture of AA portrays alcoholics as driven by pride, resentment, and dishonesty with themselves and toward others. These "defects of character" are often to be found at the roots of misbehavior and disorientation and give rise to a host of other defects. Bob, a Catholic priest, for example, tells of his once prideful lack of humility in describing his relationship in seminary to the man who would eventually become the pope:

BOB: And he's known today as Pope John Paul II. Now there was a time when I would have told you the pope went to school with me. [Audience laughs.] But since I became humble, now I just say I went to school with the pope. [Audience laughs.]

Nate narrates a story that epitomizes a "typical alky" as he might awaken from a drunken slumber. The tale is a litany of misbehavior and disorientation: sleeping in the car, vomiting against a closed window, driving on a flat tire until the tires come off, falling out of the car onto the lawn, all while maintaining prideful concern over how he might appear to others:

NATE: Then you wake up a couple of days later in the front seat of your car, you know. He's sleeping there again, we have a lot of car sleepers in AA. [Audience laughs.] Hey, it helps us get into AA, that, you know, having your head screwed up under that armrest all night and the door handle in your ear. You ever wake up about midnight and you're just sick as hell and you think your window's down but it's up? [Audience laughs.] Oooh [audience laughs], and you heave right into your window [audience laughs], and you knock the hell right out of your head. [Audience laughs.] And then a typical alcoholic, he rolls the window down squish squish squish, right? [Audience laughs.] Yeah. And then he sits there and says to himself "Why don't I roll it down before I heaved on it I wonder?" [Audience laughs.] Well these are big problems, major problems in the life of an alcoholic. But then I gotta go home. And I gotta wash the car out. But on the way home you have a flat tire. But you never change it. Well, not if you're drinking, you don't. You might hurt yourself. And no self-respecting alcoholic will change a flat tire, he'll drive on it. [Audience laughs.] Because he knows it will go away, right? Because everything that's disagreeable in our life will go away. We never face anything, it'll go away, and it does. Tire goes away. You are now driving on the rim. [Audience laughs.] We have a lot of rim drivers in AA. [Audience laughs.] And the sparks fly, and the neighbors run out, they get all the kids out of the way, you pull the car into the driveway over the lawn, open the door, and you fall out. [Audience laughs.] And then we lay out there for a while so the neighbors might inspect us [audience laughs], say, "Oh, there he is [audience laughs], yes, yes." [Audience laughs.] And then the poor old alky gets up and he says to himself, "I wonder if anybody saw me?" [Audience laughs.] Yes. Because he's worried about what people think about him. All alcoholics worry about their reputations. We never do anything about it, [audience laughs], we worry a lot about it though. [Audience laughs.]

In the following, anger and obsessiveness are featured as the sources of problematic behavior. Bob's obsessiveness—often seen as entwined with pridefulness—leads him to engage in meditation with an almost self-defeating kind of intensity. Moreover, the obsessively long period of meditation does not prevent the resurgence of anger, which asserts itself once he gets in his car. Significantly, the same qualities of the alcoholic self are present eight years into recovery.

BOB: My biggest problem probably in early recovery for a number of years was anger. And it seemed to be connected to my ignition key, for some reason. [Audience laughs.] Now I am compulsive and obsessive. You can give me something to do that's good for me and I can probably almost kill myself with it. [Audience laughs.] We will take meditation as an example. Someone said meditation is good for you. I discovered that if you meditate you can leave your body. [Audience laughs.] I had, you know, been involved in a lot of near-death situations trying to leave my body. This is a good concept, I like this concept of leaving my body. I reached a point eight years clean and sober where I would get up at 4:00 in the morning and meditate for four hours before leaving the house. After four hours in the lap of God, the thunder of silence, and beauty of spirituality, I would go downstairs, get in my car, start it up, get out the driveway, turn right on Doheny, and someone, some poor unenlightened, uninformed human being would fail to use their turn signal. [Audience laughs.] This would result in a hundred-mile-an-hour chase down Doheny Blvd [audience laughs], with me with my head hanging out the window, with foam coming out of my mouth [audience laughs], screaming obscenities like a mad dog. [Audience laughs.] If we were all fortunate, I never caught the poor son of a bitch, you know. If we weren't, I could be found standing in the middle of somebody's hood in an intersection trying to explain to them politely what the little lever on the left side of their steering wheel was for. [Audience laughs.] Which they did not seem to want to get out and talk about. But I would then proceed from there to the meeting, pull into the parking lot of the meeting, wipe off the foam [audience laughs], brush the hair back from, you know, being windblown from my head hanging out the window. Walk up to the door and there would be the greeter, who'd say, "Hey Bob, how are you?" [Audience laughs.] "Fine, thanks." [Audience laughs.]

The Trickster, Transcendence, and Laughter

A social constructionist reading of the apocryphal aphorism "You don't have to have a soul unless you really want one" (Geertz 1973, p. 108) is that a soul requires a certain kind of interpretive work through which the "soul" is posited, addressed, engaged, and cared for. So it is with other inner entities: what will be found within and what its qualities will be—and, indeed, that there is a "within" or "subjectivity" in the first place—is suffused by the interpretive and discursive resources that posit and articulate the inner world and the practices for its navigation. As they specify the substance and dynamics of subjectivity and invite attention to it, self-processing organizations constitute and colonize subjectivity (Berger 1966).

It is no surprise that humor and laughter may be mobilized as part of the technology of the construction and reconstruction of the self. Certainly, at the colloquial level, "laughing at oneself" is understood to show that one may have "transcended" one's troubles and that in laughing at oneself, one is no longer within oneself (Jefferson 1984). Ironically, humorous observations about one's own ineptness and inadequacy often yield positive gains for both the humorist and the audience. Neal Norrick (1993, p. 79) suggests that tellers "gain credit for not taking themselves too seriously" and for their capacity to manage or transcend adversity. The collective laughter and the subsequent sharing of other self-deprecating stories, in turn, contributes to rapport among participants. Thus, if, as has been suggested, the humorist is a kind of shaman (Mintz 1985), then the jocular sacrifice of his self enhances both his personal stature and the cohesion of the little tribe of laughers gathered around him. Indeed, humor and laughter may be involved in the ministrations of actual shamans in actual tribes. In traditional healing ceremonies in Sri Lanka (Amarasingham 1973), for example, the cause of physical or mental distress is represented as a demon. Often the demon's outlandish appearance and behavior in the ritual context are sufficient to evoke a mixture of apprehension and amusement. During the ceremony, the demon is derisively mocked, eliciting yet more laughter. The "Vadda" is a "dirty, wild, aggressive, and uncivilized being" whose transformation is partly achieved through "laughing at the characteristics which have made him ominous" (1973, p. 155).

For AA, the alcoholic self is also dirty, wild, aggressive, and uncivilized, a part of the alcoholic that can never be completely exorcised but must be ceaselessly transcended "one day at a time" by the recovering self. AA speakers mobilize the powers and properties of humor and laughter to disseminate and display these very understandings of the alcoholic and recovering selves. Specifically, we suggest that self-deprecating humor contributes to narratively constructing the alcoholic self as a "trickster within," facilitates the transcendence of the trickster-like alcoholic self, attunes members to AA precepts, and sustains interest and engagement by simulating the effects of alcohol.

The Trickster Within

Members' tales of impropriety and disorientation reflect, construct, and disseminate an image of the alcoholic self. There is an intriguing resemblance between the alcoholic self imaged through text, talk, and humor in AA and the amusing and amazing character found in the myth and folklore of many societies: the trickster. Blair Moffett (1979) provides a synopsis of part of the trickster's typical odyssey:

> This outlandish yet remarkable thing in human form learns, grows in understanding, changes and, at a certain point in his adventuresome blunders, is transformed. Until that moment, however, Trickster keeps changing shape and experimenting with a thousand identities including shifts in sex, in a seemingly never-ending search for himself. During all this he inflicts great damage on all those around him and also suffers innumerable blows, defeats, indignities, and dangers resulting from his thoughtless, reckless forays. On entering upon existence he is first seen as a blurred, chaotic hardly unified being having no self-knowledge or life-knowledge despite his divine parenthood.

Although qualities of the trickster vary across cultures, Mahadev Apte (1985) has identified several modal characteristics. The trickster is distinct from humans by virtue of his special origins. Similarly, the alcoholic self is understood to be distinct by virtue of the nature of the disease. As the Big Book states, the alcoholic is "bodily and mentally different from his fellows" (Alcoholics Anonymous 1976). Apte notes that "Tricksters frequently change form. They seem to switch back and forth from an anthropomorphic to a theriomorphic form" (1985, p. 226). The trickster's capacity to change from human to animal form is paralleled by the alcoholic's reversion from ostensible composure and conventionality to unrestrained impulsive and destructive actions. Moreover, even sobriety—ostensible humanness as it were—may at times take on some manifestation of the trickster-like alcoholic self. The so-called "dry drunk" is but the alcoholic self in the member who is not drinking. "Tricksters are primarily preoccupied with satisfying their basal desires and with deriving pleasure," and, as Apte (1985, p. 226–27) continues, "In pursuit of such aims, tricksters totally disregard the established social norms . . . frequently act in a haphazard manner . . . suffer injuries and pain that they try to inflict on others . . . punished for breaking taboos . . . trickster's behavior reflects a relationship of contest to the world." As we have seen, story after story in AA, humorous or otherwise, is a tale of basal desire, social impropriety, and haphazard actions that produce injury and pain for the alcoholic and for others. Finally, the trickster's personalities combine opposing traits in an unusual way: "They are powerful, clever, selfish, cruel, deceitful, cunning, and sly. They are also boastful, foolish, lazy, and ineffective" (1985, p. 227). The catalogue of contrary qualities is remarkable in its resemblance to the qualities attributed to alcoholics.

In effect, the text, talk, and self-deprecating humor of AA convey and construct an image of alcohol as "cunning, baffling, and powerful," a trickster insinuated in the alcoholic's body, mind, and spirit. Variously termed the "disease," "alcoholism," or "alcoholic thinking, " the ever-present trickster within seduces or overwhelms the capacity for prudent action and judgment. The self-deprecating humor is characteristically targeted at those episodes when the trickster—whose identity is unknown to itself—asserts itself in a buffoonish, absurd, and

destructive manner. As such, humor and laughter often occur early in the chrono-
logically ordered narratives of AA, for as the trickster within becomes aware of
itself by identifying as an alcoholic, the resources for humor diminish.

Transcending the Trickster

As AA constructs and illuminates the ways of the trickster in the lives of alcoholics, it also provides the resources for transcendence. The "trickster inside"
(Weinberg 1997) is transcended through differentiating and distancing oneself
from the source of the unmanageable behavior: the tricksterlike alcoholic self is
objectified as a part of, yet distinct from, the individual. As Denzin (1993) notes,
doubling enables the individual "to turn back on himself . . . and distance himself from who he previously was."

The self-stories told in AA contribute to doubling in several ways. The very
act of speaking about oneself (in public), for example, differentiates the speaker
from the self that is spoken about in the tale. Further, the prespecified format of
self-stories encourages if not stipulates the distinction between what she was like
before and after joining AA. Self-deprecating humor extends and (literally) am-
plifies the doubling powers of narrative for speakers (and their audience). As
Arthur Koestler (1964) has so eloquently argued, doubling is inherent in humor
itself. Humor requires simultaneously entertaining—or "bisociating"—two ordi-
narily incompatible matrices of meaning. The self-debasing humor involves the
bisociation of alcoholic and conventional frames of reference. Many of the behaviors are humorous by virtue of their contrast with conventional norms of behavior and the precepts of AA. If tellers are giving and hearers are getting the
humor, they are necessarily—if only for the instant of laughter—thrust out of the
perspective of the alcoholic self and into the perspective of the recovering self. In
giving (and getting) the humor, speakers necessarily attain an added measure of
distance from what they once were. As Nate said (in the very first excerpt): "You
see I discovered through the laughter of the program I could clear out the wreck-
age of my past. Through the laughter I discovered a way to take a thousand
pounds of guilt off my back, and I laid it down. And through the laughter I discovered that I could truly make a transition. That I no longer had to be that taker,
that hustler. I can be a giver, and by being a giver, I will have the world."

Attunement

Self-deprecating humor plays a role in imparting lessons about the trickster. Aspects of the dynamic are suggested in Frances Trix's (1993) analysis of her learning and development with her Islamic master. She proposes that at the heart of
the dialogue between herself and her teacher is the process of "attunement." One
sense of attunement is taken from Alton Becker (1984, cited in Trix 1993), who described it as the process of self-correction in the philologist's effort to decipher the
meaning and world of a distant text. A second aspect is derived from David Blum's
(1986, cited in Trix 1993) study of the Guarneri Quartet, which describes attunement as a "fifth presence" in which all members of the quartet are playing as
one: "It is as if the music is playing them." In the context of her own study of a

single exchange between herself and her teacher, Trix defined attunement as increasing coordination and convergence through "play-full" recollecting of dialogue with one another.

Although the situation of Trix and her teacher do not fully parallel the relation
of speaker and audience in AA, members are indeed encouraged to attune themselves with the precepts of the initially "distant world" of AA and old-timers are
inclined to share their wisdom (Pollner and Stein 1996). In the playful or humorous recollecting of their pasts, speakers (implicitly and explicitly) invite members
to understand themselves as alcoholic selves on a journey of recovery. To be sure,
lessons of doubling and transcendence may be imparted in a serious monologue,
but humorous formulation of the trickster allows an unusually obvious and intense
expression of attunement: precisely to the extent the hearer understands the
speaker—to the extent she "gets it"—she makes audible rhythmic noises and her
body shakes (cf. Katz 1996). She is singing and dancing. In this context, laughter *is*
the music of the message imparted through self-deprecation: "It is as though the
music is playing them." The instant of attunement attained and expressed through
laughter can be surprising and moving, as this excerpt from Penny attests:

> But I'm going to tell you what I heard the very first night at my very first meet-
> ing. I heard the strangest sound that I had heard in the last two years. And it came
> from way down in here inside of me. And it bubbled up and it came out my
> mouth. You know what it was? It was laughter. I laughed out loud. I hadn't
> laughed in so long. And I guess I laughed because I identified with the guy.

The public character of attunement has collective consequences. The construction of humor necessarily involves collective values and expectations. Humor requires background understandings about the actual or ideal nature of self
and society, if only to be subverted or critiqued. In unavoidably invoking a set of
norms or ideals, humor has a moral dimension and the comedian is a "disguised
moralist" (Coser 1959). The inadequacies of the speaker targeted in self-deprecation are constituted as such by communally shared standards regarding appropriate conduct. Every jocular reference to misbehavior, disorientation, and defect
of character is simultaneously a reference to the ideals of the recovering self. Thus,
as the speaker mocks himself, he provides occasion to celebrate the very standards by which his earlier incarnations have fallen short. Indeed, the AA humorist
plays what Lawrence Mintz (1985, p. 74) refers to as "comic spokesman" who,
"as a part of the public ritual of standup comedy, serves as shaman leading us in
a celebration of a community of shared culture, of homogeneous understanding
and expectation."

The collective response to statements of group values is a primordial sociological moment. In his seminal statement of the rituals through which societies
reaffirm, integrate, and constitute themselves as such, Emile Durkheim wrote:
"Every society feels the need to reaffirm the collective ideas and sentiments that
make up its identity. Yet this moral remaking cannot be achieved except by means
of reunions, assemblies, and meetings where the individuals, being closely united
to one another, reaffirm in common their common sentiments" (1961, p. 474–75;

see Trevino 1992). Reviewing the sparse ethnographic reports of the simple societies that he felt allowed him to witness this process in pristine form, Durkeim conjectured the high excitement at such communal gatherings: "On every side one sees nothing but violent gestures, cries, veritable howls, and deafening noises of every sort, which aid in intensifying still more the state of mind which they manifest" (1961, p. 247).

Again, a distinctive feature of the *humorous* expressions of moral stances is that they provide an opportunity for an immediate and collectively hearable response: laughter. Koestler (1964) writes that laughter is the Geiger counter of humor. In the context of an AA meeting, everyone hears everyone else's Geiger counter. Thus, in laughing (or not), participants provide one another with mutually hearable evidence of their endorsement—or lack thereof—of the norms and values implicitly evoked. It is a moment of collective attunement when everyone hears one another's tune. In this sense, humor-laughter sequences are significant vehicles through which collective identity is constructed and reaffirmed. When the response is strong, one is indeed surrounded by "cries, veritable howls, and deafening noises of every sort, which aid in intensifying still more the state of mind which they manifest."

Attractions

The personal stories of others offer insights and inspiration for understanding one's difficulties. Although the eventual dividends are great, they are relatively slow in maturing. An immediate payoff of humorous self-deprecation—tales about the trickster, as it were—is fun. Observing an AA meeting to which he accompanied a friend, Alan Bennett (1995, p. 110) observed that general tales of degradation are boring but specific stories about bad behavior are entertaining. Thus, humorous self-deprecation might serve as an incentive to "keep coming back," as Johnny explains in the next excerpt.

> JOHNNY: The thing I did like about the meeting, though I didn't let any of you know it, was that I liked that fact that you guys would laugh at inappropriate things. [Audience laughs.] I liked that. [Audience laughs.] There was a guy who was sharing that while drunk, backing out of his driveway, he accidentally ran over his wife. [Audience laughs.] And everybody laughed. [Audience laughs.] Even his wife was there, sitting in the front row, and she was laughing. [Audience laughs.] She limped a little bit, but she was laughing. [Audience laughs.] What a crazy place.

Beyond the generic appeal of fun, the attractions of humor in AA may be intensified by the intriguing isomorphism between humor and laughter and drinking and drunkenness. The embodied, experiential, and cognitive effects of humor bear an arguable similarity to those of alcohol and other psychoactive substances. Like alcohol, for example, humor affects composure and control of the body. The "punch" of a punchline literally produces paroxysms that deconstruct the body. Relatedly, just as psychoactive substances may produce euphoria—a high—the humorous mode induces its own lightness. In the humorous mode, persons experience freedom from the "gravity" of the constraints and conventions of the serious world. In other words, levity, the root of the word *levitation* (and *alleviates*) levitates: persons get a lift or get high. Finally, just as psychoactives affect the capacity or inclination for conventional reason and cognition, humor permits and even encourages reveling in the contradictory, absurd, and fantastic (Mulkay 1988). Thus, humor may be especially attractive as it simulates the very substance from which members are abstaining.

The Last Laugh

The deprivatization of experience (Gubrium and Holstein 1995) brings the inner recesses of subjectivity under the auspices of organizationally situated public discourse and practice. Indeed, the very notion of an inner recess and perhaps subjectivity itself are constituted in such discourse and practice. One expression of the deprivatization of experience is the emergence of organizations and professions proffering definitions of a new self and guidance in how it can be attained. Sometimes welded into explicit programs, they promise to transform or replace painful or pathological selves with fuller, truer, or deeper selves.

The division between profane and sacred elements of subjectivity is often "talked into being" (Heritage 1984). As participants use the local discourse to formulate (and thus form) their selves, they are tutored to distinguish the authentic, real, and positive from the (now to be seen as) superficial, false, and destructive selves. In addition to talk and texts, humor makes a distinctive contribution to self-doubling—at least in AA. Self-deprecatory humor engagingly articulates the tricksterlike qualities of the alcoholic self. One learns in an appealing way of the capacities of a dangerous "other within." Simultaneously, humor shows—not merely describes— the possibility of transcendence: the humor bifurcates the humorist into the perduring alcoholic self *and* the continuously re-created recovering self. Members in the audience, in turn, are literally and figuratively doubled over in (and by) an explosion of laughter. The collective laughter attunes participants to the version of the powers and possibilities by which they understand themselves to be inhabited. Each laugh, then, constitutes, articulates, reflects, broadcasts, and reaffirms the profane and sacred selves putatively lodged within. As members give and get the jokes, they laugh themselves into being.

REFERENCES

Alcoholics Anonymous. [1939] 1976. *Alcoholics Anonymous: The Story of How Many Thousands of Men and Women Have Recovered from Alcoholism*. 3rd ed. New York: Alcoholics Anonymous World Service.
Amarasingham, Lorna Rhodes. 1973. "Laughter as Cure: Joking and Exorcism in a Sinalese Curing Ritual." Ph.D. diss., Cornell University.
Apte, Mahadev L. 1985. *Humor and Laughter: An Anthropological Approach*. Ithaca: Cornell University Press.

Bakhtin, Mikhail. 1984. *Rabelais and His World.* Trans. Helene Iswolsky. Bloomington, Ind.: Indiana University Press.

Becker, Alton. 1984. "Philology and Logophilia: An Exploratory Essay." Henry Hoijer lecture. University of Southern California.

Bennett, Alan. 1995. *Writing Home.* New York: Random House.

Berger, Peter L. 1966. "Identity as a Problem in the Sociology of Knowledge." *Journal of Sociology* 7:105–15.

Blum, David. 1986. *The Art of Quartet Playing: The Guarneri Quartet in Conversation with David Blum.* New York: Knopf.

Coser, Rose Laub. 1959. "Some Social Functions of Laughter: A Study of Humor in a Hospital Setting." *Human Relations* 12:171–82.

Davis, Murray S. 1993. *What's So Funny: The Comic Conception of Culture and Society.* Chicago: University of Chicago Press.

Denzin, Norman. 1993. *The Alcoholic Society: Addiction and Recovery of the Self.* New Brunswick, N.J.: Transaction Publishers.

Durkheim, Emile. 1961. *The Elementary Forms of the Religious Life.* New York: Collier.

Geertz, Clifford. 1973. *The Interpretation of Cultures.* New York: Basic Books.

Gergen, Kenneth. 1991. *The Saturated Self.* New York: Basic Books.

Gruner, Charles R. 1997. *The Game of Humor: A Comprehensive Theory of Why We Laugh.* New Brunswick, N.J.: Transaction.

Gubrium, Jaber F., and James A. Holstein. 1994. "Grounding the Postmodern Self." *Sociological Quarterly* 38: 685–703.

———. 1995. "Qualitative Inquiry and the Deprivatization of Experience." *Qualitative Inquiry* 1:204–22.

Heritage, John. 1984. *Garfinkel and Ethnomethodology.* Cambridge: Polity.

Hertzler, Joyce O. 1970. *Laughter: A Socio-Scientific Analysis.* New York: Exposition Press.

James, William. [1902] 1961. *Varieties of Religious Experience.* London: Collier-Macmillan.

Jefferson, Gail. 1984. "On the Organization of Laughter in Talk About Troubles." In *Structures of Social Action,* ed. J. Maxwell Atkinson and John Heritage, 346–69 Cambridge: Cambridge University Press.

Katz, Jack. 1996. "Funny Mirrors and the Social Construction of Humor." *American Journal of Sociology* 101: 1,194–237.

Koestler, Arthur. 1964. *The Act of Creation.* New York: Dell.

Makela, Klaus, et al. 1996. *Alcoholics Anonymous as a Mutual-Help Movement.* Madison, Wisc.: University of Wisconsin Press.

Mintz, Lawrence E. 1985. "Standup Comedy as Social and Cultural Mediation." *American Quarterly* 37(1): 71–80.

Moffett, Blair A. 1979. "Mind: Trickster, Transformer." *Sunrise Magazine.* November.

Mulkay, Michael. 1988. *On Humour: Its Nature and Place in Modern Society.* Cambridge: Polity Press.

Norrick, Neal R. 1993. *Conversational Joking: Humor in Everyday Talk.* Bloomington, Ind.: Indiana University Press.

Oring, Elliott. 1992. *Jokes and Their Relations.* Lexington, Ky.: University of Kentucky Press.

Pollner, Melvin, and Jill Stein. 1996. "Narrative Mapping of Social Worlds: The Voice of Experience in Alcoholics Anonymous." *Symbolic Interaction* 19(3): 203–23.

Rose, Nikolas. 1998. *Inventing Our Selves: Psychology, Power and Personhood.* Cambridge: Cambridge University Press.

Trevino, Javier. 1992. "Alcoholics Anonymous as Durkheimian Religion." In *Research in the Social Scientific Study of Religion,* ed. Monty Lynn and David Moberg. Volume 4, 183–208. Greenwich, Conn.: JAI Press.

Trix, Frances. 1993. *Spiritual Discourse: Learning with an Islamic Master.* Philadelphia: University of Pennsylvania Press.

Weinberg, Darin. 1997. "The Social Construction of Non-Human Agency: The Case of Mental Disorder." *Social Problems* 44: 217–34.

GALE MILLER

Changing the Subject
Self-Construction in Brief Therapy

> Two psychiatrists are sitting on the beach. They notice a man
> on the horizon who seems to be drowning. The man goes un-
> der for dangerously long periods of time, only to reappear fran-
> tically waving his arms. The faint sound of "help me, help me"
> comes from the general direction of the drowning man. One psy-
> chiatrist turns to the other and says, "Now, there's a man with
> a problem," to which the other replies, "Yes, but it's good that
> he's talking about it."

This joke, told by a practitioner of brief therapy, presents an obviously absurd situation, since a drowning man clearly doesn't have time for a lengthy discussion
about his problem. How could any discussion lead to a solution to the man's immediate problem? But that's not important for the purpose of this chapter. Silly
as it may sound in the context of the joke, the psychiatrist is making a significant
point about personal problems in general: the man is talking about his troubles.
If we take this just a bit seriously, it raises the possibility that individuals actually
do construct their identities, lives, and problems in their talk. This, in turn, leads
us to the realization that discourse is a key to producing troubled selves and situations, and, just as relevant, that talk is the means through which solutions are
constituted. This chapter examines how troubled identities are discursively organized within brief therapy. It focuses, in particular, on how changing discursive
environments in a brief therapy agency altered therapy talk to produce contrasting senses of the subject and his or her troubles, as well as the solutions appropriate to them.

Brief Therapy as an Institutional Discourse

Brief therapy is an important recent development in counseling, one that does not
easily fit within the traditions of either family therapy or psychotherapy (Miller
1997a; Miller and de Shazer 1998). The distinctiveness of brief therapy is related
to its emphasis on solving clients' problems as quickly as possible. This can be
contrasted with the long-term orientation of other approaches, especially psy-
choanalysis. Brief therapists characterize the latter approaches as structuralist,
meaning that the approaches assume that the sources of clients' problems are
deep-seated—often hidden—and may be related to basic pathologies or deficits

in clients' personalities. These assumptions, brief therapists explain, make complex and extended analyses of clients' psyches and biographies necessary. Brief therapists themselves emphasize instead how clients' problems can be solved in the short term. Central to their approach is the assumption that clients are competent or normal people who effectively manage their lives most of the time. They are not sick. Rather, they are "stuck," being unable to effectively use their normal problem-solving skills and knowledge to deal with their troubles.

The following is an "ethnography of institutional discourse" (see Miller 1994, 1997b) that describes the arrangement and use of language in brief therapists' interactions with clients and other therapists. It analyzes these institutional circumstances and their discursive practices as conditions of possibility (Foucault 1977) within which some social relationships and realities—especially, particular subjects—are more likely to emerge than others. In a related fashion, the analysis treats brief therapy as an instance of what Michel Foucault (1988) calls technologies of the self. Technologies, for Foucault, are knowledge systems or "truth games" associated with techniques that people use to make sense of life experiences, to construct themselves as kinds of people, and to understand the social worlds within which they participate. Technologies of the self are distinctive because they involve knowledge and techniques that permit interacting individuals to constitute "their own bodies and souls, thoughts, conduct, and way of being, so as to transform themselves in order to attain a certain state of happiness, purity, wisdom, or perfection, or immortality" (Foucault 1988, p. 18).

This approach has affinities with some recent developments in social theory (Douglas 1986; Holstein 1992; Fox 1999; Gubrium 1989; Loseke 1989, 1993; Spencer 1994). It raises issues discussed by Ian Hacking (1986) as aspects of his dynamic nominalist approach to "making up people," which is concerned with how people construct different kinds of institutional selves by applying cultural categories to themselves and others. The approach stresses how making up people involves both situational considerations and more general discursive factors. Hacking instructs us to attend to how each instance of making up people is a discursively organized event, yet remains somewhat different from all other instances of making up people.

Hacking argues that we can better see how, in socially constructing institutional selves, we also construct horizons of possibility for our own and others' lives. What he calls making up people involves more than considering the discursively provided "facts" of persons' past and present lives. It also includes orientations to what was possible in the past, what is possible in the present, and what might be possible in the future. It isn't just that the drowning man talks through his problem, but that particular forms of talk, or discourses, shape the actual course of talk and its personal consequences. These issues are central to this chapter because brief therapists "change the subjects" of their conversations with clients and each other in response to the discursive options available to them in particular discursive environments. They do this in relation to the institutional discourse within which they conduct their activities, and the related practical contingencies of their interactions with each other.

The Shifting Discursive Environment of Brief Therapy

My analysis centers on how a shift in the discursive environment of a renowned brief therapy clinic led to a striking change in the way therapists and clients talked about clients' subjectivities. The clinic in question—here called "Northland Clinic"—shifted its therapeutic approach from an ecosystemic version of brief therapy to solution-focused brief therapy. This, in turn, led to a significant change in the way clients' selves and troubles were constructed, producing distinct institutional identities. In recent years Northland Clinic has taken a leading role in transforming the basic conceptual and discursive orientation of brief therapy (see Miller 1997a, 1997c). Many brief therapists have moved away from the ecosystemic assumptions and practices associated with family therapy (de Shazer 1982) and toward the more radical assumptions and practices known as solution-focused brief therapy (de Shazer 1988). The shift in Northland's discursive environment both fueled and responded to this change.

Ecosystemic brief therapists orient to their clients' lives, problems, and subjectivities as aspects of clients' social systems (Miller 1987). These social systems consist of the various linkages between clients' social relationships and activities, such as clients' family, work, and school relationships and activities. Clients' social systems also include clients' unique perspectives, as well as the values that clients share with others in these systems. Much of ecosystemic brief therapy involves therapists making assessments of their clients' social systems, and constructing intervention strategies designed to change the systems (Miller 1986). Within the discourse of ecosystemic therapy, clients are defined by their membership in social systems, and therapists are experts on assessing and changing the systems. Clients' institutional roles and selves involve reporting on the social systems of which they are a part, and initiating the systemic changes recommended by their therapists.

Solution-focused brief therapists, in contrast, emphasize how their clients' lives, problems, and subjectivities are socially constructed in language. They adopt a Wittgensteinian (1958) orientation to their professional relationships with clients by treating problems and solutions as language games and forms of life (de Shazer 1991, 1994; Miller and de Shazer 1998). These are socially organized ways of constructing, and living in, social worlds. Solution-focused brief therapists argue that clients and others frequently "play" the language game of "problems" by describing themselves as without resources for effectively managing their lives and as powerless to provide solutions. The therapists go on to state that a major failing of conventional structural therapy is its focus on clients' problems, not on clients' articulations of the problems. One practical effect of the conventional approach is that it risks making clients' problems bigger and more intractable than is necessary or useful for clients.

As the name suggests, solution-focused brief therapists prefer to talk with their clients about solutions. Solutions talk differs from problems talk in its focus on the times when clients' problems are not so severe, on the problem-solving skills and knowledge that clients possess, and on other reasons why clients should expect their lives to be better in the future. Solution-focused brief therapists justify this emphasis on practical grounds, stating that the solution-focused language game is a quicker and more effective route to change. As Insoo Kim Berg (1994, p. 10) explains,

> Solution-focused brief therapists believe that it is easier and more profitable to construct solutions than to dissolve problems. It is also easier to repeat already successful behavior patterns than it is to try to stop or change existing problematic behavior. Furthermore, they believe that activities that center around finding solutions are distinctively different from problem-solving activities. For example, the activities a worker may engage in to "protect a child" from his abusive or neglectful parent are quite different from those designed to "build safety" for the same child. What the worker does becomes even more different when he looks for and finds instances when the parent is already successful in insuring the safety of the child, even a little bit and even if it occurs only occasionally. Getting the client to repeat her successful method of child rearing is easier than trying to teach her totally new and foreign skills.

In addition to conveying the practical emphasis of solution-focused therapy, this statement points to some important aspects of the social construction of institutional selves in solution-focused therapy. Clients are carriers of solutions, even if they aren't yet aware of this circumstance, and therapists are specialists at helping their clients identify the solutions that are already present in clients' lives. Solution-focused therapists are, in other words, adept—even expert—"players" of the solutions language game.

Ecosystemic brief therapy and solution-focused brief therapy are related—but separate—institutional discourses and environments for doing brief therapy (Miller and Silverman 1995). They are most obviously related because solution-focused brief therapy was invented by a group of therapists seeking to develop more streamlined and effective strategies. The discourses are distinctive because they involve different epistemological assumptions about social and personal transformation, different practical strategies for creating change in clients' lives, and different therapist-client relationships. Stated another way, the institutional discourses of ecosystemic and solution-focused therapy provide brief therapists with somewhat different conversational subjects and resources for interacting about their professional activities, relationships, and selves. The decision to shift from ecosystemic to solution-focused brief therapy involves a change of subject and subjectivity that is akin to that which takes place in brief therapist-client interactions, and which has direct implications for those interactions.

Northland Clinic

Northland Clinic was a major site of this shift in institutional discourse. Indeed, it had long been a major center for brief therapy training and practices in general, and was the primary setting in which solution-focused therapy actually was invented. From here, solution-focused therapy has spread to diverse international sites in Asia, South America, Australia, Africa, and Europe. My research at Northland includes two 12-month periods of intensive observation in 1984–85 and 1988–89, and continued observations at various levels of intensity from 1989 to the present. During this time, I have observed hundreds of therapy sessions and many training workshops and seminars. I have augmented the observational data gathered at Northland by reading the professional literature on brief therapy, by attending professional conferences concerned with brief therapy, and by reviewing videotapes of therapy sessions conducted by therapists who are unaffiliated with the clinic. I draw upon each of these experiences in analyzing the changing construction of institutional selves in shifting from ecosystemic to solution-focused therapy.

Northland Clinic is located in a city in the upper Midwest region of the United States. The clinic has evolved remarkably over the years, beginning in the living room of the founder's home and eventually becoming an independent entity. During much of the research period, the clinic was located in the central city area, although the staff served clients from all parts of the metropolitan area and beyond, including some who traveled from distant regions of the United States. The clinic's clientele also represented a cross-section of social classes, ethnic groups, and ages, who presented the clinic staff with a variety of problems. For example, I have observed therapy sessions concerned with disputes between family members, incorrigible children, drug and alcohol dependence, domestic abuse, homelessness, employment problems, depression, and behaviors diagnosed by others as evidence of various mental illnesses.

At Northland, ecosystemic and solution-focused therapy are team activities made up of therapists, clients, and support teams. The teams consist of other therapists who observe sessions from rooms adjoining the interviewing rooms in which therapists and clients meet. The interviewing and observation rooms are linked by one-way mirrors and an in-house speaker system that make it possible for team members to unobtrusively observe and listen to ongoing interviews. The observation and interviewing rooms are also linked by telephone connections that team members sometimes use to intervene in ongoing therapy sessions. Team members call to ask for additional information and clarifications from clients, and to suggest new questioning strategies to therapists.

Both ecosystemic and solution-focused therapy sessions have three major parts—the interview, the team meeting, and the delivery of the intervention message. The number of clients involved in therapy interviews ranges from one client to all of the members of large families. During most of the research period, the vast majority of therapy sessions conducted at the clinic involved one to three clients. About two-thirds of the way through each session, the interviewing therapists inform clients that they are going to take a break in order to meet with their teams. The meetings take place in the observation rooms and without clients. The major focus of therapist-team meetings is on developing intervention messages that are written down and later read to the clients. Brief therapy sessions end with the reading of these intervention messages to clients.

My analysis of self-construction in brief therapy involves more than a simple contrast of one institutional discourse with the other. While I do argue that ecosystemic and solution-focused brief therapy are conditions of possibility for constructing different kinds of problems, solutions, and selves, I also believe that it is possible to overemphasize the differences between these institutional discourses to the extent that we overlook how change and continuity are simultaneous aspects of the construction of subjectivity. It is significant, for example, that the Northland Clinic therapists invented solution-focused therapy in order to more effectively achieve the practical aims of ecosystemic therapy. Equally important, both ecosystemic and solution-focused therapy involve changing clients' lives and selves by using resources and opportunities that are already present in clients' lives (Erickson 1967). I develop these analytic themes in the next two sections, which focus on the details of problems, solutions, and self-construction in ecosystemic and solution-focused therapy.

Constructing Context in Ecosystemic Therapy

Ecosystemic therapists treat their clients' subjectivities as embedded in social systems. While somewhat different for everyone, persons' social systems form social contexts within which troubles emerge, persist, and may be changed. Ecosystemic therapists also stress that the elements of persons' social systems are connected in both direct and indirect ways, making it impossible for therapists to identify single causes for clients' troubles. Rather than focus on problem causes, then, ecosystemic brief therapists ask their clients to describe the concrete details of clients' everyday lives and relationships with others, including clients' and others' perspectives on the issues at hand. Ecosystemic therapists describe these questions as aspects of mapping clients' social systems. The therapists use clients' answers to mapping questions to socially construct clients as the directs of social systems forces and themselves as professional therapists.

Consider, for example, the following exchange involving a family made up of two parents and three children (Jim and Sarah are two of the children). The parents requested the meeting to discuss problems caused by the children, whom the parents described as disrespectful. The exchange followed a discussion by the parents of their children's most troublesome behaviors and attitudes. According to the parents, their children frequently shout at others and act in disruptive ways, behaviors that the parents portrayed as signs of the children's anger and crabbiness.

THERAPIST: So how come Sarah is the crabbiest? [pause]

JIM: I know.

THERAPIST: Why?

JIM: She has a bad temper. [pause]

THERAPIST: She always has? [pause]

JIM: Yes, pretty much, she takes after my dad. [pause]

THERAPIST: She does what?

FATHER: I have a bad temper too. [pause]

THERAPIST: So, everyone agrees that Sarah's the crabbiest?

This exchange illustrates the central role played by clients in providing information that ecosystemic therapists and team members use in constructing social contexts for understanding and responding to the clients' systemic problems. Without the information provided by clients, it would be impossible for ecosystemic therapists to do their jobs. Ecosystemic therapists' questions create conditions of possibility that are given concrete shape through clients' answers and therapists' interpretations of the answers. In the above case, for example, Jim and the father provide information that might be used to justify treating the family as a social system involving two people with bad tempers. The therapists might construct the clients' social system in at least two ways. First, the therapists might treat the clients' statements as literal facts that describe actual behaviors and relationships within this social system. Or, second, ecosystemic therapists might orient to such statements as information about the shared perceptions or culture of the family's social system. Both interpretations are useful to ecosystemic therapists who assume that clients' perceptions are just as real as clients' behavior and, therefore, equally relevant to the ecosystemic therapy process.

A related emphasis in ecosystemic therapy discourse is the claim that creating effective changes in clients' social systems does not always involve making large scale changes or even directly addressing those aspects of clients' lives that therapists consider to be the most problematic. Since clients' social systems involve circular—as well as linear—connections, a small change in one aspect of clients' social systems can eventually initiate changes in other parts of the systems. Thus, in asking mapping questions of their clients, ecosystemic brief therapists also seek information that they and their team members might use in developing effective intervention—or change—strategies. The therapists characterize effective intervention strategies as responses that fit with their clients' social systems. This ecosystemic brief therapy assumption and emphasis is related to Gregory Bateson's (1979) discussion of binocular vision as a necessary condition for change. Bateson argues that change emerges in the interaction between two different—but compatible—circumstances or ideas.

Ecosystemic therapists' concern for creating intervention strategies that fit with clients' social systems points to another important aspect of this institutional discourse. Ecosystemic therapists are experts who ask questions that elicit therapeutically useful information from clients. Therapists use the information to assess clients' social systems, and develop intervention strategies that fit with clients' social systems. Two major practical issues to which ecosystemic brief therapists orient in doing these activities involve transforming clients' complaints into problems, and developing intervention strategies that disrupt and/or refocus existing troublesome patterns in clients' social systems, including clients' perceptions. Through these activities, ecosystemic therapists and clients also socially construct institutional selves for themselves and clients.

Ecosystemic Problems and Selves

Ecosystemic therapists define complaints and problems as different social realities. Complaints are vague portrayals of clients' desires and circumstances that are unconnected to any concrete solutions. They neither point to nor imply goals toward which therapists and clients might work in changing clients' lives. Ecosystemic therapists treat complaints as vicious cycles that maintain problems by focusing clients' attention on what is wrong with their lives, and the hopelessness of clients' circumstances. Within ecosystemic discourse, problems are descriptions that point to observable goals. They are circumstances that can be assessed as present or absent, as getting better or worse. Thus, one of ecosystemic therapists' major responsibilities and skills involves helping their clients to shift from talking about complaints to talking about problems. The major way in which ecosystemic therapists do this is by asking questions that clients answer. Ecosystemic therapists and clients are different—but inextricably linked—problem-solvers who are working together to solve clients' problems.

Transforming complaints into problems is also a major topic in ecosystemic therapy team members' interactions about ongoing therapy sessions. As they observe sessions, team members categorize the clients' statements as signs of complaints or problems. Team members use their portrayals of clients' responses as complaints and problems in two major ways. One use is in assessing the effectiveness of therapists' questioning strategies. When team members assess ongoing therapy sessions as unproductive, they sometimes telephone therapists to suggest new lines of questioning that team members believe will move the therapy sessions toward more therapeutically productive topics. Second, team members use their categorizations of clients' responses to assess clients' social systems, including how clients' perceptions and/or orientations (that is, subjectivities) are part of the problems at hand.

These ecosystemic team member activities are aspects of a general emphasis in ecosystemic therapy discourse on intermingling self and system. Within this institutional discourse, self and system are inextricably linked aspects of the same process and structure. Ecosystemic therapists' interest in assessing clients' perceptions, attitudes, and orientations cannot be adequately explained without considering the therapists' concern for assessing and changing clients' social systems. And, the reverse is equally true. That is, in assessing clients' social systems, ecosystemic therapists cast clients as members of distinctive social systems or contexts. Ecosystemic therapists use these contexts as relevant backgrounds in interpreting and assigning meaning to clients' behavior—including their talk—during therapy sessions.

Ecosystemic therapists at Northland Clinic sometimes used a local vocabulary of client-system types in assessing the meaning of statements made by clients in therapy sessions. The categories that constitute this local vocabulary emerged over time and in response to particular clients and therapy sessions. Thus, while the categories were frequently part of team member discussions behind the mirror, they were seldom mentioned during formal training sessions conducted at Northland Clinic. In applying the categories to actual clients and therapy sessions, team members socially constructed clients as kinds of people (or institutional selves), placed the clients within different kinds of social systems, and defined the professional task at hand for therapists and team members. Consider the following exchange that occurred between a team member and myself in the observation room at Northland Clinic. Notice, in particular, that while the team member discusses how the case is like "a fog" and "the piano," he never mentions the details of the ongoing interview or of the cases that were the sources for these categories. The focus is on the client's ability to describe his life circumstances.

TEAM MEMBER: We have half a fog here and if we brought his wife in, we'd probably have a whole fog. Ya know, they just don't know what's going on?

MILLER: A fog?

TEAM MEMBER: Yeah, a fog is when both parties of a couple don't know what's happening. Everything is unclear, fuzzy, a fog. It's not that rare either. There's a subtype of it that's called the piano.

MILLER: The piano?

TEAM MEMBER: Yeah, that's when they think they know what's going on, but they don't. They have the mistaken notion that they know what's happening to each other, but they really don't know what the other is thinking. We have to get through that before we can do anything with 'em.

This therapist's explanation provides insight into ecosystemic therapists' and team members' interest in constructing problems at the start of therapy sessions. Team members display this interest by carefully listening to clients' reasons for coming to therapy, and interpreting the reasons as complaints or as the beginnings of problems. But even as team members portray clients' statements as complaints, they continue to observe and react to the interviews as potential sources for problems. Indeed, a discussion of a client's vague or unreasonable complaints might suddenly end when one or more team members proclaims that the client has just offered a problem or, at least, the beginnings of one. The following interaction involving two Northland Clinic team members is an example of such a conversational shift.

TEAM MEMBER 1:   Ah, we now have a problem that we can work with. All these problems are signs of confusion. She doesn't know what she wants to do.

TEAM MEMBER 2:   She's going through a midlife crisis.

TEAM MEMBER 1:   It's interesting how people go through them at different times. Some people go through them 10 and some go through them 1,000 times. You know, what we have here is a female version of Dilemma [another type and local category involving a man who was confused about how to deal with his future after the dissolution of his marriage].

As with the previous exchange, this interaction displays ecosystemic therapists' practical interest in constructing problems on which they and their clients might work. It is difficult to overstate this aspect of ecosystemic therapy, since it is designed to solve problems. Without problems, there is nothing for ecosystemic therapists and clients to do and, therefore, no reason for therapy. Ecosystemic therapists' interest in constructing problems also has implications for the institutional selves that are possible within this discourse: because clients are members of distinctive, but troubled, social systems, they are partly defined by system problems.

We see this aspect of ecosystemic therapy discourse in the above interactions, beginning with team member 1 stating, "Ah, we now have a problem that we can work with. All these problems are signs of confusion. She doesn't know what she wants to do." Team member 1 and team member 2 elaborate on this assessment in the next two turns by describing the client as experiencing a midlife crisis. This interaction also shows how ecosystemic therapists' interest in developing intervention strategies that fit with clients' social systems involves treating clients as people with problems. Specifically, in linking this client with another ("she is a female version of Dilemma"), team member 1 shifts the conversation to whether the intervention strategy that fit with the other client's social system might work with this client's social system. Further, the entire interaction is an example of how ecosystemic therapists interactionally construct themselves and others as skilled assessors of clients' social systems, selves, and problems. Ecosystemic therapists display their professionalism by making assessments and creating intervention strategies that are therapeutically useful in just these terms.

But all of this is subject to change should the therapists redefine the problem at hand, and/or the client's social system. Either of these changes might provide ecosystemic therapists with reasons for reconsidering their designation of the client as a confused person. This development might also have implications for the ways in which the therapists describe themselves and each other as competent professionals. The shift might, for example, involve an accounting by the therapists about their prior "mistakes," "misunderstandings," or "confusion" about the client, her problems, and her social system.

Initiating Ecosystemic Change

Ecosystemic therapists stress that all clients' social systems are unique, and that therapists and team members must be sensitive to these differences in assessing clients' social systems. But they also stress that it is possible to develop general intervention strategies that are effective in initiating change in diverse client social systems. Steve de Shazer (1985) explains that such ecosystemic brief therapy intervention strategies work like skeleton keys, keys that may be used to open many different locks. Ecosystemic therapy skeleton keys, then, are intervention strategies that are effective in initiating change in diverse client social systems. Ecosystemic therapists explain that their interest in skeleton keys is related to their wish to be effective therapists while using a minimum of personal time and energy. This practical interest also has implications for the social construction of self in ecosystemic brief therapy.

For example, ecosystemic therapists ask questions in therapy sessions that are designed to encourage clients to think about their lives in new ways. Therapists portray these questions as part of a general strategy of reframing clients' perceptions and orientations, thus opening new possibilities for interpreting clients' past, present, and future lives. Reframings are one way in which ecosystemic therapists encourage binocular vision in clients. In suggesting alternative interpretations of clients' lives, ecosystemic therapists attempt to put clients in a position of having to reconcile the disparities between their old perspectives and the alternative possibilities suggested by the reframings. Further, because client perceptions, relationships, and behavior are treated as interrelated within this therapy discourse, ecosystemic brief therapists assume that the reframing of clients' perceptions will have implications for other aspects of clients' social systems. One reframing technique involves asking clients what positive changes have occurred in their lives since their last sessions, or between the time when they scheduled their first therapy sessions and the current session. Consider, for example, the following exchange that followed the report of a client (Eva) that she had found and started a job since the last interview.

THERAPIST: So this is a big change for you, working?

EVA: Yes, it is. Yes, it is. I've already got done furnishing and remodeling our house. That's all done.

THERAPIST: You got all that done!

EVA: Yeah, that's all done. Got the carpeting in, all the woodworking done.

THERAPIST: Wow, you're an industrious person.

EVA: Energetic, I'm energetic.

THERAPIST: Pretty hard that first week or two to uh—

EVA: [Interrupting] Yeah, I got the, the body's got to get adjusted to it. . . .

This intervention is typical of how ecosystemic therapists respond to client statements about positive change in clients' lives. The therapists express delight at the change ("You got all that done!"), provide clients with new—more positive—identities ("Wow, you're an industrious person"), and cast the changes as involving difficulties. The latter move is a way of making clients responsible for their successes by treating change as based on clients' hard work, as involving a struggle, or otherwise reflecting clients' strength and commitment to change. Each of these responses is also a way of redefining clients as competent people who are consequential in their social worlds. So defined, ecosystemic therapy clients are normal people living with normal problems that clients can manage in normal ways, similarly implicating their social systems.

A New Institutional Discourse

The ecosystemic processes discussed above were readily observable aspects of brief therapy practice at Northland Clinic during my initial fieldwork experience there. These practices were what I expected to see upon my return to the clinic in 1988. What I found was still called brief therapy, but the Northland Clinic therapists were now doing something quite different with words. They called it solution-focused brief therapy. And, since the therapists had only recently invented this therapy discourse and approach, I saw no shortcuts in doing my research. I could not go to the library and check out a textbook that would tell me whatever

I wanted to know about this development. If I wanted to know what solution-focused brief therapy was all about, I had no choice but to watch the Northland Clinic therapists at work and to talk with them about what I was seeing.

Solution-focused brief therapy is a radically new institutional discourse because it is based on different assumptions about social reality, new practical concerns about the therapy process, and new strategies for changing clients' lives. For example, within the solution-focused therapy discourse, clients' problems are treated as aspects of therapist-client interactions, not as parts of clients' social systems which presumably exist outside of therapy sessions. Solution-focused therapists maintain that all of the information that they and their clients need to solve clients' problems is available in their social interactions. These assumptions are central to solution-focused therapists' depictions of therapy sessions as getting at the surface of clients' problems (de Shazer 1994). That is, there is no practical need for therapists or clients to look behind, above, below, or beyond the surface in order to solve clients' problems. All that is needed is for the therapist to ask solution-focused questions and to listen carefully to clients' answers.

Associated with solution-focused therapists' interest in getting at the surface of clients' problems is their conceptualization of problems and solutions as different kinds of language games that need not be related in therapy. Talking about problems and about solutions are different activities within this institutional discourse. Indeed, solution-focused brief therapists state that it is possible to create solutions without specifying a problem, a claim that clearly distinguishes solution-focused therapy from its ecosystemic counterpart. This is not to say that solution-focused therapists and clients never link problems and solutions, but the linkage is established within the context of their social interactions. Sometimes they construct problems and solutions, other times they only talk about solutions.

One reason why solution-focused therapists and clients do not need to talk about problems is because solution-focused therapy discourse includes several questions that are designed to shift the conversational focus toward better times in clients' lives. The solution-focused therapy question that most obviously expresses this emphasis is the so-called miracle question. This question asks clients to imagine that a miracle happens while they are sleeping, thus the clients cannot know that their miracles have taken place. The therapists then ask clients to describe the concrete signs that the clients will notice—upon waking—that will signal to the clients that their lives have changed. In addition to changing the subjects of their conversations with clients, solution-focused therapists use the miracle question to encourage clients to clarify the concrete changes that clients would like to have happen in their lives. Once clients have clarified the changes, the task at hand for therapists and clients involves figuring out how clients' miracles might be made to happen, or—as solution-focused brief therapists prefer—figuring out how aspects of clients' miracles are already present in clients' lives.

The miracle question is partly a technique developed by the Northland Clinic therapists to address their practical interest in getting clients unstuck from problems. It is also an example of how the solution-focused therapy discourse casts clients as the carriers of solutions to their problems, and the therapists as conversational facilitators of clients' solution-building. Solution-focused therapists are willing and able to work with a wide variety of client miracles, their major concern being that clients articulate the concrete signs of change the clients will notice upon waking and discovering that their miracles have happened. The miracle question also displays solution-focused therapists interest in selectively talking about clients' lives. What is the point, solution-focused therapists ask, in talking about problems, since problems and solutions are disconnected language games and realities? They also ask, what is the point of talking about clients' deficits, pathologies, or flaws, if one assumes that clients are competent people who already know how to adequately manage their lives?

Solutions as Misreadings

De Shazer (1991) offers a deconstructive understanding of solution-focused therapy in portraying all interpretations of clients' life circumstances as misreadings. He explains that since no one—including clients—can say that he or she understands the ultimate meaning of the issues at hand, then the social realities constructed in therapy are always relative and changeable. Social realities constructed in one language game may be changed by engaging another language game. De Shazer (1991, p. 51) further states that "Misreading is not a problem to be solved, just a fact to be lived with . . . each misreading creates a new version of the text and increases both its potential usefulness and potential misunderstanding." Viewed in this way, solution-focused therapy involves the self-conscious development of misreadings that cast clients as competent persons.

Solution-focused therapists state that their efforts to misread their clients' lives are made easier by the fact that our everyday lives include a diversity of events and experiences, including some that might be interpreted as contradicting the usual ways in which we interpret who and what we are. Solution-focused brief therapists note, for example, that persons who are diagnosed as alcoholic do not drink alcohol all day long, every day of the year. Indeed, most "alcoholics" experience periods of reduced alcohol use and even abstinence, although these times are glossed over—if not denied—by the language of alcoholism that focuses attention on the times when "alcoholics" drink excessively. Put differently, the concept of alcoholism is part of a problem-focused strategy for constructing people as uncontrolled drinkers. (See Pollner and Stein, this volume.)

While not denying the problems associated with excessive alcohol use, solution-focused brief therapists stress that finding solutions to problem drinking is most easily done by identifying the times when clients have succeeded in drinking responsibly or not at all, and finding ways to recreate and extend those times (Berg and Miller 1992). As some solution-focused therapists state, they do not treat chronic alcoholics, rather they treat people who have experienced multiple sobrieties. Solution-focused therapists express this orientation in therapy sessions by asking "alcoholic" clients to describe how they are sometimes able to get and stay sober, and how they might do more of whatever helps them to remain that way. Solution-focused brief therapists emphasize similar—"contradictory"—aspects of other clients' lives, treating the events as therapeutically meaningful and asking clients to talk at length about these successes. In this way, solution-focused brief therapists implicate their clients in the misreading of clients' lives.

One way in which solution-focused brief therapists encourage their clients to identify the already present beginnings of change is by asking questions about exceptions to clients' problems. The questions focus on the times when clients' problems are absent from their lives or at least less severe. Once clients report on either circumstance, solution-focused brief therapists ask about the details associated with the exceptions and how clients might recreate the exceptions in the future. Walter and Peller (1992, pp. 95–96) offer the following example of how they invited talk about exceptions from a client who stated that he heard voices and that other people were complaining about his behavior.

THERAPIST: So, are there times when you do not listen to the voices or you do not act that way?

CLIENT: Well, the voices are there all the time.

THERAPIST: So, do you listen to them all the time?

CLIENT: No, not all the time. Sometimes, I am just too busy or I trust my own opinion rather than the voices.

THERAPIST: So, sometimes you trust your own opinion and you act differently. Those times go more the way you like?

CLIENT: Yes

THERAPIST: How do you do that?

This exchange illustrates how solution-focused brief therapists persist in asking clients about exceptions. When the client responds to the therapist's first question about exceptions by stating that "the voices are there all the time," the therapist asks her question again. Such persistence is pervasive in solution-focused brief therapy interviews. Also, notice that the therapist repeats and highlights aspects of the client's description of the circumstances associated with exceptions. The therapist states, "So, sometimes you trust your own opinion and you act differently." The therapist further pursues this solution-focused brief therapy interest by asking the client, "How did you do that?" This, too, is a frequently asked question in solution-focused brief therapy, one that displays the therapists' assumptions that clients are competent people and that clients are carriers of the solutions to their problems.

Asking clients "how did you do that" is associated with solution-focused brief therapists' use of "getting by" questions. This misreading strategy asks about the ways in which clients manage their lives despite their problems. It focuses on clients' coping knowledge and skills, casting them as signs of clients' extraordinariness, and as resources that therapists and clients might use in changing clients' lives. Solution-focused brief therapists often emphasize "getting by" questions in their interactions with clients who persist in talking about problems. The therapists begin by agreeing with the clients' descriptions of their lives as deeply troubled, and then therapists ask how the clients manage under such difficult conditions. In asking the question in this way, solution-focused brief therapists acknowledge the seriousness of the problems, while also raising the possibility that the clients already possess the knowledge and skills needed to solve their problems.

The following exchange illustrates one way in which solution-focused therapists implement this strategy. In this case, the client reported earlier in the session that her life was improving, but later talks of her sense of frustration with the seeming intractability of her problems. The client reported on her better times in responding to a scaling question asked by the therapist. The question posited a 10-point scale on which 1 represents the worst that the problem has ever been and 10 stands for the achievement of the client's miracle. Notice how the therapist uses the client's answer to this question to misread her life as getting better.

THERAPIST: So, [pause] how do you manage to keep going, [pause] when you're feeling so badly, much of the time, how do you manage to keep going?

CLIENT: I force myself to keep going.

THERAPIST: Uh, huh, so where do you get the strength to do that?

CLIENT: I always make up [pause] some reason [pause] why I have to get up and to work.

THERAPIST: Uh, huh, for instance?

CLIENT: I have to keep my job.

THERAPIST: And, uh, [pause] okay. And, uh, [pause] how long has it been this way, how long have you had this problem? [Client chronicles her problem.]

THERAPIST: Uh huh, uh huh, I see. Okay, so, it's been a difficult year.

CLIENT: Yes.

THERAPIST: But [pause] in the last two weeks, you've had four days that were at six, seven, or eight. [pause] That's better than it was [pause] before.

This exchange includes several notable features. First, notice that the therapist does not challenge the client's portrayal of her life as troubled; rather, he asks, "how do you manage to keep going," and, "where do you get the strength to do that?" Notice, also, that the client does not object to the therapist's characterization of her as strong. Indeed, she provides information that supports the emergent image by stating that she forces herself "to keep going," always makes up a reason to be strong, and gives an example of her strength ("I have to keep my job"). In some solution-focused brief therapy sessions, therapists respond to such client answers by being impressed, and by asking for more details about clients' amazing insights, strengths, and accomplishments. The therapist in this interaction pursues a different strategy by asking the client about how long she has suffered from her problems, and expresses sympathy for her plight by stating, "so, it's been a difficult year." At this point the therapist reminds the client of her earlier statement that her life has been substantially better in the last two weeks. Following the extracted exchange, he further develops this line of questioning by asking the client how she might create these better times in the future. Specifically, the therapist asks, "So, [pause] what do you think needs to happen for, [pause] oh, I don't know, let's say [pause] what would it take for everyday to be sort of six, seven, or eight?"

The misreading strategies developed by solution-focused therapists are designed to make problem-solving resources available to clients and therapists that are not available in the problems language game (deJong and Berg 1996; George et al. 1990). And, because clients know more about the details of their lives than do therapists, solution-focused brief therapists stress that clients must be centrally involved in this process. Berg (1994) describes the logic of this solution-focused brief therapy strategy in discussing a client who was referred to therapy because the client could not manage her children. The referring agencies stated that the mother was inconsistent in dealing with her children and did not hold the children accountable to household rules. During the interview, the client stated that her job involved supervising others, and that she was an effective supervisor on the job. The therapist and her team used this information in suggesting how the client might use her job-related supervisory skills and knowledge in dealing with her children, stating that many aspects of mothering might be understood as supervising.

In this way, then, the client, therapist, and team members worked together to misread the client's life and abilities in solution-focused ways. The interaction involved replacing the prior definition of the client as an incompetent mother with one emphasizing the client's supervisory skills and competence, skills that she might use on the job and in the home. This example points to another major theme in solution-focused therapy discourse, that solution-focused therapy sessions are most usefully conceptualized as conversations about change (de Shazer 1991; Furman and Aloha 1992). So defined, solution-focused brief therapy sessions involve no experts, at least not in the sense of ecosystemic brief therapy. Rather, solution-focused therapists describe therapy sessions as involving two or more people talking about how clients' lives can be improved.

Finally, we can see how ecosystemic therapy and solution-focused therapy are organized as different conditions of possibility by considering therapists' and team members' practical interests in creating appropriate intervention messages for clients. In ecosystemic therapy, these messages must fit with clients' social systems, whereas in solution-focused brief therapy appropriate intervention messages are assessed by whether they fit with client-therapist conversations. The preferred situation in solution-focused therapy is for intervention messages to affirm—and sometimes to elaborate upon—problem-solving skills and strategies mentioned by clients in therapy sessions. For example, the suggestions made by Berg (1994) and her team members in responding to the client who was portrayed as an ineffective mother but effective supervisor are cited by solution-focused therapists as an intervention message that fit with its client-therapist conversation. Solution-focused brief therapists also treat their interest in fitting intervention messages with therapy conversations as related to their interest in getting at the surface of clients' problems, and in solving clients' problems with a minimum of therapist interference.

An Altered Moral Climate

Solution-focused brief therapy discourse provides therapists, clients, and team members with different activities, responsibilities, orientations, and relationships than those provided in ecosystemic brief therapy discourse. Each of these aspects of solution-focused therapy has consequential moral implications for how participants in this language game construct their identities to themselves and for others. Further, in constructing solution-focused selves, solution-focused brief therapists and clients construct social contexts that provide their members with new life possibilities. For clients, alternative possibilities center on the ways in which clients might use their existing knowledge and skills to create new—more desirable—future lives for themselves. The new possibilities for therapists involve the ways in which solution-focused therapy reconfigures brief therapists' professional roles, responsibilities, and relationships.

Perhaps the most dramatic change associated with this discursive shift involves the importance of clients' expertise within solution-focused therapy. Simply put, the major responsibility for constructing solutions to clients' problems is shifted from the observation room to the interview room in solution-focused therapy. This task—which is shared by ecosystemic therapists and team members— is the major focus of therapist-client interactions in solution-focused therapy. Indeed, solution-focused therapists state that under ideal circumstances, therapy interviews allow clients to solve their own problems.

This preference reflects, and is a source for, the special social role provided to clients in solution-focused brief therapy. Clients are central actors in this discourse because they are the carriers of solutions. Where clients in ecosystemic therapy are informants about social systems which team members and therapists assess, solution-focused therapists treat clients as authorities themselves on both clients' problems and how solutions are already present in clients' lives. Because clients are competent people, they already know how to solve their own problems, but clients cannot use this knowledge so long as they are stuck in a problems language game. The therapist's job in solution-focused therapy, then, involves helping clients to enter the solutions language game so that clients can use their problem-solving skills and knowledge to change their own lives.

The major way in which solution-focused therapists encourage clients to enter and participate in the solutions language game is by asking questions and offering evaluations of clients' lives that are designed to help clients misread their lives and selves. The misreadings are interpretive procedures for making problem-solving resources available for practical use by clients and therapists. For solution-focused therapists, these resources are the beginnings of solutions and evidence that their clients are competent people. If clients are carriers of solutions in solution-focused therapy discourse, then therapists are curious conversationalists who are interested in finding out about the solutions that clients carry, about what clients know how to do, what clients wish for their future lives, and how clients might achieve their future goals.

Solution-focused therapists also orient to their clients as extraordinary people. They express this orientation by treating clients' answers to their questions as reasons for being impressed, and by proclaiming their amazement at clients' insights and achievements. Solution-focused therapists treat both clients' successes in changing their lives and frustrations in struggling with their problems as signs of clients' extraordinary abilities. In the latter case, solution-focused brief therapists treat clients' frustrations and struggles with problems as signs of clients' personal strength and tenacity. The frustrations and struggles are evidence of clients' amazing capacity to persist where others give up.

Conclusion

Ecosystemic therapy and solution-focused therapy discourses provide setting members with different opportunities for developing new stories of life and self. The opportunities are potentially infinite. In the abstract, there is no limit to the number of success stories, exceptions to problems, and/or miracles that solution-focused brief therapists and clients might construct. Nor is there a predetermined limit to the number of social systems and intervention strategies that ecosystemic brief therapists and team members might invent in fulfilling their professional responsibilities to clients. The potential for making up people within these institutional discourses is, it seems, only limited by the imaginations and inventiveness of brief therapists, team members, and clients.

This conclusion, however, overlooks the ways in which opportunities for displaying personal imagination and inventiveness are socially organized and provided to brief therapists and clients. The opportunities are made available within discursive environments. This is one way of understanding Hacking's (1986) paradoxical claim that the possibilities for making up people within any institutional discourse are simultaneously inexhaustible and bounded. Setting members have myriad options in using the interpretive resources provided to them within institutional discourses, but the members' creativity is still bounded by the opportunities and resources that are available within any particular institutional setting. We have seen, for example, how ecosystemic therapists' and team members' practical interest in inventing diverse, individualized intervention strategies for clients is countered by their interest in developing skeleton keys that can be effectively and efficiently used with a variety of client problems and social systems.

In order to get beyond the inexhaustible but bounded opportunities of any particular institutional discourse, then, it is necessary to engage a new institutional discourse. This is a major sociological lesson that I draw from my observations at Northland Clinic, and related studies of the evolution and transformation of brief therapy. The development of solution-focused therapy provided Northland Clinic therapists and clients with new resources and opportunities for pursing their practical interests in therapy sessions, as well as a new discursive context for evaluating the usefulness of ecosystemic therapy strategies and techniques. But, like those provided within ecosystemic therapy, the opportunities and resources provided to therapists and clients in solution-focused brief therapy are bounded.

This study also relates to Foucault's (1988) analysis of technologies of the self. Most obviously, it illustrates how two brief therapy technologies operate to produce conditions of possibility within which both clients' and therapists' subjectivities and selves are transformed. They are also different practical strategies for creating social conditions that simultaneously take account of individual differences and the social contexts within which people live their lives. Foucault (1984) analyzes such strategies as ethical practices that open up new possibilities for persons to socially construct themselves as free and autonomous subjects. Steven Best and Douglas Kellner (1991, p. 64) further explain that

> Ethics here depends not so much on moral norms as free choice and aesthetic criteria and avoids subjectivizing the individual into a normalized universal ethical subject. The task is not to "discover" oneself, one's secret inner being, but rather to continuously produce oneself.

Brief therapists and clients continuously produce themselves and each other by reconfiguring the horizons of possibility that define and organize their social relationships and lives in therapy. Analyzed as technologies of the self, ecosystemic and solution-focused brief therapy discourses are designed to construct contrastingly competent people and social worlds in which those competencies can be effectively used.

REFERENCES

Bateson, Gregory. 1979. *Mind and Nature: A Necessary Unity*. New York: E. P. Dutton.

Berg, Insoo Kim. 1994. *Family-Based Services: A Solution-Focused Approach*. New York: W. W. Norton & Company.

Berg, Insoo Kim, and Scott D. Miller. 1992. *Working with the Problem-Drinker: A Solution-Focused Approach*. New York: W. W. Norton & Company.

Best, Steven, and Douglas Kellner. 1991. *Postmodern Theory: Critical Interrogations*. New York: The Guilford Press.

deJong, Peter, and Insoo Kim Berg. 1996. *How to Interview for Client Strengths and Solutions*. Pacific Grove, Calif.: Brooks/Cole Publishers.

de Shazer, Steve. 1982. *Patterns of Brief Family Therapy: An Ecosystemic Approach*. New York: The Guilford Press.

———. 1985. *Keys to Solution in Brief Therapy*. New York: W. W. Norton & Company.

———. 1988. *Clues: Investigating Solutions in Brief Therapy*. New York: W. W. Norton & Company.

———. 1991. *Putting Difference to Work*. New York: W. W. Norton & Company.

———. 1994. *Words Were Originally Magic*. New York: W. W. Norton & Company.

Douglas, Mary. 1986. *How Institutions Think*. Syracuse, N.Y.: Syracuse University Press.

Erickson, Milton H. 1967. "A Transcript of a Trance Induction with Commentary." In *Advanced Techniques of Hypnosis and Therapy*, ed. Jay Haley, 395–97. New York: Grune and Stratton.

Foucault, Michel. 1977. *Discipline and Punish*. Trans. Alan Sheridan. New York: Pantheon.

———. 1984. "What Is Enlightenment?" In *The Foucault Reader*, ed. Paul Rabinow, New York: Pantheon.

———. 1988. "Technologies of the Self." In *Technologies of the Self: A Seminar with Michel Foucault*, ed. Luther H. Martin, Huck Gutman, and Patrick Hutton, 16–49. Amherst, Mass.: University of Massachusetts Press.

Fox, Kathryn J. 1999. "Changing Violent Minds: Discursive Correction and Resistance in the Cognitive Treatment of Violent Offenders in Prison." *Social Problems* 46 (Feb.): 88–103.

Furman, Ben, and Tapani Ahola. 1992. *Solution Talk: Hosting Therapeutic Conversations.* New York: W. W. Norton & Company.

George, Evan, Chris Iveson, and Harvey Ratner. 1990. *Problem to Solution: Brief Therapy with Individuals and Families.* London: Brief Therapy.

Gubrium, Jaber F. 1989. "Local Cultures and Service Policy" In *The Politics of Field Research,* ed. J. F. Gubrium and D. Silverman 94–112. London: Sage.

Hacking, Ian. 1986. "Making Up People." In *Reconsidering Individualism: Autonomy, Individuality, and the Self in Western Thought,* ed. Thomas C. Heller, Morton Sosna, and David E. Wellbery, 222–36. Stanford, Calif.: Stanford University Press.

Holstein, James A. 1992. "Producing People: Descriptive Practice in Human Service Work." In *Current Research on Occupations and Professions,* vol. 7, ed. Gale Miller, 23–40. Greenwich, Conn.: JAI Press.

Loseke, Donileen R. 1989. "Creating Clients: Social Problems Work in a Shelter for Battered Women." In *Perspectives on Social Problems,* vol. 1, ed. James A. Holstein and Gale Miller, 173–94. Greenwich, Conn.: JAI Press.

———. 1993. "Constructing Conditions, People, Morality, and Emotion: Expanding the Agenda of Constructionism." In *Constructionist Controversies: Issues in Social Problems Theory,* ed. Gale Miller and James A. Holstein, 207–16. New York: Aldine de Gruyter.

Miller, Gale. 1986. "Depicting Family Trouble: A Micro-Political Analysis of the Therapeutic Interview." *Journal of Strategic and Systemic Therapies,* 5 (Spring and Summer):1–136.

———. 1987. "Producing Family Problems." *Symbolic Interaction* 10(Fall):245–66.

———. 1994. "Toward Ethnographies of Institutional Discourse: Proposal and Suggestions." *Journal of Contemporary Ethnography* 23(October):280–306.

———. 1997a. *Becoming Miracle Workers: Language and Meaning in Brief Therapy.* Hawthorne, N.Y.: Aldine de Gruyter.

———. 1997b. "Building Bridges: The Possibility of Analytic Dialogue Between Ethnography, Conversation Analysis, and Foucault." In *Qualitative Analysis: Issues of Theory and Method,* ed. David Silverman, 24–44. London: Sage Publications.

———. 1997c. "Systems and Solutions: The Discourses of Brief Therapy." *Contemporary Family Therapy* 19 (March): 5–22.

Miller, Gale, and Steve de Shazer. 1998. "Have You Heard the Latest Rumor About . . . ? Solution-Focused Therapy as a Rumor," *Family Process* 37. (Fall): 363–78.

Miller, Gale, and David Silverman. 1995. "Troubles Talk and Counseling Discourse: A Comparative Study." *The Sociological Quarterly* 36 (4): 725–47.

Spencer, J. William. 1994. "Mutual Relevance of Ethnography and Discourse." *Journal of Contemporary Ethnography* (23): 267–79.

Walter, John L., and Jane E. Peller. 1992. *Becoming Solution-Focused in Brief Therapy.* New York: Brunner/Mazel Publishers.

Wittgenstein, Ludwig. 1958. *Philosophical Investigations.* Trans. G. E. M. Anscombe. New York: Macmillan Publishing Co.

DARIN WEINBERG

Self-Empowerment in Two
Therapeutic Communities

> So, it is not enough to say that the subject is constituted in a
> symbolic system. It is not just in the play of symbols that
> the subject is constituted. It is constituted in real practices—
> historically analyzable practices. There is a technology of the
> constitution of the self which cuts across symbolic systems while
> using them.
>
> —Michel Foucault, 1983

If we have grown sensitive to the fact that selves are *shaped* by the social environment, we have been slower to appreciate the diverse ways in which selves are
put to *use* in our everyday lives. As Michel Foucault intimates above, we have often emphasized the variety of ways in which selves are symbolically construed
without due attention to the fact that self-construction is fundamentally grounded
not in symbolic systems but in materially embodied practices. This chapter elaborates this perspective by comparing the work of self-empowerment in two therapeutic communities. I show how clients' selves are not only given symbolic
meaning in these settings, but are *incited* and *empowered* to accomplish the con-
stellation of practices that comprise these settings as distinctive "going concerns"
(Hughes 1971). Following Foucault, my primary thesis is that clinical treatment
in these programs was not governed by the logic of a symbolic system or treatment philosophy, but was more immediately responsive to the specific institutional contingencies under which participants were compelled to work. In
particular, it was differences in the residential status of clients (inpatient or outpatient), not differences in treatment philosophy, that most immediately shaped
the approaches taken to client self-empowerment in the settings.

Self-empowerment in both settings was viewed specifically as *therapeutic*
work. That is, it was taken up for the specific purpose of fostering clients' recoveries from the mental disorders presumed to afflict them. Thus, empowering
clients' selves was in part a project of learning to recognize when and how clients'
particular mental disorders affected them so as to better anticipate and prevent
future flare-ups. Obviously, the effects of clients' mental disorders were observed
only in their personal actions and experiences. Hence, in the course of being col-
laboratively constructed and empowered, clients' selves were indeed routinely *installed* and *removed* as the effective agents of their own personal behavior and

experiences. A second thesis, then, is that beyond their being variously constructed for use in therapeutic work, clients' selves were occasionally supplanted entirely. That is, clients' mental disorders were sometimes socially constructed and used as surrogates for clients' selves.

The Communities

The therapeutic communities I studied served homeless adults diagnosed with both severe mental illnesses and substance abuse disorders. I call these communities "Canyon House" and "Twilights," both of which are pseudonyms. Canyon House was a residential facility administered by a private nonprofit corporation but funded primarily by a joint grant from Los Angeles county mental health and substance abuse services. I conducted fieldwork there for nine months. Twilights was expressly established as a nonresidential copy of Canyon House. A nonprofit research corporation founded and administered this program as part of a federally funded study intended to investigate the comparative costs and benefits of residential and nonresidential care for dually diagnosed homeless adults. I studied Twilights for seven months.

Originally, Twilights was envisioned to provide a regimen of treatment identical in every respect to that provided at Canyon House, but in a nonresidential setting. This was to facilitate rigorous quantitative comparisons between the programs. However, early in the study it became clear that despite the best efforts of everyone involved, preserving comparability was no easy task. This fact is important to keep in mind. Twilights was founded with the specific intention of replicating the Canyon House program design in a nonresidential setting. Indeed, given the fact that the validity of the study (and its continued funding) hinged in large part on maintaining the comparability of the two programs, both researchers and clinicians had powerful incentives to ensure that therapeutic practice in the programs remained as similar as possible. The dissimilarities that emerged between the two programs, then, were emphatically not the results of differences in the programs' respective treatment philosophies. These remained identical. Rather, such differences resulted from the programs' contrasting organizational environments.

My research was primarily intended to consider ways in which the two programs differed that were not discernable by quantitative indicators. I was to observe the manner in which treatment was actually put into practice at Canyon House and Twilights in order to shed light on processes that either impeded or facilitated clients' recoveries (cf. Weinberg and Koegel 1995, 1996). The fieldwork consisted of both participant observation and unstructured interviews with clients and counselors. I visited the sites weekly, spending the day with program members and going through their daily routines. I attended all formal group sessions, participated in informal and recreational activities, and talked individually with both clients and counselors regarding their activities and experiences in the programs and related topics.[1] I had abundant opportunity to witness the close relationship between the specific organizational parameters of program practice and

the distinctive ways in which clients' selves were empowered and held accountable for progress in recovery. I also witnessed the close relationship between therapeutic self-empowerment and the construction of clients' mental disorders as
autonomous agents of clients' personal behavior and experiences.

Both programs borrowed heavily from the 12-step approach to recovery ad-
vocated by Alcoholics Anonymous (AA). Each strove to empower program clients
as the primary ministers of their own recoveries (see Alcoholics Anonymous 1976).
In stark contrast to medical and psychiatric models of care that construe "patients"
as essentially raw material for the work of clinically trained professionals, clients
at Canyon House and Twilights were told in no uncertain terms that recovery was
impossible if they were not themselves "ready" and "willing to go to any length
to get it" (Alcoholics Anonymous 1976, p. 58). The construction of clients as responsible for their own recoveries was considered to be absolutely essential to
therapeutic practice in both programs. Likewise, in both programs, the fundamental objective was to transmit "tools" with which clients might themselves more
effectively engage the work of recovery. Undoubtedly, staff exercised greater control than did clients in designating the character and proper use of those tools.
But this does not change the fact that *empowerment*, or the cultivation of clients'
self-control over their respective personal beings, was both the expressly sought
outcome of therapy *and* an explicitly avowed resource for accomplishing that goal.

Though focused principally on self-empowerment, program participants were
also convinced that their psychiatric disorders and addictions were genuine medical afflictions, nefarious disease agents distinct from themselves and eminently
capable of periodically intruding into their lives despite efforts to prevent them
from doing so. This is evident in the following exchange in a community meeting at Twilights. Claire, a counselor, began this exchange by asking a client, Roger,
about his recent episode of depression. Russell, another client, joined in the
discussion:[2]

CLAIRE: How did you deal with it Roger?

ROGER: . . . as far as dealing with it I guess I just stuck it out. There's really
           not much you can do other than hope it'll go away after a while.

RUSSELL: Yeah, that's what I usually do. I just wait and after a while it goes away
           . . . It ain't no fun though. It's just that it feels so big that you think
           there's no point in fighting it. For a while I try to fight it but after a
           while I just give up. It's too big to fight.

In this excerpt both Roger and Russell attribute independent causal force to
their depressions, describing them as pernicious entities against which they often
feel helpless. Similarly, in the following excerpt, Stephen describes his addiction
to cocaine as a noxious internal entity that he does not understand, and with
which he struggles in an almost Jekyll-and-Hyde fashion for control over his conduct:

I've promised myself I wouldn't use a thousand times and really meant it. And
then I use. I mean it's like there are two sides of me: the rational reasonable per-

son who knows he's gonna die if he keeps on living this way and the insane one who just doesn't care. My reasonable side of me can be as sure as it wants to be but when those drugs appear in front of me the insane one takes over and all those reasons I had not to use are just gone. They just disappear. And I use. It's like my mind just goes dead and my addiction takes over. I hate myself right afterward and I'm completely confused by the fact that I just used. I didn't want to but I did.

In sum, the institutional order that linked members of these communities flowed from the premises that 1) community participants genuinely suffered from severe mental disorders, and 2) clinical treatment for these disorders entailed empowering clients as the primary agents of their own recoveries. Hence, the programs called for clients' *selves* to be realized in subjective opposition, and objective contrast, to the mental disorders presumed to lurk within them. In effect, intervention was intended to empower clients to control the disease agents that, in the past, were found to have chronically controlled them.

Contrasting Environments of Self-Empowerment

Though they shared these premises, the two programs operationalized them in distinct ways, and, as a result, constructed clients' selves differently. Again, it is important to note that this dissimilarity of therapeutic practice occurred despite the fact that Twilights' program was conceived as an *exact* duplicate of the Canyon House program. The fact that Twilights did not provide clients with housing ultimately forced a variety of changes in program practice, distinguishing treatment at Twilights in some important respects from the ways treatment was accomplished at Canyon House. These changes, coupled with basic differences between their homeless clients' orientations to the prospective benefits promised by residential and nonresidential modes of treatment, systematically differentiated how both clients' selves and their mental disorders were realized and managed in the programs.

Right Living Versus Tenable Community Living

By providing room and board and removing clients to the remote hills above Los Angeles, Canyon House insulated clients from the pressures they might have faced before to their admission. Thanks to its comparatively luxurious provisions, Canyon House enjoyed a lengthy waiting list. Many on the list were homeless, or nearly so, and this alone made entry into the program attractive merely for the subsistence it promised. But this did not come without a price in commitment. Admission was contingent upon prospective residents persuading Canyon House staff that they were, in fact, genuinely dedicated to recovery from their mental disorders and that they were personally equipped to participate in the facility's recovery activities. As clients became integrated into the community, they were called upon to persuade their peers of this as well. In the beginning, this could be accomplished through little more than verbal avowals of one's commitment to recovery (Weinberg 1996). In the case of newcomers, failures to adequately participate in the program's work might be chalked up to honest ignorance, as in the following extract from a community meeting. Edgar, the client in charge of chores, speaks to a new client, David:

EDGAR: There were cigarette butts on the ground outside the rec room. Who was
          that?

DAVID: It was me, but . . .

EDGAR: [Interrupting] Okay, I don't know your name. What's your name?

[David said his name and Edgar continued.]

EDGAR: I don't know you so I guess you're new . . . Anyway, I don't know how
          much people have told you about what needs doing but you probably
          should take it upon yourself to find out what needs to be done, okay?

As clients continued in the program, however, simple ignorance became a less plausible account for lapses from adequate participation. Furthermore, mere verbal avowals of commitment became less convincing. In the language often heard in the programs, clients were progressively required not only to "talk the talk," but to "walk the walk" that indicated conformity to the locally approved methods for pursuing recovery from one's mental disorders (see also Bloor, McKaganey, and Fonkert 1988; Denzin 1993; Skoll 1992; Sugarman 1974; Yablonsky 1965).

All told, at Canyon House, the promotion of self-empowerment consisted basically in morally enforcing proper participation in the collective life of the house, or what I am calling "right living." As it happened, the substance of right living was subject to a good deal of negotiation but generally required the following: complete abstinence from illicit drugs and alcohol;[3] nonviolence; candor regarding one's actions, thoughts, and emotions; contribution to the maintenance of the facility; attendance and participation in community functions (including, of course, therapy groups); and investment in the recovery of one's peers. In recognition of the variability of clients' particular needs and capabilities, the enforcement of right living was also tailored to the expectations program members had of one another as unique individuals (e.g., their level of commitment to the shared work of the program, their unique personal temperaments, and the specific "issues" they were presumed to need work on). Through the exhibition and enforcement of right living, Canyon House members strove to include themselves and one another as members of the distinctive institutional order they presumed to unite them as a community. Beyond fostering a sense of collective identity, the exhibition and enforcement of right living also was a humanizing endeavor in the sense that it was through this work that the human selves of Canyon House members were empowered against the disease agents they believed had periodically taken hold of them in the past.

Following admission, program members at Canyon House soon learned that right living was, in effect, the toll to be exacted from them for the privilege of lodging at Canyon House. Though the substance of right living was subject to negotiation, it nevertheless involved living in accordance with the locally enforced morality of the house. Whether or not one agreed with the suitability of their judgments, one was generally compelled to live by the dictates of one's coparticipants in the program. As will be seen shortly, such prescriptions were far more easily enforced at Canyon House than at Twilights. Given the usual meagerness of their prospects outside the program, clients generally tried, at least, to appear that they were contributing to the collective life of the house and affably abiding by the reasonable expectations of their peers.

In contrast, Twilights had little leverage over its clients' compliance. Because it was nonresidential and offered clients far less in the way of subsistence needs, Twilights participants had less incentive for holding themselves accountable to the program. Furthermore, program administrators at Twilights were compelled for the sake of the study to keep enough clients participating in the program to gather meaningful outcome data. Once individuals had screened appropriate for the study and were assigned to participate in the Twilights program, vigorous outreach campaigns were mounted to bring them into the program and to keep them participating. Instead of enforcing right living among program clients, staff members at Twilights often had to cajole candidates to participate by stressing the tangible benefits they stood to gain from participation. Suffice it to say that most candidate participants did not regard the promise of sobriety and psychiatric care as especially enticing. Much more crucial to them were matters of immediate relevance to their day-to-day survival on the streets. Thus, as much as they could, staff members emphasized these practical benefits of participation.

Prospective clients were told that the Twilights program entitled them to genial companionship, a free dinner every weeknight, a free bus pass, coupons for free meals at McDonald's, access to the free laundry facilities, and use of the shower at no charge. They also were informed of the vigorous case management services that Twilights offered. Prospective clients were told that Twilights could help them determine their eligibility and sign up for a variety of public entitlement programs (e.g., General Relief, AFDC, SSI, SSDI). They were told that staff could help them to find temporary and permanent housing. And depending upon clients' individual circumstances, Twilights staff also held out the possibility of assistance with other matters such as legal problems, medical difficulties, employment problems, clothing needs, and storage needs. These incentives for joining the program were, of course, also incentives for remaining in the program. But rather than being incidental enticements to submit to clinical treatment, these services comprised the bulk of the substance abuse and psychiatric treatment that Twilights clients received. Thus, instead of self-empowerment being fostered through the moral enforcement of right living, at Twilights, self-empowerment became entrenched in promoting what I call "tenable community living" (see Emerson 1989; Holstein 1993).

Analyzing the work of Psychiatric Emergency Teams (PET) and involuntary commitment hearings respectively, Robert Emerson (1989) and James Holstein (1993) have shown the extent to which decisions to release candidate mental patients into the community hinged upon determinations as to whether candidate patients' community living arrangements were tenable.[4] They also showed that these determinations were intrinsically negotiated outcomes, subject to discretionary assessments of a wide variety of contingencies specific to individual cases. But in PET work and involuntary commitment hearings, candidate patients do not normally exercise much control over these negotiations. Their own actions figure primarily as raw material for *professional* diagnoses of tenability or untenability rather than as direct contributions to the work of defining tenability. At Twilights, in contrast, program clients were themselves extremely influential in determining whether their own community living arrangements were tenable as well as how they might go about making them more tenable. Hence, therapeutic practice consisted in empowering clients by helping them develop their own "programs" for contending with life in the community.

Of course, I am not arguing here that the types of concerns attendant to professional diagnoses and treatment of mental disorders were completely irrelevant to therapeutic practice at Twilights. As I have said, there was a very lively sense among program participants that Twilights clients were being treated for discrete mental disorders. My point is that because Twilights was not residential, and its clients were so destitute, considerations of more narrowly "clinical" issues were almost always embedded in broader determinations of tenability. Furthermore, despite their lack of professional training in the conduct of clinical assessments, clients were themselves integral players in the work of defining what in their lives was, and was not, an appropriate focus of therapy. This can be clearly seen in the following exchange from a meeting at Twilights between Sean, a client, and counselor Eve:

SEAN: I don't think I've been that fucked up in the head since Maureen died.

EVE: You've been havin' a hard time off and on ever since then haven't you?

[Sean nodded and Eve continued.]

EVE: How often do you still think about her?

SEAN: There ain't a day goes by I don't think about her. She's always with me.

[Sean turned to me, pointed to his prominent tattoo of her name on his neck, and continued.]

SEAN: She's always with me.

[Sean then turned to Eve and continued.]

SEAN: I think things'd be a lot worse than they are if she wasn't.

EVE: Does she ever talk to you?

SEAN: Yeah, I hear her voice sometimes but that's a blessing man. That's a blessing.

EVE: [Nodding] Do you think you still mourn her death? I mean, do you ever still get depressed about her death?

SEAN: I don't think I'll ever be as happy as I was when she was alive if that's what you mean. She was my everything and now she's gone. I don't think I'm as messed up about it as I used to be though. I've accepted it but I won't ever get over it.

[Eve nodded.]

In this episode, Eve speculates that Maureen's death triggered Sean's psychiatric breakdown and asks about Sean's experiences in a decidedly diagnostic tone. For his part, Sean is evidently aware of Eve's agenda, and despite a general willingness to accept the reality of his mental illness ("I haven't been that fucked up in the head since Maureen died"), he declines to ratify Eve's diagnostic musings regarding hearing Maureen's voice and his current sadness about her absence. Sean says Maureen's voice is a "blessing," not a symptom, and likewise refuses to pathologize his missing her. In both cases, Sean suggests he regards these candidate symptoms as reasonable features of his life and hence not as symptoms of any mental disorder. Rather than taking his assessments as evidence of denial, Eve acquiesces.

The pharmacological management of mental disorder was also conceived broadly in terms of enhancing the overall tenability of individual clients' lives (see also Kramer 1993). This approach can be seen in the following account Charlie gave regarding his current medication regimen. His remarks are clearly focused on finding medications that help enhance the overall tenability of his life rather than merely alleviating a professionally specified set of biopsychological symptoms:

> At first you don't even really realize you feel any different, you know they tell ya it takes a little while to kick in. But after a while I knew that shit wasn't doing *anything* for me. I'd feel jittery, I'd sleep late. Usually I wake up at 8:00 A.M. without fail but with this stuff I'm wakin' up at 10 still tired. I can't get a hard-on to save my life. I mean it's not that I'm needin' one too often but you know Rosie gets lonely [laughs]. Also I'm incredibly irritable. I was in the Winchell's yesterday and I couldn't believe myself. I was waitin' there at the counter and this chick who works there is doin' a bunch of other stuff. And I'm gettin' a little impatient and finally I scream, "You think I can get that donut today or you think I should come back tomorrow!!" I mean I was pissed!! Over a fuckin' donut, you know? And it wasn't like I had anywhere I needed to be. I looked at the situation and realized what an asshole I was being [laughs] and I said to myself, "I'm not usually *this* much of an asshole." I apologized to her and said I hadn't really been myself lately. Boy, was that embarrassing though. Right after I got outta there I said forget it. I don't want to keep takin' those meds. They are not doing me one bit of good. So I saw my doctor today and told him how I felt about it and he tried to get me to give it another chance but I just said, "It ain't worth it to me, Doc." So he's gonna put me on something else.

The same emphasis on overall tenability could also be seen in discussions of recovery work aimed at subduing people's addictions. Members of the Twilights treatment program did not regard recovery from addiction merely in terms of living drug free. One often heard reiterations of AA slogans in this regard. The most common of these involved references to what were known as "dry drunks," or episodes during which people were said to be off drugs and alcohol but not genuinely recovering from addiction. Beyond abstinence, the work of recovery entailed changing one's life sufficiently so that drug use no longer seemed necessary. If people failed to cultivate satisfying lives without drugs, their sobriety was generally regarded as vulnerable and relapse was thought to be inevitable. This orientation is illustrated in the following excerpt wherein Layla expresses her sentiments regarding the untenability of her life without drugs and hence the unlikelihood of abstaining for any extended period of time:

> See, Darin, it's hard for me to stay clean, because my life when I'm clean is so horrible. They say it gets better but for me it never got better. I knew when I relapsed that it wasn't the answer, that I was gonna be even worse off, but I didn't care. I just wanted relief from that misery, even if it was only going to be a temporary fix and was going to make things worse in the end. I just said, "Give me the temporary fix."

In the case of both psychiatric disorders and drug problems, then, recovery was sought and fostered at Twilights through the promotion of tenable community living rather than by way of narrowly focused efforts to subdue biopsychological symptoms. Efforts to promote tenable community living arrangements focused on a wide variety of issues including housing, work, entitlements, medical care, legal aid, and sundry other challenges attendant to clients' efforts to subsist.

As one might expect, Twilights members pursued a variety of personally distinctive approaches to achieving and sustaining tenability. In the following exchange, for example, Eric describes his move from a temporary shelter into his car as, in fact, an improvement in the tenability of his community living arrangements. The passage also sharply illustrates how Twilights staff generally yielded to clients' definitions of tenable community living rather than imposing their own definitions. Claire, a counselor, had just asked Eric why he had gotten himself kicked out of a local shelter. This led to the following conversation:

ERIC: I just couldn't take bein' around all those people all the time. I told you I'm basically a loner and I just got too paranoid around all those people there. Bein' sober made it even worse. I was startin' to get thoughts like if I don't get out of here I'm gonna get drunk and so I was gonna leave anyway before they kicked me out. I don't mind that they kicked me out at all.

CLAIRE: So what are you gonna do now? Where you sleepin' now?

ERIC: I got my brother's car. It's kinda like my car. It's his but he lets me use it. I been sleepin' in it a long time so I'm used to it. I don't have no problem with it. At least for now anyway. It's better for me than the shelter. I didn't get along with them anyway.

CLAIRE: Okay, it's up to you Eric. I just hope this isn't an excuse for you being irresponsible. I mean I did a bit of footwork gettin' you in there and it was a bit of a disappointment for me to find out you got kicked out. I mean that's not such a big deal but I just hope this isn't a bigger problem than just Jumpstreet [the shelter].

ERIC: It's not. I mean I ain't gonna say that things are goin' well for me but I don't think Jumpstreet has anything to do with my troubles. If anything it's a little better now that I'm outta there.

CLAIRE: Okay.

Retrospection Versus Realistic Planning

The fact that Canyon House was residential and Twilights nonresidential also forced another rather dramatic difference in the character of therapeutic self-empowerment in the two programs. This difference concerned the temporal focus of self-empowerment efforts. In addition to fostering self-empowerment by enforcing right living among themselves, Canyon House members also sought to empower themselves by retrospectively identifying the specific patterns in which clients' mental disorders had assailed them in the past. Given clients' current enjoyment of room, board, and an extremely rarified social environment, there was little incentive to attend to the details of ensuring one's own livelihood or to fortify oneself against the kinds of obstacles to recovery that lurked beyond the confines of the program. In this atmosphere, residents were relatively free to contemplate their pasts, to formulate the particular patterns their distinctive troubles had taken in their lives, and to parse these troubles into those for which people were properly held morally accountable and those that had been foisted upon people by their mental disorders. In contrast, Twilights clients were not nearly as free. They returned to their lives outside the program each evening at 9:00 P.M. And, of course, they remained deeply concerned with exigencies attendant to their outside lives throughout the time they spent at Twilights. John, a counselor at Canyon House for several years and now the director at Twilights, made the point this way:

> We [at Twilights] tend to be more focused on what's going on for a person outside the program—finding housing, getting benefits, getting a sponsor, getting a relationship going with an outside psychiatrist, finding a home meeting, those kinds of things. Whereas in a program like Canyon House the focus tends to be a little more on internal issues like problems between residents, chores problems, and stuff like that. Our goal plans are more in terms of concrete practical issues that people need to address, and the Canyon focuses a little more on feelings issues and patterns that residents have in dealing with people and their denial of responsibility for their problems. We deal with those things too but maybe not as much as an inpatient. I think that stuff comes up no matter what but for us it comes up in dealing with the more practical stuff.

At Twilights the temporal focus of self-empowerment was trained less upon grasping the characteristics of the specific disorders presumed to have assailed clients in the past, than on the specific practical issues that emerged as obstacles to, or as opportunities for, promoting the current and future tenability of their lives in the community. The work of self-empowerment thus consisted more in looking forward than backward, more in the work of realistic planning than in the work of therapeutic retrospection. This is not to say that realistic planning entailed no retrospective assessments of client troubles. Rather, whatever retrospection took place was driven primarily by efforts to enhance the tenability of people's community living arrangements and only secondarily by efforts to diagnose the characteristic actions and identities of the mental disorders presumed to afflict them. Furthermore, the concrete efforts associated with realistic planning did not necessarily implicate past troubles at all. Often this work consisted of putting people in touch with opportunities they may not have known about or in addressing obstacles to recovery that loomed exclusively in the future rather than those that were suggested by the patterns in one's past.

Perhaps the most important thing to remember when comparing self-empowerment at Twilights and Canyon House is Twilights' proximity to the environments in which Twilights clients experienced their troubles. In the following excerpt Eve, who had worked at Canyon House before to coming to Twilights, testifies to this while discussing the types of people who need inpatient treatment:

> Some people are just chronic relapsers and can't stay clean by themselves on the outside. They need to be completely removed from that environment for a little while so that they can get some distance and some insight on what's going on for them. When they're on the outside it's all just too close and they can't really detach themselves from it. Like I think Eric might be better in inpatient [Claire nodded in agreement]. I think he really wants to quit but it's just too hard for him when he's outside.

More than anything, this proximity to the circumstances of daily suffering drew attention to the specific details of people's community living arrangements as opposed to the problematic patterns in their past personal actions and experiences. Above all, realistic planning entailed sensitizing people to the effects their community living arrangements had on their actions and getting them to behave in accordance with that sensitivity. Though this was in some sense a retrospective project of detecting personal patterns, the primary focus was decidedly prospective, extrapersonal, and concerned with tenability in contrast with Canyon House's focus on detecting the patterns characteristic of clients' past troubles.

This contrast may be seen in the juxtaposition of a typical therapeutic exercise at Canyon House with a piece of advice John, a counselor, gave clients during a group session at Twilights. The following exchange is from a feeling-good group at Canyon House. Participants had been given a handout that listed 10 kinds of "twisted thinking" that often produce anxiety. After giving people time to read the handout, Ron, a recovery specialist, asked for a volunteer to begin the discussion by applying the information in the handout to times when she or he had experienced serious anxiety. Lonny, a client, raised his hand and replied that he would start:

LONNY: I feel anxious a lot when I speak in front of big groups like here and at AA meetings.

RON: Okay, and what kinds of twisted thinking were you using that made you feel anxious, that made you feel that fear?

LONNY: [Looking over the handout] Well let's see. "Four: discounting the positive." I would think that I didn't have anything important to say and that nobody would want to hear it. "Five: jumping to conclusions." I didn't think about the possibility that some people *would* want to hear what I had to say. "Magnification: six." I would exaggerate the importance of the moment and think that if I made a fool out of myself it would be the worst thing in the world when really it wouldn't be that bad. It would be bad, but not the worst thing in the world. "Seven: emotional reasoning." I assumed my negative emotions reflected the way things really were. And "Nine: labeling." I thought I *was* a fool and so it was unavoidable that I would make a fool out of myself.

RON: Okay, that's real good. Looks like you spotted a lot of twisted thinking in the way you were approaching those situations. What do you think you could do to *solve* some of these problems, these sources of fear—you know, Feeling Good, this is a problem-solving group. [Many laughed as if this characterization of the group was getting a bit tired. One could hear that Ron anticipated such a reaction in the tone of his voice.]

LONNY: [Responding to Ron's question] Well I think I'm improving on this one. One of the things I do is just to raise my hand and get it over with, not dwell on it too long. That's what I just did for this assignment. I also try to think about myself as having important things to say.

We can see in this exchange the retrospective quality of the exercise as well as its promotion in the interest of Lonny's self-empowerment.

Now compare this to an excerpt from John's comments during a community meeting at Twilights:

You know, in that sense it's just like any other disease. Once you know you have diabetes it's the same thing. You learn how the disease affects you and you take precautions to stay out of the situations that might be dangerous for you, like eating wrong or not having insulin handy. With alcoholism or drug addiction you work on discovering your triggers and what we call your slippery places and once you know what those are it becomes your responsibility to avoid those places. Working a program is about living your life intelligently, given the knowledge you have about your disease.

More than simply casting therapeutic practice in terms of helping people develop a personal past as it relates to their disease, John specifies self-knowledge in distinctly prospective and environmental terms ("You learn how the disease affects you and you take precautions to stay out of the situations that might be dangerous for you").

An important therapeutic consequence of the difference in temporal orientation is that different kinds of evidence were used to document clients' disorders. Thus, learning about one's disorders and how to control them unfolded in very different ways. Fostering knowledge about one's disease at Canyon House consisted primarily of efforts to discover and articulate the characteristic personal, *internal* patterns of action and reaction that created problems for particular people in their lives. At Twilights, in contrast, knowing one's disease primarily involved efforts to discover and articulate the various environmental, *external* "triggers" and "slippery places" that people needed to avoid if they were to sustain their recoveries. No doubt, the various internal and external processes through which people's disorders were exhibited in these settings were often closely related to one another. Nevertheless, the greater emphasis on triggers and slippery places at Twilights as opposed to patterns of personal action and reaction at Canyon House produced systematic differences in the ways mental disorders were construed and managed in each of these settings.

Constructing Moral Accountability

Strange as it might seem from medical and psychiatric perspectives, therapeutic practice at Canyon House and at Twilights was more fundamentally concerned with the routine production and maintenance of normal social orders than with the detection and repression of clinical "symptoms." In the residential setting of Canyon House this involved the collective embodiment and enforcement of right living among program members. In the outpatient setting of Twilights it consisted mainly in the collective cultivation and achievement of tenable community living. In both instances, mental disorders were invoked and elaborated only as collateral resources in the more basic work of empowering clients as effective participants in their respective communities. Likewise, in both cases the empowerment of clients' selves was not only an explicit treatment goal but also an explicitly avowed resource for treatment. Thus, therapeutic practice at Canyon House and at Twilights was fundamentally concerned with equipping clients themselves to become the primary ministers of their own recoveries.

This required that clients' selves be constructed as *morally accountable human subjects*[5] capable of contributing effectively to their own recoveries. Therefore, the ability to recognize and sanction people's particular successes and failures in the work of recovery was a necessary feature of therapeutic practice at both Canyon House and Twilights. This often required program members to *distinguish* between the actions and identities of the various human subjects who collaborated in the therapeutic enterprise and the actions and identities of the mental disorders that participants found to obstruct and interfere with that enterprise. In this section of the chapter, I address how mental disorders were constructed as tangible worldly entities in their own right, or as nonhuman determinants of program affairs. I also describe how the contrasting dynamics of therapeutic practice at Canyon House and Twilights systematically altered the patterns according to which mental disorders were installed as the causal agents of clients' actions.

Institutionally contingent differences in the construction of moral agency at each of these programs produced systematic differences in how Canyon House and Twilights members (both staff and clients) constructed the mental disorders presumed to afflict clients. Though I found no strict formulas for distinguishing specific mental illnesses and addictions as such,[6] disparate tendencies in the ways mental disorders were designated at Canyon House and at Twilights were very plainly evident. In both cases these tendencies were heavily influenced by the distinctive manner in which efforts were made to foster community and empower program clients.

Using Mental Disorder at Canyon House

As I have shown elsewhere (Weinberg 1997, 1998), there was a basic preference in both programs for holding clients—and not their mental disorders—accountable for their personal behavior and experiences. Mental disorders were used as surrogate explanations of people's troubles or troublesome behavior only when those troubles were found to resist[7] being construed as deliberate rejections of program decorum. At Canyon House, this type of resistance was found in personal behavior and experiences that departed from right living in ways that program members found irreconcilable with their sense of a given offender's self. Hence, determinations that program participants were not acting or feeling "themselves" were often grounds for the finding that mental disorder was causing their behavior or experience. This may be seen in the following exchange from a meeting in which Sherry's "willfulness" is attributed to her disease. Paula, a counselor, had been surprised when she saw the list of people with three or more "6:15" transgressions because it was so long.[8] She said she saw a lot of names she didn't expect to see on it, people who she had thought were doing really well:

PAULA: Let's start with you Sherry. I was surprised to see your name on this list. What's up?

SHERRY: I'm surprised too, I don't know.

[Sherry mentioned what she thought she had gotten them for—things like not going to meetings and refusing to get to her kitchen assignment on time.]

PAULA: Sounds like a lot of 'em you got behind that willful behavior of yours.

SHERRY: [Nodding and smiling] Yep, it does look like that. I think it is my being willful.

PAULA: When you start having good ideas, when you start thinking that you know better than everybody else what's good for you, that's a good time to start getting suspicious and to check yourself. When you start saying, "I don't think I need to go to group," or "I don't think I need to get up and do my chore," that's the kind of thing that's gonna get you kicked out of here and you'll be right back out there where you were. *That's your disease talkin' and tryin' to get you to relapse.* It's real important that when you start getting those willful feelings that you find somebody to talk to and check yourself.

[Sherry nodded sheepishly.]

It was only by virtue of Sherry's otherwise encouraging performance of late that it became reasonable to attribute her recent and "willful" accumulation of "6:15s" to her disease rather than deliberate misconduct. If we view the diagnosis of mental disorder as a strictly "technical rational" enterprise (see Kirk and Kutchins 1992, pp. 220–23), then clinical judgments like this may be viewed as aberrations; at best they are mistakes and at worst they are deeply disturbing instances of personal oppression carried out under the auspices of clinical medicine (cf. Szasz 1961). However, if we view such diagnoses as fundamentally responsive to an institutionally contingent moral order, things don't appear quite so grave. Seen in this light, Sherry's "willfulness" was a departure from right living. It resisted being understood as a product of her self because it was inconsistent with the self Paula perceived Sherry to have become ("I was surprised to see your name on this list"). Paula goes on to interpret this departure from right living as evidence that Sherry's "disease" was "tryin' to get [her] to relapse." "Willfulness" may seem an odd category of personal behavior to attribute to a disease, but the practical circumstances in which Paula and Sherry found themselves allowed for this attribution, simply and unremarkably. In this exchange Sherry's disease is invoked to replace her self—as a surrogate cause of her behavior, absolving her of moral accountability for her uncharacteristic departure from right living without absolving her of the moral duty to more vigilantly attend to her recovery in the future.

Using Mental Disorder at Twilights

I have mentioned that Canyon House residents had strong material incentives to comply with house policies and programs. I should also mention that because Canyon House residents were together nearly all day, every day, and were required to collaborate with one another on chore teams and meal crews, there was abundant opportunity for Canyon House clients to get to know one another personally and to participate in the enforcement of one another's right living. Hence, opportunities to detect, construe, and manage one another's departures from right living were also abundant. In contrast, Twilights clients had only minimal incentive to comply with any moral demands that might be made of them by others in the program. They were together as a therapeutic community only five days a week, eight hours a day, and only very rarely did they spend time together outside the program. Nor were Twilights clients required to collaborate with one another in the preparation of meals or the maintenance of the facility. And, as we have seen, the aim of therapeutic practice at Twilights was largely focused outward, on clients' living arrangements outside the program, not on the adequacy of their participation within the program.

Given the greater precariousness of Twilights clients' investment in participating in the program, the greater weight placed on mere attendance as an indicator of investment,[9] staff's concern to retain clients, and the comparative superficiality of clients' relationships with one another, departures from right living were less often registered and more ambiguous at Twilights than at Canyon House. If and when a departure from right living was registered at Twilights, clients were generally left to decide for themselves whether such departures indicated mental disorder or not. When collective efforts were made to formulate the characteristics of particular clients' mental disorders, these efforts consisted primarily in discovering the specific "triggers" and "slippery places" that posed threats to the tenability of clients' community living arrangements beyond the confines of the program.

Because departures from right living were rarely registered at Twilights, the bulk of evidence for clients' mental disorders was found elsewhere. Typically, it was found in the behavior and experiences people undertook *between* the periods they were present in the program. That is, evidence was drawn primarily from clients' personal behavior and experiences outside the program setting itself. Indeed, both Twilights staff and clients often attributed client absences from the program to clients' disorders.[10] Clients' mental disorders were often held to have caused their literal disappearance or complete estrangement from the program. This can be seen in the following discussion between Clarise, a counselor, and Bob, a client, regarding Bob's roommate, Mack. I arrived at Twilights to discover Bob and Clarise immersed in conversation. I asked what they were talking about:

CLARISE: [Replying to me] Mack relapsed.

DARIN: What happened?

CLARISE: Well, Mack finally got his retroactive SSI check. I guess they owed him several thousand dollars or something. Bob, how much was it for?

BOB: [Shrugging] I dunno. I never saw it. A lot though.

CLARISE: Anyway as soon as he got it he took off, disappeared as soon as he got it.

BOB: [Laughing sarcastically] Figures, don't it? He left me holdin' the bill to the cable too. He's got all this money all of a sudden and he goes off leavin' me with the bill for the cable.

CLARISE: It was his turn?

BOB: Think he'd leave when it was my turn? No way. That motherfucker was goin' for all he could get. Dope fiend motherfucker is all he is.

CLARISE: We've all done things like this, but that doesn't mean it ain't a shame. I thought Mack was doin' real good. I guess it just goes to show you doesn't it, how destructive this disease can be?

BOB: Yep.

Disappearances were not always this complete. Often they took the form of only temporary absences or disengagements from the shared recovery work of the program. This can be seen in the following passage where Bill, a counselor, describes a particular client's failures to return to the program. When I asked Bill about Stephen, the client, and his friend Alicia, another client, he said:

They haven't been back for about a week and a half. I was supposed to bring Stephen to the doctor on Monday but I went to his apartment and he wasn't there. We went by on Tuesday too and he wasn't there . . . Stephen is a very sick guy. He is very paranoid, very delusional and he won't stay on his meds. I don't think he's the kind of person that can make it in a program like this one. It's just too much for him. When I was supposed to pick him up on Monday we were going to see the doctor about getting him placed in a residential program. I think he needs more than Twilights can give him. Stephen was one of those people who would come in for a day or two days and quit. The only reason he came back was because Alicia was coming and we physically went and brought him back in. He doesn't have much commitment to this program at all. The last time a Rand interviewer knocked on his door he wouldn't open it. He just yelled to them to leave him alone and go away. I mean, what are you supposed to do about someone like that? There's not a lot you can do, short of kidnapping them.

While Bill does speak to Stephen's lack of commitment, he also emphasizes the severity of Stephen's disorder and Stephen's having greater "needs" than Twilights can meet. Hence, Stephen's absence from the program is explained as a product of both his own lack of resolve (as a morally accountable human self) and the severity of his affliction (by a mental disorder). As was the case at Canyon House, being found to be controlled by a mental disorder did not entail being found to have been completely deprived of one's humanity (see also Gubrium 1986). Instead, it only entailed being found *incapable* of adequate participation in the program.

If and when program members were held accountable for such troubles, they were not found to have rejected the program but to have lacked the resolve to remain connected in spite of their disorders. Thus, the primary causes of their troubles were held to be their mental disorders (above which they could not, or would not, rise) rather than their own morally accountable human selves. Therefore we cannot understand the social construction of mental disorders to consist entirely of processes through which persons' selves are assembled and transformed. Participants in both Canyon House and Twilights were often simultaneously found accountable for their lack of resolve and not accountable for the specific behavioral and experiential effects of their disorders. Behavioral transgressions were routinely attributed not to clients' selves but to their disorders—as distinct causal agents. This fact cannot be explained unless we acknowledge that at least two categorically distinct types of intrapersonal agents were held to be capable of governing clients' personal behavior and experience—a morally accountable self and an amoral mental disorder with which clients chronically struggled.

Self-Empowerment, Institutional Order, and Mental Disorder

I have argued that therapeutic practice at Canyon House and Twilights consisted of the incitement and empowerment of clients' selves in relation to their distinctive institutional environments. Though Twilights was intended to exactly replicate the Canyon House program in a nonresidential setting, its lack of institutional encapsulation forced significant changes in how the therapeutic work of self-empowerment was actually conducted. These changes were not caused by differences at the level of what Foucault called the "symbolic system," or what we might call the programs' respective "treatment philosophies," but by the material and organizational parameters of therapeutic practice itself. Self-empowerment at Canyon House consisted fundamentally of morally enforcing right living among clients and in collaborative efforts to retrospectively assess the specific causes and characteristics of the troubles they had suffered in the past. Despite its identical treatment philosophy, therapeutic self-empowerment at Twilights involved fostering tenable community living arrangements for clients, promoting realistic planning for the immediate future, and developing clients' abilities to accomplish these tasks for themselves. In each instance, these therapeutic practices were directly responsive to the distinctive institutional environments in which they took place—most notably clients' status as inpatient or outpatient.

Of course, this is not to argue that therapeutic practice at Canyon House and Twilights occurred without resort to any more enduring therapeutic discourse or symbolic system. Various narrative resources drawn from the 12-step fellowship, psychiatry, clinical psychology, and social work were indeed abundantly invoked in both programs. But it was the decidedly *practical* logic of empowering clients' particular selves in light of their respective material circumstances—not the *conceptual* logic of a given therapeutic discourse—that most powerfully governed if, when, and how these resources were appropriated. Thus, to borrow Foucault's (1983, p. 250) phrase, each of these programs embodied a distinctive "technology of the constitution of the self which cuts across symbolic systems while using them." At Canyon House and Twilights, fostering recovery was not simply a matter of training clients to "talk the talk" that indicated fluency in a locally endorsed therapeutic discourse. It was more fundamentally concerned with ensuring that clients learn to "walk the walk" that marked their empowerment as effective, self-governing participants in their respective institutional environments.

At Canyon House this meant empowering clients' selves through immersion in a communally shared regimen of right living and pushing clients to scrutinize their pasts so as to better understand and control both their selves and their unique mental disorders. Hence, clients' selves were constructed and empowered at Canyon House through a combination of domestic cooperation and retrospective biographical work (see Gubrium and Holstein 1995; Holstein and Gubrium 2000). These selves were cast in subjective opposition, and objective contrast to the disorders presumed to afflict them but because clients resided full time at Canyon House they were not required to confront the demands of subsisting in the wider community. In contrast, because Twilights was nonresidential and its clients were homeless and destitute, coping with the demands of subsistence in the wider community emerged as the central focus of self-empowerment there. Despite all efforts to replicate the regimen of treatment provided at Canyon House, the selves of Twilights clients were, of necessity, constructed and empowered less through right living and retrospection than through collective efforts to anticipate and manage the relentlessly pressing vicissitudes of life on the streets.

Of course, the selves constructed in both of these settings contended with the ever-present prospect of being overwhelmed by the distinctive mental disorders presumed to afflict them. Selves in Canyon House were empowered, figuratively speaking, through efforts to understand their enemies in order to conquer them; accumulating knowledge of the distinctive characteristics their disorders had manifest in the past would help clients fully master their personal actions, thoughts, and emotions. For Twilights clients, however, self-empowerment basically entailed cultivating the ability to avoid their mental disorders through realistic planning for the immediate future—identifying and avoiding those events and environments they anticipated as "triggers" and "slippery places" respectively. In both sites, the work of self-empowerment constructed client selves that were instrumental in dealing with mental disorders in the specific ways that the respective institutions came to address these troubles.

Finally, members of these programs took very seriously the capacities of mental disorders to actively intervene in people's lives, and to obstinately resist people's efforts to prevent the disorders from doing so. Though no doubt ancillary to the more basic work of self-empowerment, the construction and management of clients' mental disorders as surrogates for clients' selves was nonetheless a very important feature of therapeutic practice. Therefore, in addition to analyzing the parameters of therapeutic self-empowerment, I have also sought to provide for the specific ways in which clients' disorders were made to figure not only as labels, roles, or accounts, but as causally influential nonhuman agents in the course of program affairs.

NOTES

1. Following my site visits, I wrote narrative fieldnotes, extensively elaborating hastily written notes I had jotted down during the day. I completed these fieldnotes as soon as possible, normally within a few days of each site visit. In addition to about 700 pages of single-spaced typewritten fieldnotes, I also collected written materials used in the programs and about 40 hours of audiotape recordings depicting group therapy sessions, private counseling sessions, and staff meetings. I collected audiotapes only in the residential program. Due to the rapid turnover, sporadic attendance, and organizational dynamics of the nonresidential program, I was unable to secure informed consent from clients for taping there. Though these data would have certainly been useful, their absence does not shortchange the analysis that is offered here.

2. The exchanges extracted throughout the paper are reconstructions of events recorded in my fieldnotes.

3. The fundamentally negotiated character of right living at Canyon House was made vividly apparent to me when I learned of the following case. One day, soon after arriving upon site, I learned that a resident who was a self-professed recovering heroin addict had been hospitalized with a kidney stone and put on a morphine drip to ease his pain. Though the news of his morphine drip was met with some concern among both clients and counselors at Canyon House, it did not for a moment threaten this resident's status in the program nor was it counted against his days of having remained clean and sober. By Canyon House lights, this manner of opiate use clearly fell within the bounds of right living.

4. The defining characteristics of *tenable* community living arrangements often vary widely from one case to the next. Holstein (1993, pp. 128–29) aptly writes in this regard, "[a]s a practical matter, tenable living circumstances are established in terms of the fit between the particular *needs* and *demands* of the patient in question and the *accommodations* available in a proposed living situation. The adequacy of a proposed living situation's accommodations can be interpreted only in light of its proposed occupant's needs and demands. A tenable situation is one that matches a patient's needs and demands with a living situation that satisfies those needs."

5. In using the expression *morally accountable human subjects* I am drawing upon an understanding of moral accountability that includes not only the demands we make of ourselves and of one another to behave virtuously, but also the moral demands we make upon one another and upon our selves to think and behave *intelligibly* (see Coulter 1973, 1979; Garfinkel 1963, 1984; Heritage 1984; Ingleby 1982).

6. Of course, many people had an abstract appreciation of the kinds of symptoms that are normally associated with specific varieties of disorder. But in practice, these sortings were governed by myriad concerns specific to the activities and participants at hand. Depending on the particular conditions under which assessments were made, putative paranoias, hallucinations, depressions, and the like were sometimes understood as induced by psychiatric disorders but they were sometimes also understood as drug induced. Likewise, professed drug cravings were held to exhibit bona fide addictions but were held to exhibit compulsions to self-medicate underlying psychiatric disorders as

well. Sometimes, neither psychiatric disorders nor addictions were implicated by the findings of hallucinations, paranoias, depressions, and other such candidate "symptoms." Such candidate symptoms were sometimes attributed to the effects of particular medications, to exhaustion, and to other causes that did not directly implicate the agency of people's putative mental disorders.

7. The expression *resist*, as I am using it here, derives from Pickering (1995, p. 22), who writes of a "dialectic of resistance and accommodation" through which physicists become acquainted with and manipulate the physical world. The *resistance* a putative object (e.g., a segment of personal conduct) might present to practical projects undertaken by human beings does not refer in any way to the realist's essential properties constitutive of an object. Instead, the expression refers to the *empirically evident* breakdowns in procedure that often occur when people encounter unanticipated outcomes in their engagements with the world's objects *as they know them*. When such breakdowns occur, they can force people to undertake accommodative reformulations of the putative objects with which they feel they have ineffectively engaged, but they do not in any way provide insight into the "essence" of objects.

8. "6:15s" were a form of punishment meted out in response to sanctioned behavior: the resident was required to awaken the morning following a transgression at 6:15 A.M. and write/reflect on a topic deemed relevant to his or her personal recovery.

9. Unlike at Canyon House, Twilights clients had to personally undertake to get themselves to the program each day. It was widely acknowledged that this in itself often entailed a good deal of exertion. Hence, clients' very presence was usually taken as more indicative of commitment to the program and recovery than was mere attendance at Canyon House, where no effort need be expended to attend.

10. In contrast, due to the remoteness of the residential facility, people almost never went AWOL from Canyon House. Because Canyon House clients did not just disappear, their mental disorders were never held to have caused a client's disappearance.

REFERENCES

Alcoholics Anonymous. 1976. *Alcoholics Anonymous.* 3d ed. New York: Alcoholics Anonymous World Services.

Bloor, Michael, Neal McKeganey, and Dick Fonkert. 1988. *One Foot in Eden: A Sociological Study of the Range of Therapeutic Community Practice.* London: Routledge.

Coulter, Jeff. 1973. *Approaches to Insanity: A Philosophical & Sociological Study.* New York: John Wiley & Sons.

———. 1979. *The Social Construction of Mind.* London: MacMillan.

Denzin, Norman K. 1993. *The Alcoholic Society: Addiction and Recovery of the Self.* New Brunswick, N.J.: Transaction Publishers.

Emerson, Robert M. 1989. "Tenability and Troubles: The Construction of Accomodative Relations by Psychiatric Emergency Teams." In *Perspectives on Social Problems,* vol. 1, ed. Gale Miller and James A. Holstein, 215–37. Greenwich, Conn.: JAI Press.

Foucault, Michel. 1983. "On the Genealogy of Ethics: An Overview of Work in Progress." In *Michel Foucault: Beyond Structuralism and Hermeneutics,* 2d ed. Hubert L. Dreyfus and Paul Rabinow, 229–52. Chicago: University of Chicago Press.

Garfinkel, Harold. 1963. "A Conception of, and Experiments with, 'Trust' as a Condition of Stable Concerted Actions." In *Motivation and Social Interaction,* ed. O. J. Harvey, 187–238. New York: Ronald Press.

———. 1984. *Studies in Ethnomethodology.* London: Polity Press.

Gubrium, Jaber F. 1986. "The Social Preservation of Mind: The Alzheimer's Disease Experience." *Symbolic Interaction* 6(1): 37–51.

Gubrium, Jaber F., and James A. Holstein. 1995. "Biographical Work and New Ethnography." In *Interpreting Experience: The Narrative Study of Lives,* vol. 3, ed. Ruthellen Josselson and Amia Lieblich, 45–58. Thousand Oaks, Calif.: Sage Publications.

Heritage, John. 1984. *Garfinkel and Ethnomethodology.* London: Polity Press.

Holstein, James A. 1993. *Court-Ordered Insanity: Interpretive Practice and Involuntary Commitment.* New York: Aldine de Gruyter.

Holstein, James A., and Jaber F. Gubrium. 2000. *Constructing the Life Course.* 2d ed. Dix Hills, N.Y.: General Hall.

Hughes, Everett C. 1971. "Going Concerns: The Study of American Institutions." In *The Sociological Eye: Selected Papers,* Everett C. Hughes, 52–64. Chicago: Aldine de Gruyter.

Ingleby, David. 1982. "The Social Construction of Mental Illness." In *The Problem of Medical Knowledge: Examining the Social Construction of Medicine,* ed. Peter Wright and Andrew Treacher, 123–43. Edinburgh: Edinburgh University Press.

Kirk, Stuart A., and Herb Kutchins. 1992. *The Selling of DSM: The Rhetoric of Science in Psychiatry.* New York: Aldine de Gruyter.

Kramer, Peter D. 1993. *Listening to Prozac: A Psychiatrist Explores Antidepressant Drugs and the Remaking of the Self.* New York: Viking.

Pickering, Andrew. 1995. *The Mangle of Practice: Time, Agency, & Science.* Chicago: University of Chicago Press.

Skoll, Geoffrey R. 1992. *Walk the Walk and Talk the Talk: An Ethnography of a Drug Abuse Treatment Facility.* Philadelphia: Temple University Press.

Sugarman, Barry. 1974. *Daytop Village: A Therapeutic Community.* New York: Holt, Rinehardt and Winston.

Szasz, Thomas. 1961. *The Myth of Mental Illness: Foundations of a Theory of Personal Conduct.* New York: Hoeber-Harper.

Weinberg, Darin. 1996. "The Enactment and Appraisal of Authenticity in a Skid Row Therapeutic Community." *Symbolic Interaction* 19(2): 137–62.

———. 1997. "The Social Construction of Nonhuman Agency: The Case of Mental Disorder." *Social Problems* 44(2): 217–34.

———. 1998. "Of Others Inside: Insanities, Addictions, and Recoveries Among Homeless Americans." Ph.D. diss. UCLA.

Weinberg, Darin, and Paul Koegel. 1995. "Impediments to Recovery in Treatment Programs for Dually Diagnosed Homeless Adults: An Ethnographic Analysis." *Contemporary Drug Problems* 22(2): 193–236.

———. 1996. "Social Model Treatment and Individuals with Dual Diagnoses: An Ethnographic Analysis of Therapeutic Practice." *Journal of Mental Health Administration* 23(3): 272–87.

Yablonsky, Lewis. 1965. *The Tunnel Back: Synanon.* New York: Macmillan.

PART 2

Constructing Institutional Selves

DONILEEN R. LOSEKE

Lived Realities and Formula Stories of "Battered Women"

Thirty years ago "wife abuse" didn't exist; there were no "battered women" or "abusive men." Of course that doesn't mean that men were not being violent toward women. Rather, it means that the *social problem* of "wife abuse" was not yet in public consciousness; the "battered woman" and the "abusive man" were not publicly recognizable identities (see Loseke 1992; Tierney 1982). This problem and these identities appeared on the social scene only as the result of successful social problems claims-making (Spector and Kitsuse 1987).

Part of establishing the social problem of "wife abuse" was creating new *formula stories* (Berger 1997) that placed "battered women" and "abusive men" at the center of depictions of domestic violence. Formula stories are narratives about types of experiences (such as "wife abuse") involving distinctive types of characters (such as the "battered woman" and the "abusive man.") As such stories become widely acknowledged ways of interpreting and conveying experience, they can become virtual templates for how lived experience may be defined. As formula stories pervade a culture, people increasingly use them to make sense of their lives and experiences.

The wife abuse formula story that has flourished in recent decades is told in terms of clearly immoral behavior, with pure victims and evil villains (Loseke 1999). This formula story can be an interpretive resource for women, showing them how to understand their experiences in ways that resonate with the story of typical "wife abuse." In turn, the formula story helps women conceive of themselves in terms of the identity or type of person that has come to be called the "battered woman." Similarly, the formula story promotes the use of the category "abusive man" to describe women's assailants.

Lived experience, however, isn't easily categorized. Indeed, "troubles" in lived experience tend to be unpredictable in emergence, irregular in progression, ambiguous in meaning, and uncertain in development (Merry 1990). While formula stories can help make sense of such troubles, in the process such stories tend to leave the complexity and indeterminacy of lived experience in the background, glossing over them in favor of lurid accounts of heinous behavior, depraved perpetrators, and helpless victims. The mundane complications of everyday social relations and interpretation may virtually disappear as the formula story presents troubles in bold relief. Hence, the relationship between formula stories and lived experience can be quite ambiguous; we can't merely assume that formula stories offer an actual recipe for making sense of everyday experiences.

This chapter explores how formula stories shape the experiences of women who participate in support groups for those who have experienced violence at the hands of their male partners. In addition to providing compassion and understanding for their members, support groups are designed to promote particular ways of understanding experiences (Dean 1998). In the process, they work to transform women's identities. In a sense, support groups are storytelling groups (Maines 1991; Mason-Schrock 1996) that provide members with "better" stories, populated with familiar institutional identities.

But the institutional mediation of the battered woman identity is not a straightforward or deterministic process. Support groups do not simply assert identities and definitions for their members. Members undertake considerable narrative *identity work* in order to articulate the battered woman image with the lived experiences of group members. Moreover, women often find alternate ways of conveying their experiences. As the analysis unfolds, it will become clear that while support groups are in the business of promoting particular definitions and personas, group members do not necessarily rely upon the groups' interpretive blueprints to format their identities and experience. Indeed, the complexity of lived experience has a way of resisting formulaic presentation.

The Complexity of Lived Experience

In lived experience, troubles do not come to us with labels describing their names, meanings, seriousness, and so forth. Assigning meaning to the lived experience of *all* troubles is complex because "perception of 'something wrong' is often vague at the onset . . . on first apprehension troubles often involve little more than vague unease . . . [t]he understandings of the problem's dimensions may only begin to emerge as the troubled person thinks about them" (Emerson and Messenger 1977, pp. 121–22). We might begin by thinking of women in support groups for battered women as women in "failing relationships." The lived experience of failing relationships most often is of a "bewilderingly complex tangle of events" (Weiss 1975, p. 16), of a "bewildering complexity of events," of "ambiguities and contradictions," and a "fundamental uncertainty" (Hopper 1993, p. 804). Women *and* men in failing relationships often cite many simultaneous troubles that might include perceptions that the partner is unfaithful, an alcoholic, suffering from mental illness, stingy, irresponsible, or sexually inadequate (Weiss 1975). People in failing relationships can talk about troubles with in-laws, disagreements about children, differences in hobbies, and/or conflicts over television (Hopper 1993). At times, there might not even be an identifiable trouble or fault, but rather a vague perception that partners have "grown apart," are "psychologically distant," or "failing to communicate" (Weiss 1975). The conceptual category of failing relationships can be the lived experience of many simultaneous, interrelated, and vaguely defined troubles.

While failing relationships is a conceptual category for relationships that are troubled for *any* reason, support groups for battered women are concerned only with troubled relationships that contain "wife abuse." The formula story of wife abuse has abuse as its central organizing theme. As a social construction, "abusive" violence is morally intolerable; it is extreme and continuing violence done intentionally by men creating women as pure victims (Loseke 1992). Yet violence in people's lived realities is not always so easy to name as the violence of abuse. Naming an experience as abuse is complicated by the presence in our culture of a category of experience called "normal violence," a folk category organized around the assumption that not all violence is morally reprehensible, that some violence on some occasions for some purposes is understandable (Merry 1990). Therefore, while the formula story of wife abuse has a central plot organized around extreme and long-lasting violence done for "no good reason," violence in lived realities can be experienced as more or less extreme, more or less consequential, more or less justifiable and, therefore, more or less intolerable.

This is further complicated because lived realities can lead women to tell stories that might seem implausible. Women's stories of their lived experiences, in other words, sometimes defy narrative conventions (see Bruner 1987; Gergen 1994; Linde 1993; Maines 1991; Riessman 1990 for examples of narrative conventions). For instance, the lived experience of violence can include characters who are *not* easily understood. Women experiencing something potentially tellable as a story of wife abuse often describe partners who simultaneously act loving and hateful; they tell stories of partners characterized by an almost complete lack of predictability. And the women themselves can seem incomprehensible as they describe their victimization in excruciating detail yet simultaneously declare their love for the victimizers.

Further, culturally acceptable stories in our historical era typically contain events connected to the story theme; there is generally some sense of temporality and causality. But women's lived experiences with violence can lead them to tell stories containing seemingly unconnected and random events; women often do not see *any* connections between their behaviors and their experiences with violence. They can talk of periods of violence followed by periods of kindness that revert again to violence for no particular reason. Hence, according to Laura Lempert (1996a, p. 27), women's talk of their experiences with violence is "punctuated by halts, hesitations, repetitions, false starts and the use of non-standard English. It is a realm of experience that is difficult, if not impossible, for the narrators to articulate." The experience of wife abuse can lead to a "crisis of ambiguity."

Stories told by women approach what Arthur Frank (1995) calls a *chaos narrative*, a type of narrative that has no sequence or discernible causality, a narrative that is about vulnerability, futility, impotence. Such stories often are heard by others as rambling or incoherent; stories repeatedly alternating love and hate, tenderness and violence are heard as illogical. Audiences tire of hearing such women talk of how they are planning to "leave," "stay," "leave," "stay." Clearly, women *need* a culturally acceptable narrative. While narratives are the ways we make sense of our selves and our lives (Gergen 1994), a chaos narrative is a "non-self story" (Frank 1995). Chaos narratives can lead listeners to reject the stories and, in so doing, reject the storyteller's reality. Furthermore, a chaos narrative leads to an immediate response of others to "drag the teller out of the story" (Frank 1995).

This is the work of shelters and support groups. Such places encourage women to make sense of their nonunderstandable lived realities by narrating their practical experiences as those of wife abuse, and simultaneously to think of their selves as battered women and their partners as abusive men.

Using data from four support groups[1] held in a shelter for battered women as well as from ten consecutive weekly meetings sponsored by an outreach group for such women, this chapter addresses the contents (the "whats") of stories told by women as well as the interactional techniques (the "hows") of these groups that encourage women's confusions to take on the particular meanings of the formula story of wife abuse (see Gubrium and Holstein 1997). This simultaneously produces the institutionalized selves of the battered woman and the abusive man. This analysis, however, presents a sometimes untidy picture. As with any good story, the formula story of wife abuse has both a *plot* (the victimization of women) and *characters* (the battered woman as victim, the abusive man as villain). The interactional production of plot and characters cannot be separated because they are simultaneously constructed. As plots and characters emerge, women's talk about their lived realities often complicates—even subverts—the straightforward narratives of the formula story of wife abuse. Showing how this happens sometimes results in a less than tidy analytic presentation, but this messiness *is* my point because within these support groups formula stories and the messiness of lived realities constantly collide.

The Narrative Plot of Violence: "Tell Us What He Did to You"

Because women seeking entry to a battered women's shelter needed to convince workers that they had experienced wife abuse (Loseke 1992), the fact of their abuse was often simply taken for granted in groups for shelter residents. In comparison, women came to the outreach groups without organizational screening. These groups were characterized by a frequent change in facilitators (six facilitators in 10 weeks), and an unpredictable, constantly changing group membership (a total of 14 women attended any of the 10 groups but only seven women attended more than one). Within such structural conditions creating unknown women with unknown biographies, facilitators most often started the hour-long meetings with questions such as: "I don't know everyone here. Just so I can get an idea of where everyone is, would you each tell me a little about yourself and why you're here?" Such instructions asked women to tell a particular type of story: why you're *here*, with "here" being a support group for battered women.

Not surprisingly, because the experience of abuse is the central plot of the formula story of wife abuse, group members often would competently narrate the violence in their lives. Consider the first two sentences offered by each of three women (pseudonyms throughout) in response to a facilitator's question "Tell us why you're here":

> I'm Patti. My husband was physically and emotionally abusive. I always put up with his crap because I didn't think I had any other options.

I'm Betty. I'm here because this is the first chance I got to get out. Last week I knew if I didn't do something I'd be dead.

I'm Doris. I was living with this guy who beat me for eight years. The last time I ended up blind in this eye.

In their first two sentences telling others "why you're here," each of these three women constructs herself as a woman who has experienced *extreme* violence: Patti told not of violence but of the morally pejorative "abuse"; Betty feared for her life; Doris suffered blindness because of violence. Notice also how two of these women go beyond their experiences in order to add a characteristic about their selves: Patti stayed because she didn't think she had options; Betty also had been trapped and left the first time she could.

While women often competently narrated the experience of extreme violence as the reason why they were "here," sometimes their initial stories didn't offer the formulaic depiction of violence. They might fail to include the *necessary* element of violence, fail to construct violence as the *central organizing story theme*, or fail to narrate the *seriousness* of violence experienced.

New members sometimes offered stories not containing violence. Consider the following example that starts when a facilitator asks Megan, a new group member, to "tell us a little about yourself and why you're here." Megan replied:

I'm Megan. I got my divorce, I have my boys. We're living in [another county] and things are really going good. I'm on probation because of him but I'm dealing with it. I beat up his girlfriend and slashed the tires on her car—and I'd do it again if I had to do it all over [laughing]. I admit to that—they got me on B and E [breaking and entering]; that's why I'm on probation. I still don't know why he left me for her. He had everything. I worked, he never did. He took off for months at a time on his bike and that was okay. The kids are doing good. They were always used to him being gone a lot anyway. He pays his child support.

When prompted to "tell us why you're here," Megan first constructs her self as a woman for whom "things are really going good." Her story does not contain an element of the violence she experienced—it includes only a component of her violence toward the woman now with her former partner. Further, her characterization of her former partner is not that of an abusive man. Others learn only that he was irresponsible in the past (he never worked, he took off for months at a time), yet is responsible in the present (he pays his child support). Nothing in her first comments characterizes her experiences as those of wife abuse. Another group member, Jessie, specifically asks Megan to enlarge her story to include violence.

JESSIE: Was he physically abusive?

MEGAN: You name it, he did it. Physically, emotionally, sexually. But I wouldn't have left. In fact, I tried to reconcile for months after he left. I guess I just couldn't handle the fact that I had always done everything for him, supported him, put up with everything he did and he left me for her.

While Megan competently answers Jessie's question by specifying several forms of abuse, she does not elaborate. Rather, she immediately returns to her preferred theme of how much she had given her partner, how much she had "put up with," and the unfairness of being left for another woman. The interaction continues as the facilitator transforms these themes into a narrative about "emotional abuse": "Emotional abuse can certainly be as damaging as physical abuse. Most people don't realize that. [Group continues to discuss the problems of emotional abuse.]"

In brief, in the interest of establishing a formula story, women whose narratives do not contain obvious violence can be directly asked to include it. Megan's story, which can be heard as one of infidelity and betrayal, is transformed into a story of emotional abuse. The battered woman is a woman who has experienced abuse; women were encouraged to include this plot.

Furthermore, desired stories have violence as a central organizing theme. Consider the following story offered by a new member, Margarite. Notice how violence *is* embedded in the story (we argued and he got violent) but how it does *not* seem to be the major story theme:

MARGARITE: I don't know if I should be in a group like this. I thought my life was pretty normal. I just got sick of doing it all and not being respected. I never worked outside the home; my husband has a good job and I didn't have to work. I always did everything at home [elaborates at some length]. He never appreciated it. Never sent me flowers or bought me a gift. Never took me out to dinner. I've been doing everything I could to make a wonderful home for us. Cooking his dinner late because he worked late and it turns out he wasn't working late—he was with another woman!! I found out and confronted him and he said I wasn't going to break up our home. We argued and he got violent. That's the first time he ever touched me, but it will be the last. I filed for a divorce and I found out when he got served he broke down and cried. That really surprised me because I thought he'd be angry. He sent me flowers for Valentine's Day. She didn't get flowers, only me.

MEGAN: I give you a lot of credit. My husband was always running around but I kept trying to get him back [two minutes detailing the unfaithfulness of her own partner].

FACILITATOR: So, Margarite, you say he got violent. Can you tell me exactly what he did to you?

While the work of support groups, in theory, is accomplished when group members make links between their own experiences and those of others, we can see in this extract how the group—more specifically, its facilitator—asserts the theme of violence, even when group members favor other themes. In this case, while Margarite's story might reasonably be read as one of a "not appreciated wife " and "marital infidelity," and while Megan makes such links between her own story and Margarite's story, the group facilitator ignores Megan's talk and the substance of Margarite's story. Margarite is not a betrayed wife or an unappreciated wife, she is a victim of violence, of what her husband *did to her*.

DI: He would take me to the door and scream at me and the neighbors heard and they wouldn't talk to me.

constructing responsibility, group interactions also constructed *motiva*. Consider the following exchange where a group member, who had just story of extreme violence, continues by narrating her understanding of use (*I used his credit card*), and immediate relational context (*we'd* been ng). She concludes by raising an explicit question about her own implica- n the abuse:

PEG: I went to bingo and used his credit card for cash advances. The night I ended up in the emergency room, I didn't expect it. He found out about the credit card a few days before and we'd been arguing ever since. Maybe I shouldn't have used his credit card?

FACILITATOR: How much did you spend?

PEG: Over $2,000. I really don't know exactly how much.

FACILITATOR: What he did to you was wrong. Financial control is one of the ways men deny women power in relationships.

In this instance, although the facilitator was inquisitive about the amount of oney Peg used, her response was unequivocal: What *he did to you* was wrong. e second sentence of the facilitator's response, "financial control is one of the ays men deny women power in relationships," depicts Peg's husband's behav- ors as indicating his desire for "financial control." It transforms Peg's husband nto an instance of a category of people: men. It constructs a motive for men's fi- nancial control: to deny women power.

The narrative of the battered woman contains the theme of control which is something men *have done* to women. Furthermore, this theme of control can describe what men *continue to do* to women. Consider the following exchange that happened during a support group for former shelter residents. In this ex- ample, group members claim that control—or at least attempts to control—is the reason that "men give gifts." The interaction begins when Velma proudly displays to the group two ceramic plaques made by a male admirer of hers, an inmate at a local prison:

VELMA: Now there's two men that want me to move to [another city]. The other one, he called the other night and wanted my daughter and me to move to [another city], and said he'd pay our way and get us a place to stay. He's a pimp. And this one is getting out soon and he asked me how I would feel about moving to [another city]. I don't know, what do you think?

MAGGIE: Yeah, men always give us gifts.

JOAN: My ex gave me a ring. He wanted me back.

JANET: My ex bought [my daughter] a dress for Easter. Then it was only an hour before it started again and it was a real hassle getting him out. [General conversation about the problems of "men and gifts."]

At other times, these groups can encourage women to understand the vio- lence they experience as *dangerous*. Consider Jane's initial narrative:

I'm Jane. I'm just getting out of an abusive relationship with a man I've been liv- ing with for four years. I was doing so good. I had a good job until I got laid off two weeks ago. We got a new car because he said he didn't want me driving all the way to the job in the old van. I thought that was good—that he was worried about me. But then when I had to get to work he was out in the new car and I couldn't get to work. I'd been off the booze for four years, I met him at AA. It was the same when we got the horse. [Tells a story about how they got a horse but he didn't let her ride it nor did he pay for the horse's cost of boarding.] Now the rent's due and so is the horse board and I know the rent won't get paid. I knew it wasn't going to get any better a couple of weeks ago when I ended up in the emergency room with broken ribs and black eyes. He just came at me and started punching. It was always the same. He starts asking questions and I never have the right answers. [Tells a story of how he found a man's business card in her purse and wouldn't believe it was a man who merely wanted Jane to attend his church.] He wouldn't believe anything but that I was having an affair. Usu- ally I don't even say anything, it doesn't matter what I say. He doesn't hear what I say. I woke up in the bedroom, I was confused, he told me I'd been drinking, that I got drunk and fell. I couldn't remember. I did start drinking then and didn't stop for a few days, then it started coming back. I remembered about the busi- ness card and him hitting me. I remember him hitting me in the kitchen then I must have blacked out. I remembered trying to explain then, bam! And my fam- ily was only too ready to believe I was drinking again. They don't want anything to do with me. I screwed up again and they don't want to know about it. So I called here. I'm not crazy but I feel like I'm crazy. Why is this happening to me? It was such a long battle to stop drinking. I'm an alcoholic but I'm not crazy. Now I'm babbling again.

Clearly, Jane's story includes several elements of the formula story of wife abuse: She once believed her partner cared for her (we got a new car because he didn't want me driving in the old van), but disappointed her (he took the car, he didn't let her ride the horse). The violence was extreme (I ended up with broken ribs and black eyes), long-lasting (it was always the same) unpredictable (he just came at me), and had nothing to do with her (it doesn't matter what I say). At the same time, Jane's story includes another strong theme of her past and current problems with alcohol (I met him at AA, I did start drinking, I'm an alcoholic). She talks of her immediate problems with finances (now the rent's due), her nonsupportive family (they don't want anything to do with me), doubts about her abilities (I screwed up again), and doubts about her sanity (I feel like I'm crazy). Yet of myriad possible themes to develop, when Jane con- cludes her story the facilitator repeatedly directs her to focus on her danger- ous situation:

FACILITATOR: So, he's gone now?

JANE: I told him I was going to press charges and he left. He'll be back to get his things. I have to find a way to pay the rent, find a job. It'll work out.

FACILITATOR:	Do you feel in danger? Do you worry about him coming back?
JANE:	No, if he comes back I'll call the police.
FACILITATOR:	Do you need help in filing a restraining order?
JANE:	I don't think I want to do that now. I don't want to think about it now.
FACILITATOR:	I'd feel better if you got a restraining order. You know you can call the crisis line day or night.

In this exchange, Jane seemingly ignores the facilitator's repeated prompting to focus on the danger she is experiencing. Jane remains focused on what *she* perceives as immediate problems (find a way to pay the rent, find a job) and her optimism (it'll work out, I'll call the police). But at another meeting, a woman tells others how these support groups *had* changed the way she defines her experiences. In introducing herself to new group members, Jessie said:

> I'm a regular, my name is Jessie. I've come a long way. You should have heard me when I started coming. I'd look around the room and think "you need to be here but I don't need to be here." I didn't think I was abused, that's what I thought. But I do need to be here, because my husband has this sweet face, I always go for the ones with a sweet face. We had everything but I was miserable. He called me every name in the book. I never thought I was abused because I thought you had to be injured to be abused [continues to document her experiences].

In brief, these women knew they were attending support groups for women experiencing wife abuse, yet they did not invariably tell stories that fit a discursive environment privileging stories featuring the centrality of dangerous violence. Redirections and questions from facilitators or other group members encourage this type of story. The formula story of wife abuse is about extreme violence; the battered woman is a victimized woman.

The Narrative Plot of Responsibility and Control: "He's Still Controlling You"

While violence forms the core of the story of "what he did to you," the plot of the formula story of wife abuse assigns *responsibility* for the violence to men and it assigns a *motive* for this violence: Men do violence in order to control women. This plot simultaneously develops the characters of the battered woman and the abusive man.

In the formula story of wife abuse, women are acted upon; things are *done to them*. Facilitators could directly ask women, for example, "Opal, what did your husband *do to you?*" or "Doris, would you mind telling [a new group member] what *he did to you*," or "what *did he do* to make you realize you had to leave?" or "try to focus on the things that were *done to you* in your relationships." The formula story of wife abuse is not one of "relational troubles" that raises questions about the "distribution of rights and responsibilities" (Emerson and Messenger,

1977, p. 123). So when Margarite (above) included in her s[...] confronted him," and "*we argued*," the facilitator ignored [...] narrative and transformed it to "you say *he* got violent," an[...] talk about "what he *did to you*." Or, in another meeting wh[...] that the authorities took away her children who were not [...] neighbors phoned the police when "*he and I* were going a[...] claimed Sara's partner nonetheless was "abusive to your child[...] them to see him hurt you" (all emphases added). Things are do[...] woman; such a character is not the author of her own experien[...]

Consider the following interaction that begins when a supp[...] ber, who was a shelter resident, seems perplexed that any wom[...] she was responsible for violence. Two other group members agre[...] do not feel responsible for the violence they had experienced. Beca[...] of the formula story of wife abuse and because there was no dis[...] facilitator could have agreed that women were not responsible and [...] other topic. Yet the facilitator moves the conversation to a more [...] which seemingly encourages women to understand their experienc[...] within a larger culture that *does* promote their responsibility.

CAROL:	I have something to ask. I was taking a sociology class and [...] fessor said that many women believed they deserved to be b[...] that it was their fault. How can anyone think that?
RANDI:	I didn't think that I deserved it.
SOPHIE:	I can't see how anyone would think that.
FACILITATOR:	In our society women are brought up to believe we should a[...] the responsibility. Like if you called your mom and she told yo[...] work on it and not leave.
CAROL:	Oh, yeah. We're the homemakers. It's our responsibility.
RANDI:	My family always told me to work on it.

At another support group meeting for shelter residents the conversa[...] for some minutes had drifted around the general topic of problems of tra[...] portation. This was a very real, immediate, and practical problem because th[...] shelter was geographically isolated; there was no decent public transportatio[...] to it. Notice in the following exchange how the facilitator transforms a woman'[...] statement about a *current* and *personal* condition (I feel isolated) to a *prior* and[...] *general* condition (how many of you felt isolated). This transformation from cur[...] rent and personal to prior and general obviously was heard by other women[...] as sensible. Sara responded that isolation is what "they" do, which constructs [...] the character of the abusive man. Randi offers a specific example from her past [...] experiences:

CATHY:	I really need a car, I feel isolated.
FACILITATOR:	How many of you felt isolated?
SARA:	Oh yes, they isolate you.

At other times, these groups can encourage women to understand the violence they experience as *dangerous*. Consider Jane's initial narrative:

I'm Jane. I'm just getting out of an abusive relationship with a man I've been living with for four years. I was doing so good. I had a good job until I got laid off two weeks ago. We got a new car because he said he didn't want me driving all the way to the job in the old van. I thought that was good—that he was worried about me. But then when I had to get to work he was out in the new car and I couldn't get to work. I'd been off the booze for four years, I met him at AA. It was the same when we got the horse. [Tells a story about how they got a horse but he didn't let her ride it nor did he pay for the horse's cost of boarding.] Now the rent's due and so is the horse board and I know the rent won't get paid. I knew it wasn't going to get any better a couple of weeks ago when I ended up in the emergency room with broken ribs and black eyes. He just came at me and started punching. It was always the same. He starts asking questions and I never have the right answers. [Tells a story of how he found a man's business card in her purse and wouldn't believe it was a man who merely wanted Jane to attend his church.] He wouldn't believe anything but that I was having an affair. Usually I don't even say anything, it doesn't matter what I say. He doesn't hear what I say. I woke up in the bedroom, I was confused, he told me I'd been drinking, that I got drunk and fell. I couldn't remember. I did start drinking then and didn't stop for a few days, then it started coming back. I remembered about the business card and him hitting me. I remember him hitting me in the kitchen then I must have blacked out. I remembered trying to explain then, bam! And my family was only too ready to believe I was drinking again. They don't want anything to do with me. I screwed up again and they don't want to know about it. So I called here. I'm not crazy but I feel like I'm crazy. Why is this happening to me? It was such a long battle to stop drinking. I'm an alcoholic but I'm not crazy. Now I'm babbling again.

Clearly, Jane's story includes several elements of the formula story of wife abuse: She once believed her partner cared for her (we got a new car because he didn't want me driving in the old van), but disappointed her (he took the car, he didn't let her ride the horse). The violence was extreme (I ended up with broken ribs and black eyes), long-lasting (it was always the same) unpredictable (he just came at me), and had nothing to do with her (it doesn't matter what I say). At the same time, Jane's story includes another strong theme of her past and current problems with alcohol (I met him at AA, I did start drinking, I'm an alcoholic). She talks of her immediate problems with finances (now the rent's due), her nonsupportive family (they don't want anything to do with me), doubts about her abilities (I screwed up again), and doubts about her sanity (I feel like I'm crazy). Yet of myriad possible themes to develop, when Jane concludes her story the facilitator repeatedly directs her to focus on her dangerous situation:

FACILITATOR: So, he's gone now?

JANE: I told him I was going to press charges and he left. He'll be back to get his things. I have to find a way to pay the rent, find a job. It'll work out.

FACILITATOR: Do you feel in danger? Do you worry about him coming back?

JANE: No, if he comes back I'll call the police.

FACILITATOR: Do you need help in filing a restraining order?

JANE: I don't think I want to do that now. I don't want to think about it now.

FACILITATOR: I'd feel better if you got a restraining order. You know you can call the crisis line day or night.

In this exchange, Jane seemingly ignores the facilitator's repeated prompting to focus on the danger she is experiencing. Jane remains focused on what *she* perceives as immediate problems (find a way to pay the rent, find a job) and her optimism (it'll work out, I'll call the police). But at another meeting, a woman tells others how these support groups *had* changed the way she defines her experiences. In introducing herself to new group members, Jessie said:

I'm a regular, my name is Jessie. I've come a long way. You should have heard me when I started coming. I'd look around the room and think "you need to be here but I don't need to be here." I didn't think I was abused, that's what I thought. But I do need to be here, because my husband has this sweet face, I always go for the ones with a sweet face. We had everything but I was miserable. He called me every name in the book. I never thought I was abused because I thought you had to be injured to be abused [continues to document her experiences].

In brief, these women knew they were attending support groups for women experiencing wife abuse, yet they did not invariably tell stories that fit a discursive environment privileging stories featuring the centrality of dangerous violence. Redirections and questions from facilitators or other group members encourage this type of story. The formula story of wife abuse is about extreme violence; the battered woman is a victimized woman.

The Narrative Plot of Responsibility and Control: "He's Still Controlling You"

While violence forms the core of the story of "what he did to you," the plot of the formula story of wife abuse assigns *responsibility* for the violence to men and it assigns a *motive* for this violence: Men do violence in order to control women. This plot simultaneously develops the characters of the battered woman and the abusive man.

In the formula story of wife abuse, women are acted upon; things are *done to them*. Facilitators could directly ask women, for example, "Opal, what did your husband *do to you?*" or "Doris, would you mind telling [a new group member] what *he did to you*," or "what *did he do* to make you realize you had to leave?" or "try to focus on the things that were *done to you* in your relationships." The formula story of wife abuse is not one of "relational troubles" that raises questions about the "distribution of rights and responsibilities" (Emerson and Messenger,

1977, p. 123). So when Margarite (above) included in her story the theme that "*I confronted him,*" and "*we argued,*" the facilitator ignored Margarite's relational narrative and transformed it to "you say *he* got violent," and asked Margarite to talk about "what he *did to you.*" Or, in another meeting when Sara complained that the authorities took away her children who were not abused because the neighbors phoned the police when "*he and I* were going at it," the facilitator claimed Sara's partner nonetheless was "abusive to your children because it hurt them to see him hurt you" (all emphases added). Things are done to the battered woman; such a character is not the author of her own experiences.

Consider the following interaction that begins when a support group member, who was a shelter resident, seems perplexed that any woman could believe she was responsible for violence. Two other group members agree that they, too, do not feel responsible for the violence they had experienced. Because this is part of the formula story of wife abuse and because there was no disagreement, the facilitator could have agreed that women were not responsible and moved to another topic. Yet the facilitator moves the conversation to a more abstract level, which seemingly encourages women to understand their experiences as located within a larger culture that *does* promote their responsibility.

CAROL: I have something to ask. I was taking a sociology class and the professor said that many women believed they deserved to be battered, that it was their fault. How can anyone think that?

RANDI: I didn't think that I deserved it.

SOPHIE: I can't see how anyone would think that.

FACILITATOR: In our society women are brought up to believe we should accept the responsibility. Like if you called your mom and she told you to work on it and not leave.

CAROL: Oh, yeah. We're the homemakers. It's our responsibility.

RANDI: My family always told me to work on it.

At another support group meeting for shelter residents the conversation for some minutes had drifted around the general topic of problems of transportation. This was a very real, immediate, and practical problem because this shelter was geographically isolated; there was no decent public transportation to it. Notice in the following exchange how the facilitator transforms a woman's statement about a *current* and *personal* condition (I feel isolated) to a *prior* and *general* condition (how many of you felt isolated). This transformation from current and personal to prior and general obviously was heard by other women as sensible. Sara responded that isolation is what "they" do, which constructs the character of the abusive man. Randi offers a specific example from her past experiences:

CATHY: I really need a car, I feel isolated.

FACILITATOR: How many of you felt isolated?

SARA: Oh yes, they isolate you.

RANDI: He would take me to the door and scream at me and the neighbors
                heard and they wouldn't talk to me.

In constructing responsibility, group interactions also constructed *motiva-tions*. Consider the following exchange where a group member, who had just told a story of extreme violence, continues by narrating her understanding of its cause (*I used his credit card*), and immediate relational context (*we'd* been arguing). She concludes by raising an explicit question about her own implication in the abuse:

PEG: I went to bingo and used his credit card for cash advances. The
                night I ended up in the emergency room, I didn't expect it. He found
                out about the credit card a few days before and we'd been arguing
                ever since. Maybe I shouldn't have used his credit card?
FACILITATOR: How much did you spend?
PEG: Over $2,000. I really don't know exactly how much.
FACILITATOR: What he did to you was wrong. Financial control is one of the ways
                men deny women power in relationships.

In this instance, although the facilitator was inquisitive about the amount of money Peg used, her response was unequivocal: What *he did to you* was wrong. The second sentence of the facilitator's response, "financial control is one of the ways men deny women power in relationships," depicts Peg's husband's behaviors as indicating his desire for "financial control." It transforms Peg's husband into an instance of a category of people: men. It constructs a motive for men's financial control: to deny women power.

The narrative of the battered woman contains the theme of control which is something men *have done* to women. Furthermore, this theme of control can describe what men *continue to do* to women. Consider the following exchange that happened during a support group for former shelter residents. In this example, group members claim that control—or at least attempts to control—is the reason that "men give gifts." The interaction begins when Velma proudly displays to the group two ceramic plaques made by a male admirer of hers, an inmate at a local prison:

VELMA: Now there's two men that want me to move to [another city]. The other
                one, he called the other night and wanted my daughter and me to move
                to [another city], and said he'd pay our way and get us a place to stay.
                He's a pimp. And this one is getting out soon and he asked me how I
                would feel about moving to [another city]. I don't know, what do you
                think?
MAGGIE: Yeah, men always give us gifts.
JOAN: My ex gave me a ring. He wanted me back.
JANET: My ex bought [my daughter] a dress for Easter. Then it was only an
                hour before it started again and it was a real hassle getting him out.
                [General conversation about the problems of "men and gifts."]

Here, the other women in the group ignore the substance of Velma's story and they ignore her direct question to them about whether or not she and her daughter should move to another city to be with a man she calls a "pimp." By returning to Velma's opening display of "gifts" she had received, Maggie moves the conversation to something appropriate to the formula story of wife abuse— *what men do.* Joan then offers a specific example of this gift-giving and ties it to men's motives to control women (he wanted me back). Janet follows with her specific example and links this with continued problems (it started again).

This narrative plot of control also can be used to construct women as out of control of their own *emotions* while simultaneously constructing men as in control of women's emotions. Consider another interaction involving Megan, the woman who was disturbed because she could not understand why her husband left her for another woman. At her second group meeting, Megan offered a fairly long narrative about what she called her "awful experience" in court that week for a child custody hearing. She ended with her recurring theme of longing for her lost love and jealousy toward his current partner:

MEGAN: What does she have that I don't have? That's what I can't take. She went to court in a white knit low-cut dress that showed everything, slit all the way up one side. I'll be okay, it's just that it makes me so mad to think about him with her. Why do I still care?

FACILITATOR: He's still controlling you. He knows he can control you through the children and by lying about you in court.

In this instance, the facilitator transforms what might be heard as a mundane narrative of jealously or lost love into a story of wife abuse. The facilitator's comment also constructed the identity of the abusive man: he is smart and manipulative because he *knows* he can control Megan. Simultaneously, this forms the troubled identity of a battered woman: Megan feels jealousy and continues to care only because she is being manipulated.

Hence, the character of the battered woman is out of control of her own emotions even after her abusive partner has departed from her life. Consider Karen, a group member, who challenges Doris's self-conception during an exercise promoting increased self-esteem:

DORIS: I guess I'd have to say that I'm pretty self-confident now because I think I can do what I need to do but I have low self-esteem. I really don't like myself!

KAREN: That surprises me. You always seem so fun-loving and happy. I think you still see yourself as Frank [Doris's former partner] saw you.

At another outreach meeting, another woman directly complained about her inability to "know herself." Although she already had formed the analysis that her problems were due to her former partner's continuing control, the facilitator uses this as an opportunity to promote the general characterization of the battered woman and what such a woman must do:

JANICE: Although I'm a tiny size four, when I look in a mirror I feel fat; I
               hear this voice saying, "you should do something to tighten up that
               tummy," and it's his voice.
FACILITATOR: We have to learn not to see ourselves through their [abusers'] eyes.

In brief, the wife abuse formula story is about violence not created by women; it is a story where men control women. The plots of responsibility and control simultaneously construct the characters of the battered woman and abusive man: she is a victim who is not the author of her experiences or her emotions; he is a villain who knowingly seeks and actively maintains control over all aspects of her life.

The Narrative Plot of the Future: "It Won't Be Easy"

The formula story of wife abuse has a happy ending when a woman leaves her abusive partner. Yet most women in these support groups already had left their partners or at least were in the process of leaving them, so their experiences went beyond the "and she lived happily ever after" public image. Facilitators and other members in these groups could offer women encouragement about how much better it was to be away from their abusive partners. Facilitators, for example, could praise women for leaving abusive relationships: "I'm glad you finally got out of that relationship. You were in real danger." Facilitators also could encourage women to remain independent, saying "you can make it, you can stand on your feet and make it by yourself." They could listen to women's stories and praise them by saying "it sounds like all of you are on the right track." Women in these groups could share the small victories they had achieved during the past week. Yet the great majority of stories group members and facilitators told one another were about troubles.

Much of the interaction in these groups was about women's *current* problems. During one outreach group, Doris asked if anyone knew if her former partner would be in court when child custody questions would be settled. Jessie replied, "Yes, and I can tell you it's awful." Jessie continued for some minutes elaborating on these awful details. During another group, Joyce told her story of how she left her husband but that "things are more horrible than ever," because of problems with joint child custody. Likewise, women residing in the shelter could be horrified about what they would do when they left the shelter. One woman feared: "I don't think there's hope for me. What do I do when the 21st of this month arrives [the end of her eligibility for shelter residence]. Go home? Then what?" Another shelter resident also pondered her life after the shelter when she asked others: "I just had an operation and I'm not supposed to even lift my 10-month-old. What am I going to do?" Women's lived realities after separation from their partners could be chaotic and such stories circulated in all groups. Indeed, groups tended to dramatize these stories as women each offered details of her own hardships.

Facilitators also could spread doom when they told newly separated women, "it won't be easy," or "it seems like an impossible hill to climb," or "it gets better, but it's never gone." Facilitators also offered less than cheerful narratives when they responded to questions raised by individual women. For example, one woman questioned her ability to be a good parent. Rather than encouraging the woman to look at what she was doing *right*, the facilitator referenced her own experiences, implicitly agreeing about the woman's failure when she said, "I felt that was another thing my ex-husband robbed me of—the ability to be an effective parent." Or, at a meeting of shelter residents, a woman asked a question about her child's suddenly troublesome behavior. The facilitator might have responded by calming the woman with the possibility that these were expectable problems from recently leaving home and from living with strangers. Yet the facilitator led the woman to expect continuing problems with her child when she said, "Children often repress the violence and many times it comes out years later."

While life without former partners was often portrayed as unhappy, the discursive environment of support groups did not allow women to improve their stories by bringing back their partners as narrative characters in their lives. By definition, these women's partners were abusive men and such a type of character could not be believed. Hence, a woman talking about going back to her partner is told that abusive men "are usually clever and have a very charming side and use it to keep the relationship going." Such men might "give gifts," but only to regain control. Or a woman might be optimistic that her partner is going to Alcoholics Anonymous, say, and therefore will change, but other women in the group form a chorus of "sure he will," "that's what they all say," or "I've heard that before."

How groups can dampen optimism is clear in the following exchange with Melanie, a new outreach group member who had sat on the couch crying, refusing to speak. The interactions start when Doris, another group member who had just talked about her week, turned to Melanie:

DORIS: Can I ask you a question? [Melanie nods yes.] Are you still with the guy? [Melanie nods yes.] That's why you can't talk. Do you want to leave? [Melanie shrugs her shoulders.] Are you married to him? [Melanie shakes her head no.] Does he hit you?

Melanie responds to this question with a very formulaic story of wife abuse: she does not understand why he is violent; she has experienced chaos for three years; she does not feel safe in her own home:

MELANIE: Only once in a while. He'll be okay for a few months then something will happen. It's like a Dr. Jekyll and Mr. Hyde thing. It can be anything that sets it off. I never know when, like putting the pillow on a different spot on the bed. You're supposed feel safe in your home but I can't feel safe. It's been happening for three years.

DORIS: If you're not married, why don't you just leave? You need to get out. You're a beautiful woman, you could do better; you could do a lot better.

Notice that Doris hears Melanie's narrative as that of a battered woman, which has an accompanying agenda for action: Melanie must leave. Doris asserts the positive aspects of this option: Melanie is a beautiful woman who can do better if she leaves her partner. But Melanie rejects the idea, offering a list of reasons why she cannot leave:

MELANIE: I don't want to leave. I love him. I know he loves me. Besides, it's my home, my pets are there, my things are there. I don't want to leave my home. He's going to counseling, he wants to change. Does it work? Can men change?

FACILITATOR: I don't think he understands what love is. He may not be capable of love. But he's gone [to counseling] voluntarily, that's a good sign. It might be fine. I don't mean to sound negative, but I want to prepare you for what might be a difficult time. You should have a plan in place. Will you go to your mom's? It's best to think it out ahead of time.

While Melanie inserts narrative optimism into her story (I know he loves me, he's going to counseling, he wants to change), she ends with hesitation: can men change? The facilitator responds that it "might" be fine but she emphasizes the negative, extinguishing Melanie's optimism. The prognosis is bleak that an abusive man will change.

While the formula story of wife abuse has a happy ending when women leave their abusive partners, the stories actually told in support groups were often far less uplifting. Certainly, women who left were now safer from the experience of abuse in their own homes, and that could *not* be discounted. But there remain the mundane problems of daily life. There are new problems with money, housing, and child custody. There can be very ambivalent emotions about former partners. For such problems there is only "support," the talk of women in these groups. What is lacking, it seems, are success stories. As wished by Sarah, a shelter resident: "I'd like to see a woman who's been in this situation and who's gotten out and who's happy. I don't know any and it scares the hell out of me." A battered woman character has been a victim in the past but "leaving home" does not promise a happy ending to her story.

Interpretive Complexity and Identity

Clearly, while support groups promote the wife abuse formula story as a template for understanding and narrating participants' experiences, the complications of lived experience thwart the formula's uniform application. This, of course, makes for a somewhat untidy description of how support groups mediate the construction of troubled identities (see also Fox, this volume). Women experience their lives in ways that often contradict or collide with the formula story and this leads to stories that vary significantly from the institutionally preferred narrative. While group meetings rely upon both the plot and the characters of the wife abuse formula story, they cannot unilaterally impose these identities upon the lives of women in the groups. This prompts several observations.

First, support groups for battered women seem to be like other groups formed for similar purposes. From Weight Watchers promoting a thin self to Alcoholics Anonymous promoting an alcoholic self (see Pollner and Stein, this volume), to groups for battered women promoting the battered woman self, these groups are about *transforming identity* so that participants display institutionally preferred personas. These groups are thus involved in the *deprivatization* of personal troubles and the institutionalization of the selves we live by (Gubrium and Holstein 1995, 1997, 1998; Holstein and Gubrium 2000).

Not surprisingly, given similarity in purpose, support groups can be similar in their interactional dynamics, even when the content of talk is much different. For example, in comparison to the *structural power* held by judges and attorneys in courtrooms (Holstein 1993), facilitators in support groups hold *interactional power*. Hence, the institutional technologies of narrative work in these places are subtle techniques such as asking questions, rephrasing stories, ignoring some aspects of women's stories and dramatizing other aspects. Women's stories in these groups are interactionally shaped in ways compatible with the discursive environment informed by the formula story of wife abuse (see Hopper, Fox, Spencer in this volume).

Second, groups for victims of wife abuse, as well those for alcoholics (Pollner and Stein 1996) and transsexuals (Mason-Schrock 1996), privilege the voice of experience rather than the voice of professional knowledge. At the same time, not just any voice of experience will do: each of these groups begins its work within a local culture that honors only some types of experiences. For example, women in groups for battered women who told stories of wife abuse were accorded the right to speak from the voice of experience; women telling other types of stories were not allowed to speak with that voice.

Third, whether in groups for victims of wife abuse, for wife abuse offenders (McKendy 1992), or Alzheimer's caregivers (Gubrium and Holstein 1998), members and facilitators keep storytellers on track. Stories are not allowed to veer much from institutionally preferred themes, plots, and characters. These groups thus are involved in the *collaborative production of narratives* and therefore the *collaborative production of identities*. It is group interaction that "unfolds to produce acceptable stories" (Mason-Schrock 1996). Hence, the process of narrative work in support groups might be very similar even when the content of these groups' preferred stories is much different.

Another observation centers on the particular content of the wife abuse formula story. This is a story about a type of phonenemon—wife abuse—with types of characters—the battered woman and the abusive man. The formula story dramatizes the severity and immorality of abuse, the purity of the female victim, and the extreme evil of the male offender. Although it is clear that much more needs to be done to resolve the social problem of wife abuse, this formula story has been instrumental in encouraging the public to take violence against women seriously. It has led to the creation of shelters, special counseling techniques, and special laws and court procedures.

But the rise to prominence of this formula story did not extinguish other narratives that potentially also make sense of women's lived experiences with violence. For example, the wife abuse formula story competes with a narrative of "marital troubles." While the wife abuse story constructs violence as the central plot, the marital troubles narrative frames violence as a consequence of larger troubles. While the wife abuse story defines women as victims and men as villains, the marital troubles narrative specifies a relational core to troubles. The battered woman character who is a pure victim trapped in her victimization also competes with other types of characters such as the "masochistic wife," who secretly desires the violence she experiences; the "shrewish wife," who acts in ways that create the violence she reaps; or the "long suffering wife" who willingly sacrifices herself in order to save her marriage. The "abusive man" in the wife abuse story also contends with other types of characters such as the "mentally ill" or "alcoholic" husband whose violence is a consequence of illness, or the "man in charge of the house" who "rightfully" uses violence because he is a "man." The wife abuse story also interpretively competes with the narrative of "mutual combat," which is centered on violence, but which has no clear victims or villains because both women and men are constructed as characters jointly engaged in the production of violence.

While there are multiple ways to make sense of the lived experience of violence, the wife abuse narrative offers much to women who embrace it as their own story. Clearly, the long-suffering wife story that promotes the goodness of saving marriages can be very dangerous for women who are in life-threatening relationships. Also, consider that within our cultural understandings, victims deserve sympathy and support (Loseke 1999), but only the battered woman is a victim. The woman characters in the masochistic or shrewish wife narratives are portrayed as responsible for the violence they experience; there are no victims or villains in the mutual combat or marital troubles narratives, which are stories of troubles with relational cores.

Yet, while the wife abuse story often benefits women, it is not a story embraced by all women experiencing something potentially tellable as a story of wife abuse. Why do some women fail to use this narrative although it has so much to offer? Social workers and shelter workers often answer this question by asking: what is wrong with *women* who do not want to understand themselves as a character in the wife abuse story? As an alternative, I ask what is it about the *formula story* of wife abuse that might encourage women to reject it as their own story?

One reason to reject the wife abuse story might be that this narrative does not easily encompass the messiness of the lived experience of troubles in general (Emerson and Messenger 1977) or of marital troubles in particular (Hopper 1993; Merry 1990; Riessman 1990; Weiss 1975). For example, the wife abuse narrative focuses exclusively on the experience of abuse; it leaves little space to include the complexities, indeterminacies, and situated nature of marital troubles. Furthermore, unless the abuse is experienced as extreme, there are questions about whether or not it is an example of morally intolerable "abuse" or of the more common—and less pejorative—cultural category of "normal violence." Still further, unless the partner can be constructed as a man with no redeeming qualities, it might be difficult to cast him as an abuser who is nothing but evil.

The coherence system (Linde 1993) of the wife abuse story is located in feminism. In that regard, it can be a theoretically coherent narrative, a symbolic story of men's abuse of women. Yet at the level of practical experience women might find it difficult to see themselves as an example of the battered woman. The lived experience of women can be one where love and hate, caring and violence are perceived as coexisting simultaneously, where the violence is difficult to classify given folk understandings of "normal" violence, where designating pure victims and pure villains ignores perceived relational cores of trouble. It might be that some women reject the wife abuse narrative because assigning theoretical meanings to violence, to selves, and to partners is not an easy task given the complexity of lived experience. Perhaps the formula story is just too neat, with too many pat answers and not enough ambiguity.

In addition, we can ask why a woman would want to understand herself as a character in the story of wife abuse. Clearly, embracing this identity offers the sympathy of others because such a woman is a victim. Yet the victim of wife abuse is known primarily by her deficiencies as read within a culture prizing individualism and independence. Such a woman is dependent and confused; she is a character in a script controlled by her abusive partner. While dramatizing the victim status of the battered woman no doubt was necessary on the public stage of social problem construction (Loseke 1999), such victim status remains disempowering (Lempert 1996b; Holstein and Miller 1990). It is possible that some women do not want to embrace the status of victim with its accompanying images of weakness. Consider, for example, the alternatives. If a woman understands herself as a long-suffering wife, she is a heroine if read through traditional notions about the sanctity of marriage. Or if a woman identifies herself as a shrewish wife or as a partner in mutual combat, she is a character who acts and who has some measure of control over her experiences. If she casts herself as a character in a script of marital troubles, she need not totally condemn the partner she still loves. In brief, Joel Best (1997) argues that our social order now rapidly creates new categories of victims as well as encourages people to come forth as victims. While this social promotion of a victim status no doubt has encouraged many women to embrace the status of battered woman, it remains that deep in our culture there are strong evaluations prizing strength. Women experiencing something potentially tellable as a story of wife abuse might reject this story because they do not want to cast themselves as "powerless" and "passive" (Lempert 1996b).

Furthermore, some women might reject the wife abuse story because the hope of happiness through independence that it offers might be judged as impossible to achieve. The wife abuse formula story is characterized by what Susan Chase (1995) calls "discursive disjunctions," which are incompatible systems of meaning. In this case, the woman character in the wife abuse story is powerless, confused, and controlled; she is a cultural symbol of what is wrong with the sex/gender system. At the same time, she is required to leave her abusive partner and become independent and such actions can require remarkable personal strength. Of course, acknowledging personal weakness as a way to strength is not a new idea; it is at the core of Alcoholics Anonymous, which takes its lead from biblical teachings that strength comes from admitting weakness and by turning over lives to a "high power." Yet the wife abuse story is a secular story; it does not contain a higher power that promises to lead women from their confusions and powerlessness to strength. The wife abuse formula story is one where women *should* be strong and independent yet where women *are* weak and dependent. Perhaps when support group facilitators warn women that it "seems an impossible hill to climb," they are making the hill seem too foreboding to try.

Finally, support groups for the battered woman tend to focus on narrating women's pasts; women's presents and futures are understood primarily as these are read through their pasts. The battered woman identity thus tends to become a master status or a pervasive identity influencing all aspects of life in the past, the present, and the future. While advocates for battered women can argue that this is a necessary step in moving from the identity of a victim toward the identity of a "former" victim (Mills 1985), it might be that some women prefer to construct new identities not tied to old, painful memories.

In conclusion, *clearly, most certainly, and without a doubt,* I do not want these remarks to be interpreted as meaning that the wife abuse formula story should be discarded because it is not useful. Countless women *do* see themselves in this narrative and for those women the wife abuse formula story can be nothing less than lifesaving. Indeed, there are myriad empirical examples of how this particular narrative encourages women to leave life-threatening relationships (Riessman 1989, 1990) The narrative of wife abuse often is successful—and its success can be measured in the number of women's lives it has saved. Yet it remains that other women whose stories are potentially tellable as those of wife abuse resist this narrative as a way to understand their lives and their selves. Rather than simply assuming that some form of individual psychopathology underlies these women's resistance, it seems beneficial to examine characteristics of the narrative itself as it relates to their particular circumstances.

NOTE

1. My data are from support groups of two types. First, I have 15 pages of notes from four support group meetings for current or recent shelter residents that I attended. Second, I have 80 single-spaced pages of notes from 10 consecutive weekly support groups for women victims of wife abuse collected by an intern for an outreach program. While there were many differences between the shelter and outreach groups, the local cultures in these groups were strikingly similar in three ways. First, at no time did facilitators in either of these places reveal their educational credentials. Rather, facilitators displayed their competence to help by narrating their own experiences with wife abuse: "I know how easy it is to go back. I went back to my second husband five times," or "I know how much it hurts because I went through the same thing." Second, both shelter and outreach groups were for women only—they were not for couples; they were not for men. Third—and the focus of this analysis—both shelter and outreach groups explicitly promoted the relevance of the "wife abuse" formula story.

REFERENCES

Berger, Arthur Asa. 1997. *Narratives in Popular Culture, Media, and Everyday Life.* Thousand Oaks, Calif.: Sage

Best, Joel. 1997. "Victimization and the Victim Industry." *Society* 34: 9–17.

Bruner, Jerome. 1987. "Life as Narrative." *Social Research* 54: 11–32.

Chase, Susan E. 1995. *Ambiguous Empowerment: The Work Narratives of Women School Superintendents.* Amherst: University of Massachusetts Press.

Dean, Ruth Grossman. 1998. "A Narrative Approach to Groups." *Clinical Social Work Journal* 26: 23–37.

Emerson, Robert M., and Sheldon L. Messenger. 1977. "The Micro-Politics of Trouble." *Social Problems* 25: 121–34.

Frank, Arthur W. 1995. *The Wounded Storyteller: Body, Illness, and Ethics.* Chicago: University of Chicago Press.

Gergen, Kenneth J. 1994. *Realities and Relationships: Soundings in Social Construction.* Cambridge: Harvard University Press.

Gubrium, Jaber F., and James A. Holstein. 1995. "Qualitative Inquiry and the Deprivatization of Experience." *Qualitative Inquiry* 1: 204–22.

———. 1997. *The New Language of Qualitative Method.* New York: Oxford University Press.

———. 1998. "Narrative Practice and the Coherence of Personal Stories." *The Sociological Quarterly.* 39: 163–87.

Holstein, James A. 1993. *Court-Ordered Insanity: Interpretive Practice and Involuntary Commitment.* Hawthorne, N.Y.: Aldine.

Holstein, James A., and Jaber F. Gubrium. 2000. *The Self We Live By: Narrative Identity in a Postmodern World.* New York: Oxford University Press.

Holstein, James A., and Gale Miller. 1990. "Rethinking Victimization: An Interactional Approach to Victimology." *Symbolic Interaction* 1: 103–22.

Hopper, Joseph. 1993. "The Rhetoric of Motives in Divorce." *Journal of Marriage and the Family* 55: 801–13.

Lempert, Lora Bex. 1996a. "Language Obstacles in the Narratives of Abused Women." *Mid-American Review of Sociology*: 19: 15–32.

———. 1996b. "Women's Strategies for Survival: Developing Agency in Abusive Relationships." *Journal of Family Violence* 11: 269–89.

Linde, Charlotte. 1993. *Life Stories: The Creation of Coherence.* New York: Oxford University Press.

Loseke, Donileen R. 1992. *The Battered Woman and Shelters: The Social Construction of Wife Abuse.* Albany: State University of New York Press.

———. 1999. *Thinking About Social Problems: An Introduction to Constructionist Perspectives.* New York: Aldine de Gruyter.

Maines, David R. 1991. "The Storied Nature of Health and Diabetic Self-Help Groups." In *Advances in Medical Sociology*, vol. 2, ed. Gary L. Albrecht and Judith A. Levy, 185–202. Greenwich, Conn.: JAI Press.

Mason-Schrock, Douglas. 1996. "Transsexuals' Narrative Construction of the 'True Self.'" *Social Psychology Quarterly* 59: 176–192.

McKendy, John P. 1992. "Ideological Practices and the Management of Emotions: The Case of 'Wife Abusers.'" *Critical Sociology* 19: 61–80.

Merry, Sally Engle. 1990. *Getting Justice and Getting Even: Legal Consciousness among Working-Class Americans.* Chicago: University of Chicago Press.

Mills, Trudy. 1985. "The Assault on the Self: Stages in Coping with Battering Husbands." *Qualitative Sociology* 8: 103–23.

Pollner, Melvin, and Jill Stein. 1996. "Narrative Mapping of Social Worlds: The Voice of Experience in Alcoholics Anonymous." *Symbolic Interaction* 19: 203–23.

Riessman, Catherine Kohler. 1989. "From Victim to Survivor: A Woman's Narrative Reconstruction of Marital Sexual Abuse. *Smith College Studies in Social Work* 59 (3): 232–51.

———. 1990. *Divorce Talk: Women and Men Make Sense of Personal Relationships.* New Brunswick, N.J.: Rutgers University Press.

Spector, Malcolm, and John I. Kitsuse. 1987. *Constructing Social Problems.* New York: Aldine de Gruyter.

Tierney, Kathleen. 1982. "The Battered Women Movement and the Creation of the Wife Beating Problem." *Social Problems* 29: 207–17.

Weiss, Robert S. 1975. *Marital Separation.* New York: Basic Books.

JOSEPH HOPPER

Contested Selves in Divorce Proceedings

Since selves are socially constructed and situationally located, the social world is populated with more selves than people. Each of us moves from work to home, from the doctor's office to the grocery store, from our immediate family to our extended family, and different selves emerge that continually shape and are shaped by the interactions and practical activities of each location. This is the crux of what some describe as the postmodern condition: multiplying sites of interaction create multiple selves; we shift rapidly from one to another and in doing so we become agglomerations of many different selves (Gergen 1991; Gubrium and Holstein 1994; Holstein and Gubrium 2000).

There is, however, a phenomenological unity to our experience and to our sense of self that we carry from one situation to the next. For the most part, we do not experience the world as a disconnected collection of behavioral roles appropriately invoked in various circumstances. Rather, we experience the world as continuous, and we feel a unitary self that is the locus of such continuity and experience. There is thus a tension in our everyday lives as we work to maintain a unified, continuous sense of self in a social world that fosters multiple selves, a world that operates as if we had and could act with different, separable selves.

Divorce provides a dramatic and instructive example of this phenomenon. Divorcing people develop strong and distinct notions of themselves *as* divorcing people in ways that help to preserve their moral standing, and they carry that sense of self into the many situations and conversations in which divorce is relevant. When they seek legal help, however, they encounter a system that denies the relevance of the "moral self." Instead, they find professionals who must work with them in terms of a "legal self"—a self that is grounded not in the particulars of their own situations and in terms of who did what to whom, but in a system of generalized, bureaucratic rules focused on apportioning money and property so as to maximize the material well-being of divorcing spouses and their children.

This chapter examines the legal self that attorneys and other professionals involved in the legal process attempt to construct against the efforts of divorcing people who maintain quite different conceptions of self. I suggest that the clash between these two exacerbates the legal difficulties of divorce, whatever the conciliatory intentions of attorneys may be.

My description is based on field observations and interviews gathered via a four-year study of divorce that began in 1991. (The research was supported by a grant from the National Institute of Mental Health, 1F31MH10797-01, and by a grant from the Fahs-Beck Fund for Research and Experimentation.) The study started as a broadly defined fieldwork effort to understand the experiences of divorcing people, and two years later it expanded to include the family, friends, attorneys, counselors, and ministers of divorcing people. I observed multiple settings relevant to divorce, attending workshops and seminars given by local service agencies, taking part in a 10-week group therapy program with 30 divorcing women and men, and attending a single father's support group. I also attended a two-month lawyer development program in which two attorneys who specialized in divorce taught a large group of other attorneys how to work with domestic relations cases in their own practices. I interviewed willing participants from each of the settings, and supplemented these interviews with several solicited from fliers and contacts at social service agencies. In all, I interviewed 99 people: 41 divorcing people; four married people who were trying to avoid divorce but who were willing to talk with me about their marital difficulties; 22 professionals (attorneys, mediators, counselors, custody evaluators, ministers, and a financial consultant); 16 family members (parents, adult children, and siblings); and 16 friends and neighbors.

The material in this chapter derives particularly from interviews with nine of the 22 professionals whose work focused on legal aspects of divorce. These nine professionals includes six attorneys, two psychologists, and one financial consultant. Of the attorneys, two taught the lawyer development program I attended, and of the remaining four, one was working as a private divorce mediator. The two psychologists were both state-certified professional counselors who devoted substantial portions of their practices to conducting custody evaluations. The financial consultant was a certified financial planner who worked primarily with divorcing women and who was often called to court as an expert witness.

The Moral Self

Divorcing persons in our culture have a pervasive and weighty set of concerns shaped by a wider institutional context of marriage and family: marriage and family provide the central place where most members of our society anchor their identity, their social and kinship ties, their child rearing, and their bases of financial and emotional support (Mead 1971); nearly all persons in our culture seek to get married, cherish the idea of marriage, and indeed get married. Not surprisingly, then, one's self in marriage gets articulated in moral terms via a discourse of kinship and domestic life, and also not surprisingly, so does one's self as a divorcing person.

Once divorce begins, people usually identify themselves as either the partner who wants the divorce or as the partner who does not (Buehler 1987; Nevaldine 1978; Pettit and Bloom 1984; Spanier and Thompson 1984; Vaughan 1986). Although the distinction conceals a great deal of complexity as to what is "really" going on in any divorce (Riessman 1990; Weiss 1975), understanding the initiator and noninitiator identities is central because they are the symbolic poles in relation to which agency gets organized. Taking on an identity in divorce as either the person who left or the person who got left imposes order and meaning upon behaviors, circumstances, and events that would otherwise seem chaotic and inexplicable (Hopper 1993a, 1993b; see also Loseke, this volume).

One component of the order thus imposed is a moral order. Marriage is vaulted both as an institution and as a personal accomplishment, and it is a relationship that is supposed to last forever. Divorce violates the profound value we attach to marriage, and it represents a personal failure for both spouses. The initiator/noninitiator distinction helps divorcing people account for that violation, and it helps them repair damage to their identities for having failed. In short, focusing on themselves as either initiators in divorce or as noninitiating partners helps divorcing persons formulate cogent explanations that emphasize compelling cultural values, and that help neutralize their own culpability. In the end, divorcing people thus constitute selves in expressly moral terms (cf. Spencer, this volume).

Noninitiators, for example, do this by articulating a rhetoric of family and commitment that shifts blame for the divorce onto initiators for having given up. They talk with considerable bitterness about their spouses not being willing to work at their marriages: "That's the part I don't like," said one noninitiator, "somebody walking out on that commitment." Even when they acknowledge the poor quality of their marriages or their own doubts about whether it could last, noninitiators uphold the sanctity of marriage and they present themselves as its defenders:

> My father came to the same place. He either had a choice of abandoning his family and going off and doing his own thing, or doing what I would like to say is right, and hanging in there and sticking it out and working on it. And I felt like I had to do that. That maybe it would have been better for me 11 years ago to have left. But that I had a commitment. I made a commitment to marry.

Initiators, on the other hand, articulate a rhetoric of individual and personal needs within marriage that shifts blame onto noninitiators for having failed to provide for a "real" marriage:

> There were needs that weren't being met, like there was no relationship there. Emotionally there wasn't any understanding and support. The fact that he isolated himself so much and the fact that he treated me with such contempt. The attitude was that he didn't really care about anybody but himself.

Initiators often describe their spouses as verbally and emotionally abusive, selfish, overinvolved in other activities, uncommunicative, and unaffectionate, and with this they begin reconceptualizing their marriages into "marriages that never were," in effect symbolically annulling their marriages and arguing that they were not marriages at all (Hopper 1998). They talk about their relationships being fundamentally flawed such that divorce becomes something not chosen, but something that happens inevitably to remedy the mistake of a "false" marriage. Deciding to divorce, then, is something not worthy of blame:

I was the dumper. But it's one of those situations where it's because I was the one who had the nerve to do it. And I always wind up saying, "Well, it doesn't mean it was my fault." He tried to turn it into, "It's your fault, you wouldn't try." And I don't buy into that.

Thus the selves that divorcing people created for themselves are, among other things, bound up with matters of fault and blame. And for good reasons: disentangling one's self from a relationship that profoundly defines the self in our culture is difficult indeed (Berger and Kellner 1964; Vaughan 1986). Add to that the moral significance of marriage, and it is easy to understand why who left whom and the dynamics that emerge around the distinction should figure so prominently in divorcing people's self-constructions.

Now when divorcing people approach the legal system, they do not approach it as a realm separate from these concerns; rather, they approach it hoping to air these concerns so that the truth of their marriages, their divorces, and who did what to whom will have consequences in how their dissolved relationships will be configured. Divorce professionals know this well: "People expect to go to court and have the judge know . . . about their relationship, about their children, about what happened in their breakup, you name it," one attorney explained. And the *truth* divorcing people want known is expressed for them via the moral self vis-à-vis the other, blamed spouse (Sarat and Felstiner 1988). One custody evaluator explained: "Everyone wants validation that their perception is the correct one and that the other person is an asshole." And an attorney said, "That's what I am dealing with a lot. The response that's coming from that chair has something to do with how rotten somebody was to them five years ago more than anything else."

Thus, however fragmented our institutional worlds may be, divorcing people presume a constant relevance to who they are as either initiator or noninitiating partner. They want and expect the moral failings, commitments, and courses of action that are now manifest in one person leaving the other to matter, and they approach the legal system expecting to find sympathetic professionals who will process their cases in such terms. The financial planner I interviewed gave an example of a client who had been left by her husband, and who expected a disproportionate financial settlement as a result: "She says, 'Well, yeah, but I deserve it. He's caused this divorce. He's the one that walked out.' I hear that a lot."

The Legal Self

The legal self of a divorcing person that lawyers and other professionals create differs sharply from the moral self that clients create. As with other institutional agents in other settings, they need particular selves to do their work. The legal self I describe in this section is an abstract person, subject to general rules laid down by a legislature—a person who has a definable and calculable future set of interests that can be determined by such rules. Divorce professionals see their clients in bureaucratic terms and interact with them, sometimes forcefully, expecting clients to take on similar understandings of self and to act accordingly.

They do this by simultaneously denying the moral self and proffering an alternative, and, when pressed, by insisting that institutional realities prevent them from doing otherwise. Erving Goffman's (1961) observations about how selves are constructed and transformed, though derived from his analysis of total institutions, are relevant here: the old self is denied its usual means of expression and affirmation, and at the same time a new self is constructed by subjecting persons to new sets of rules and behavioral criteria that get incorporated into their ongoing sense of how to get through divorce intact.

The process is facilitated by the temporal framework of divorce; it is not a singular event, but a drawn-out process. "Unlike any other piece of litigation, a divorce is made as it goes along," explained one attorney, "It's a plastic thing, it's a living thing." Another attorney explained:

> We get to sort of make our case during the case. As opposed to, like, a traffic light. The light was red, or the light wasn't, when the car went through it. And the case freezes in time. But with divorce, you work with the people throughout. That process is . . . in the beginning, I'm assessing where that person's going to be, where they're going to need to end up, and what's it going to take to get them there. Not only to present to the court, but also for them. So they can go on.

Clients are seen as part of the malleable process, as evidenced by attorneys telling me that part of their job is to "rehabilitate" clients. One attorney spoke of a client she was seeing that afternoon:

> I'm working like crazy to rehabilitate her. Quickly. To let her know that as smart as she is, she looks like such an idiot. That if I took her to court tomorrow, which is when the hearing is scheduled, I'm not only going to lose, she's going to be penalized in some way in her parenting for the rest of her life. I have to somehow get that across, that the consequence is real, immediate, and perpetual. And then I'll get some cooperation, even in the face of terrible resistance.

Denying the Moral Self

The first step for divorce professionals involves denying the moral self and the particulars of who left whom typically presented. Most simply emphasize to their clients the irrelevance of who left whom to the legal matters at hand, some saying they refuse to talk with clients about it. One attorney explained: "There are times when you have to say, 'You really don't want to talk to me about this. This is not important in the whole scheme of things as far as the divorce is concerned.'" The financial planner elaborated: "It's not that I don't care. I would rather not hear it all, because it doesn't affect what I'm doing." If noninitiators hope to use the legal system to contest the divorce itself, attorneys explain to them its futility:

> Our society doesn't recognize that. As far as our laws are concerned, there's no way to avoid a divorce in a nonfault state where the only grounds for dissolution is irretrievable breakdown of marriage. You got to tell them, "Look, that may be your belief system, and it may be the important law for you, but this state does not agree with that."

Even the more dramatic and seemingly relevant moral aspects of divorce, such as spouses having affairs, squandering family income, or acting cruelly or emotionally abusive are considered unimportant.

In many cases, professionals see the moral contours of divorce as not only irrelevant to the legal process, but as potentially damaging as well. It can be damaging if professionals know and work with clients in moral terms, as the financial consultant described:

> I have found that when I go to court, when the other side cross-examines me, if I haven't heard a lot of that stuff, I'm better off. Because they really get into it. They'll say, "Well, did you know that?" And if I can say, "No, I didn't," there's nothing else they can question me on. If I say, "Yes, I did," they really dig in. And if it has nothing to do with the financial issues, there's no reason for them to be asking me those questions. And I would rather not be entrapped. Because those are attorneys who really know how to trap you with questions. So I would rather not mess with that stuff.

It can be disadvantageous, too, if clients themselves insist on pursuing moral claims. Custody evaluators described listening for whether divorcing spouses are preoccupied with laying blame, as this would reflect poorly on their abilities to attend to a child's needs; lawyers know that this, in turn, will likely affect an evaluator's recommendation to a court regarding custody. Thus, as one attorney told me:

> I perceive any client's interests as having me sit on them more than in some other kinds of cases. By that I mean, I think it is in my client's interests to have them not pursue their obsession with getting even.

Defining Clients' Best Interests

As the moral self is denied, a new legal self is preferred, one that is tailored to the requirements of legal institutions. As such, it is a self that divorce professionals conceptualize in terms of "interests" quite apart from the moral dynamics of divorce. Lawyers in particular see themselves as having an obligation to process cases and clients in ways that may contradict their clients' wishes. And they see it as their job to help clients understand themselves—and therefore what they need and want—in terms of such interests:

> My obligation is to do what's in their best interest, not necessarily do what they want to do. Because they don't necessarily know what's in their best interest at the time they're in there because of their emotional state. . . . I know what they need and I know why they need it.

Another attorney said:

> Part of my job is to help them get to know what's right and what they want. And when I say, "what's right"—I'm talking about their legal . . . what is potentially out there for them legally.

How do these interests, needs, and wants get built up and defined? It happens through conversations and interactions by which professionals continually broaden, shift, and refocus cases by emphasizing the contexts, rules, and standards that govern divorce as a legal proceeding. They explain, for example, that "there is no divorce without the system," as one attorney put it:

> Some people would like to just do it their own way even if they shouldn't. Or even if they are going to pay a terrible price. One of the things that I do when I'm talking to people like that is that I tell them that the court is going to have to review their agreement and it might not be approved.

Another attorney said:

> [I] show them the larger context in which their case, their life, their relationship is going to proceed. Especially if you start talking about a new divorce client. Many people will come in and say I need X, Y, Z, whatever. And they just are never going to get it. You better tell them. Or if they want it, you may have to tell them that it has to come in this way, in this context, you have to ask for it this way or you'll never get it. To reframe their experience from being one of a simply personal and relational problem, to now one that is going to include me, it's going to include someone else's lawyer, usually, it's going to include a system. It's going to include much more than they ever anticipated.

The working assumption among professionals is that every divorce will go to a full-blown trial: "I assume every case will go to court . . . even though 90 percent of them don't," one custody evaluator said. Thus they remain attentive to how cases and clients must be configured for future institutional scrutiny. As one attorney described:

> I'm always building the faces that I have to prove to a judge sometime later. . . . You have to be thinking from the moment you first sit down, that this person, even if he's here, how you're going to present it to a judge someday.

Professionals explain that within the broader context thus laid out is a set of dispassionate, clearly articulated rules that are fault-blind and that will determine outcomes, be they "right, wrong, or indifferent." "You're stuck with the state system, so here is the range that this state is going to deal with," one attorney explained. Many used language as if they were working with algebraic formulas: "The marriage has been X amount of time, she has made X amount of sacrifices." Another put it this way:

> The court is going to say, "Okay, here's the deal: the marriage is X amount of years time, it was this kind of marriage, here's what you did, here's what the other person did during the course of the marriage. Here's what you need, here's what they need. Here's what you can afford, here's what they can afford." So that's what we've got to talk about. We've got to talk about what your expenses are. We got to talk about what your needs are and we've got to talk about what your in-

come is. We've got to talk about what the future is going to be for you under
whatever the scenario might be.

Several emphasized that the rules are general rules, the procedures are bureaucratic, and so the particulars of each case are emphatically pushed to the background:

> I give a lecture . . . that goes through every element of domestic relations, whether
> it's applicable to this particular situation or not. So they understand the general
> foundations and rules, and also they understand the grounds for dissolution, they
> understand the longevity of the proceeding, on a minimal basis what has to be
> done, what procedures we go through, the collection of data, collection of evi-
> dence if we're in that type of case, and what they can expect.

Hence for professionals, the self of a client is a generalized self. It is a self that
expresses something more abstract, an outcome achieved by applying universal
rules within a legal context to the situation at hand. One lawyer, in fact, complained about divorce mediation because it is premised on the opposing idea that
spouses know best their own situations and can therefore craft better and more
particular solutions:

> Mediation [is] a narcissistic hangover of values from the '80s: "What I want and
> how I want to do it is very important; it doesn't matter about the social context
> in which it arose or in which it's going to die—the legal ramifications of it. No,
> it's personal to me. Me me me me me. And therefore, I I I I I want to do it my
> my my my way. And so we are going to make this a very personalized kind of a
> thing."

The result is that lawyers and other divorce professionals work with clients
and construct notions of who clients are in calculable terms that focus on matters
of money, property, and time with children. They collect information about income and expenditures, property, bank accounts, retirement plans, and debts.
They work out the specifics of who will get what and when and how two house-
holds can be maintained, apportioning cars and houses and in some cases trifling
items like Zippo lighters and blue Corning pots. They haggle over maintenance
(alimony) and child support payments, which are themselves calculated with formulas laid out by the law. Even the issue of custody is handled not in terms of
who left whom (i.e., who "betrayed" the family) or in terms of who is the better
parent (as divorcing people typically argue) but in terms of "the best interests of
the child." Interests of children are, in turn, determinable according to financial
formulas and according to the scientific canons of developmental psychology.

There is a way in which this legal self is still related to questions of morality,
but the grounds shift decisively. First, what is "right" is what conforms to the
rules, precisely because the rules are designed to ensure equitable outcomes despite the whims of divorcing spouses, attorneys, and judges. Second, what is
"right" has to do with the future and how that future must be mapped out, rather
than having to do with the past and how grievances might be redressed. Third,

what is right has essentially to do with matters of "fairness" in terms of clients' legally defined interests. "If it's one person getting everything and the other person getting nothing," a mediator explained to me, "or an agreement is very detrimental to the child, then I wouldn't be able to participate in it. I would say, 'Sorry, I can't work with you anymore. And here's why.'" An attorney described his job thusly:

> You're extricating people from a legal binding relationship, and you want them to be happy as you can. You want them to be under the last strain that they can be in. You want to make sure the children are cared for, so maybe there's a joint caring of the kids. You want to make sure there's a fair disposition of the money accumulated during the course of the marriage, i.e., marital assets. You want to make sure the payments are fair and commensurate with ability to pay and need. And you want to make sure that, hopefully, that everybody goes on with their lives and is happy. That's really the job.

Asserting Ownership of the Legal Self

The legal self constructed by divorce professionals, though constructed in response to institutional demands about how cases and clients must be processed, is more than a heuristic that allows professionals to accomplish their work. It is something they believe in, and they see this legal self as a self that clients can and should adopt for their own good. Most attorneys thus insist that clients take "ownership" of the process and of the decisions finally made:

> I want it to be from his heart, too. For him, it's better that it's real. . . . The last thing I want him to say is, "Yeah, I went to a parenting class because my lawyer told me I had to." And the truth is, I want . . . if my client wants custody, my client has to show *me* that he's committed in that kind of scenario. You show me how committed you are to making some changes, because what I'm trying to sort out is: is this just a power struggle? or this guy doesn't want custody, he just wants to zing the wife?

Most attorneys want their clients to move on with their lives, and most want to spare them the trauma and expense of a court trial. "Winning" cases thus involves settling them, I was told. And settling cases is a matter of having clients internalize an understanding of the legal rules and procedures according to which their cases will be processed, then having clients arrive at the kinds of decisions a court would arrive at were their divorces actually to go to trial. This is not always easy. It is facilitated in part by the fact that most clients pay for the legal services rendered, giving them an incentive to work out fair solutions quickly and agreeably. It is also accomplished strategically when attorneys solicit decisions about how cases should proceed. Some present clients with a narrow range of choices, letting clients then choose from among them. Others offer clients a kind of veto power: "I tell them my posture, my position and why, and then they make a decision as to whether or not they want to go along with it." One attorney described the process in these terms:

> I start saying, "This is what is really going on out there and these are your choices, and my recommendation on here and here . . . "I don't get many clients at that point that don't agree with me. I'm not saying I'm imposing my will on them. I let them make decisions, but we come to it together.

Sometimes attorneys and clients decide to fight the other side and to litigate all the way to a trial, but what really matters are not the particulars of what attorneys and clients decide or how they proceed; what matters is that their actions remain consistent with, and motivated by, clients' legal selves. As the attorney quoted above suggested, she will fight for custody, but not if it is just a power struggle. Another lawyer told me that he was always willing to "kick the living hell" out of the other side, but he refused to work with clients "if they're here to hurt somebody just to hurt them and it isn't logical and fair."

There is an interesting element of self-interest on the part of attorneys in having clients adopt the legal self, as well. If clients do not make their own legally sound decisions, if, as one attorney explained, "Instead of making their decision they just let somebody else make it for them, [then] that puts the lawyer in a lot of risk." Several said that they try to protect themselves from lawsuits by refusing to work with clients who are unduly influenced by others or who ignore their legal advice. Attorneys are also sensitive to the fact that their *own* selves as legal professionals are at stake, and so frequently they lean hard on their clients to elicit the cooperation they need:

> I'm telling them that if they don't get their act together, here are the consequences. The legal consequences are: you lose. Pure and simple. That's one good thing about being a lawyer—I don't have to go into all this stuff. I know pretty much how the courts are going to act if no one does anything to deal with their problems and I'll just say, "Fine, then you lose." [Interviewer: What's the response?] Some people will say, "Well, it's your job to make this come out better for me." And I'll say, "No. . . . You don't do it, I may not be your attorney either. Because I don't like to lose cases and you're making me a loser. I won't do it." I'll say that. "Go to somebody else. You want someone else to tell you this is all right? Go ahead. But I have my own personal investment in not going to court with stupid-looking or losing cases. Because my reputation is my life work. So I'm just not going to mess around."

The Unifying Intrusions of the Moral Self

As professionals work with their clients in divorce cases, they construct working models of who their clients are in terms of tangible interests with determinate rights and obligations as specified by the legal institution within which they must work. Meanwhile, divorcing people construct moral selves that provide, among other things, some means of defense against the ignominy of divorce. Thus, people getting divorced have at least two "divorcing selves" that get constructed in at least two different contexts according to the institutional demands of each.

I suggested earlier, however, that within the lived experienced of most divorcing persons there are not multiple selves but a unified self—a self that cannot easily shed its various assemblages depending upon institutional contexts. Hence, professionals come to discover that their clients usually expect the legal system to serve the moral self, and that clients often transform dispassionate discussions of interests, legal rights, and contractual obligations squarely back into moral terms. This is part of what makes the process so complicated and potentially difficult. Clients must be able to "separate their own stuff from the business end of the divorce," one attorney explained, and when they cannot, "when the relationship issues are just so overwhelming, oftentimes you can't reach agreement."

A number of factors make it particularly difficult for divorcing people to separate out different selves for the sake of getting the legal work done. First, divorcing people are not separated from the everyday world and institutional sources that shape the moral self. Goffman (1961) suggests that total institutions are able to reconstruct inmates' selves in part because total institutions separate inmates almost entirely from their "home worlds." (See Weinberg, this volume, for a parallel discussion.) Divorce lawyers cannot do this; in fact divorcing people are often pulled more tightly into the social worlds that define the moral self as they turn to parents and family members for financial, practical, and emotional help, even as they seek out attorneys for legal help.

Lawyers recognize this and the difficulties it creates. "There's very often parental influence," one attorney explained, and every lawyer I interviewed said that having a client's parents somehow involved in the process made the job more difficult. "It's just a bad situation," one said. "You're trying to get them to see things impartially and Mom or Dad or both are coming in and saying, 'You ought to do this, you ought to do that.'" Another attorney described: "Those pulls are incredible on them. And quite often very destructive in the legal case as well as to that person who can't deal with that right then." This same attorney noted that professionals, too, can get swept into the familiar context that shapes moral selves and lose sight of their clients' legal selves as a result. The more an attorney knows the detailed story of a client's life, she told me, the more "you want to react emotionally, just like the client does":

> You begin to get strong feelings about the other attorney, and about the other client. It happens frequently in divorce cases, but it's even more of an issue when you're handling postdecree cases, cases that you've been on for years and years and years. That person is like an aunt or an uncle. You know everything about the family. You know what's going on. And you really get entrenched there.

A second factor that makes it difficult for clients to separate the legal self from the moral self is that attorneys may work in ways that actually reinforce the strength and clarity of clients' moral identities in divorce. When attorneys have clients who are wavering about whether or not to get divorced, they often push their clients toward taking a more resolute stand—not necessarily because divorce attorneys have an interest in clients pursuing divorce, but because they can not work effectively within ambiguously defined situations. Ambiguity and ambivalence "just drive you crazy," said one attorney as he related to me a story about a client he was working with:

> I had a discussion with her, "Look, damn it, you've got to make a decision. I can't do this and this at the same time. Tell me which one you want to do." [Interviewer: What can't you do at the same time?] I can't pursue this case in litigation and not pursue. I can't do discovery and not do discovery. Tell me which one. [Interviewer: And what does she say?] Well, it depends on what moment you catch her. We executed a very unusual order that allowed us to go into his business and inventory everything without his knowledge. So we went in last Sunday and did all of that. And she calls me up Monday and says, "Do you think I'm walking away from this relationship too soon?"

But it is precisely when resolute decisions are made and ambivalence resolved that the moral identities in divorce take form and become important phenomena in divorce (Hopper 1993a, 1993b). The either-or nature of the legal system effectively pushes people toward resolving the ambivalence they might have had, and, as most attorneys know, few clients turn back once legal action is begun. Attorneys also sometimes strengthen the salience of clients' moral selves by maneuvering them into doing the "right" thing—what is required of the legal self—by drawing upon clients' moralistic interpretations of how a divorce is playing out. "You sometimes have to play into their craziness," one attorney explained:

> For example, "You don't want him to see the kids because you think this bad thing is going to happen?" And the bad thing is not too bad. I mean I wouldn't do it with any safety issues. Sometimes you have to say, "Well, you know I really believe you, but we don't have the evidence. So what we need to do is we have to try it, and then if he does it then your case is going to be made." And you kind of feed into the sort of craziness and suspiciousness and paranoia in a way to get them to do the right thing. And it's not totally dishonest—I don't feel that good about having to do it—but a lot of times you have to do it. Especially at critical stages. And then later you can talk to them about it. But especially if they are doing something really destructive for their case. Sometimes you have to give them okay reasons to do the right thing.

In short, though the legal system technically nullifies questions of fault—questions that are at the heart of clients' moral selves—the practical realities of how lawyers and other professionals get their clients processed through that system often intensifies the moral selves of clients. One might think that the dual constructions of self would cause confusion among divorcing people as they work to manage competing versions of the self in various contexts, and this on top of the crisis in meaning that divorce itself would seem to present. But as one custody evaluator observed, there does not seem to be much in terms of confusion:

Usually, they're arguing their case to me and arguing their case to their attorney, and as they do that they become more and more convinced that what they're saying is right and the way it should be.

For many divorcing people, then, the unifying intrusions of the moral self beckon strongly. "They need fault. They want fault. They want somebody to pay when they're bad," one attorney explained, and they want that somebody to pay in tangible ways via a penalty imposed by the court. A number of attorneys suggested to me that one result is that many more clients than ever before are playing out matters of fault in battles over custody. One said:

> That's the only place where the whole system seems to let fault be played out. I think that if parents could—and I'm talking about marriages with children—if parents could get in the court and say why they think they were wronged, and there might be legal consequences to it to the other parent, they probably would not use their children as the go-betweens as much.

There may be no-fault divorce in a technical sense, but for divorcing people the issue of fault does not go away. And the issue of fault in divorce can easily translate into the domain of parenting and custody, for the central issues about who left whom and why still get expressed, as one divorcing woman explained to me:

> Morally, are you being a bad parent because you're having an affair with this man? What are you going to teach the child if you're doing this during our marriage? Or, the child's going to get hurt if he stays with you because you beat me; what's going to make it to where you don't beat them?

Clients thus reassert their moral selves, bringing matters of fault back into the legal process by linking their identity in divorce with their identity as a parent. The legal system may thus exacerbate divorce conflict in a rather surprising way. It may generate conflict not because it is structured as an adversarial system rather than as a cooperative one, as some divorce researchers have suggested (Johnston and Campbell 1988; Knox 1990; Sprey 1979; Felstiner, Abel, and Sarat 1981), but because it refuses to allow matters of fault within the purview of divorce proceedings. In the end, since the legal system has no place for fault to play out within the domain of the dissolving marital relationship itself, the moral battle may get displaced into arenas like custody where divorcing partners can fight over who is at fault the marriage's failure by fighting over who is the better parent. As courts have tried to remove matters of fault and blame even from custody considerations, hoping instead to rely on the scientific formulations of child psychology and expert opinion, one attorney hypothesized that the custody battles would get even worse:

> There are more allegations of spousal and child abuse made to get custody. It's upped the ante so that if someone really wants to show someone else is at fault,

and they'll do anything to do it, they've just upped the ante. So now you say "This person has abused me." Whereas before all you had to say was they were mean.

Selves in Conflict

There are at least two selves in divorce that I have called the moral self and the legal self; they are constructed in different institutional spheres by social actors who attend to the ongoing concerns of those institutions. From one perspective, the two selves in divorce give evidence that theorists of self in postmodernity are right that we are each constituted by multiple selves—that the self in our post-modern society, with its burgeoning possibilities for interactions contextualized within multiple institutions, has become a "saturated" self, as Kenneth Gergen (1991) has put it.

But the descriptions in this chapter suggest a more distressing possibility as well: perhaps it is not so much that we have become saturated with multiple selves, but that we have become fragmented into partial selves. As we become increasingly subject to diverse and disparate encounters in various spheres, our attempts to pull our experiences into some semblance of unity through a singular point of reference become more precarious. This chapter has emphasized, in particular, the unifying attempts of the moral self, as divorcing persons seek to bring the legal system into line with their everyday moralistic expectations. The legal self has unifying tendencies as well: witness legal professionals insisting that the legal self is the good self, the fair self, the self that ought to come from one's heart so that one can move on. Either way, it seems that as institutional spheres proliferate in number and scope, according to a logic that does not necessarily serve the living persons who comprise them, the self is frustrated in its unifying efforts. In the case of divorce, each competing self attempts to incorporate the other under its own terms, and neither seems to accomplish it. The legal self requires objectivity and compromise, which the moral self refuses and stymies; the moral self requires justice, not scientific administration, and thus seeks ever new ways to use the legal system to fight its battles.

No doubt the conflict in divorce between two competing selves can take its toll on two levels. First, since the two constructions of self presumably inhere in one and the same person, the conflict may be internalized as an existential struggle in personal terms. Second, it can be externalized and manifest in social terms, as battles over custody attest. In this, perhaps the social theorists of modernity were more prescient than postmodern theorists appreciate. Translated into language about the self, we might say that Marx wrote about the alienated self, Durkheim the anomic self, Weber the self trapped in an iron cage of rationality, and Simmel the subjective self outpaced by objective culture. Each suggested in his own way that we face the danger of becoming fragmented, impoverished, and frustrated at the partial demands multiple institutions put upon us and the limited possibilities they give for unitary self-expression.

REFERENCES

Berger, Peter, and Hansfried Kellner. 1964. "Marriage and the Construction of Reality: An Exercise in the Microsociology of Knowledge." *Diogenes* 46:1–23.

Buehler, Cheryl. 1987. "Initiator Status and the Divorce Transition." *Family Relations* 36:82–86.

Felstiner, William L. F., Richard L. Abel, and Austin Sarat. 1981. "The Emergence and Transformation of Disputes: Naming, Blaming and Claiming . . . "*Law and Society Review* 15:631–54.

Gergen, Kenneth J. 1991. *The Saturated Self: Dilemmas of Identity in Contemporary Life.* New York: Basic Books.

Goffman, Erving. 1961. *Asylums.* New York: Anchor Books.

Gubrium, Jaber F., and James A. Holstein. 1994. "Grounding the Postmodern Self." *The Sociological Quarterly* 34:685–703.

Holstein, James A., and Jaber F. Gubrium. 2000. *The Self We Live By: Narrative Identity in a Postmodern World.* New York: Oxford University Press.

Hopper, Joseph. 1993a. "Oppositional Identities and Rhetoric in Divorce." *Qualitative Sociology* 16:133–56.

———. 1993b. "The Rhetoric of Motives in Divorce." *Journal of Marriage and the Family* 55:801–13.

———. 1998. "The Symbolic Origins of Conflict in Divorce." Paper presented at the annual meeting of the American Sociological Association, San Francisco.

Johnston, Janet R., and Linda E. G. Campbell. 1988. *Impasses of Divorce.* New York: Free Press.

Knox, David. 1990. "A Sociologist's Encounter with Divorce Lawyers." *Free Inquiry in Creative Sociology* 18:197–98.

Mead, Margaret. 1971. "Anomalies in American Postdivorce Relationships." In *Divorce and After,* ed. Paul Bohannan, 107–25. Garden City, N.Y.: Anchor Books.

Nevaldine, Anne. 1978. "Divorce: The Leaver and the Left." Ph.D. diss., University of Minnesota.

Pettit, Ellen J., and Bernard L. Bloom. 1984. "Whose Decision Was It? The Effects of Initiator Status on Adjustment to Marital Disruption." *Journal of Marriage and the Family* 46:587–95.

Riessman, Catherine Kohler. 1990. *Divorce Talk: Women and Men Make Sense of Personal Relationships.* New Brunswick, N.J.: Rutgers University Press.

Sarat, Austin, and Felstiner, William L. F. 1988. "Law and Social Relations: Vocabularies of Motive in Lawyer/Client Interaction." *Law and Society Review* 22:737–69.

Spanier, Graham B., and Linda Thompson. 1984. *Parting: The Aftermath of Separation and Divorce.* Beverly Hills: Sage Publications.

Sprey, Jetse. 1979. "Conflict Theory and the Study of Marriage and the Family." In *Contemporary Theories About the Family,* vol. 2, ed. Wesley R. Burr et al., 130–59. New York: Free Press.

Vaughan, Diane. 1986. *Uncoupling.* New York: Oxford University Press.

Weiss, Robert S. 1975. *Marital Separation.* New York: Basic Books.

SUSAN E. CHASE

Universities as Discursive Environments for Sexual Identity Construction

Not long ago, a student at my university committed suicide after coming out as a lesbian to herself, a few friends, and her mother. Her death, of course, was a personal tragedy for the people close to her. At the same time, some members of the university community found themselves responding to this terrible event by raising questions about their university as an institutional context in which lives are lived and shaped. What kinds of personal identities—sexual or otherwise— does our university welcome? What kinds of public dialogue do we have—or fail to have—about various forms of diversity? What is the effect of our dialogue or silence on the personal identities that students—and for that matter, faculty and other employees—can comfortably develop? What resources are available for students who are struggling with new understandings of their race, ethnicity, nationality, gender, sexual orientation, or religion?

A common response to such questions is that a university is an educational institution, not a therapeutic setting or a family. As such, it is not responsible for the psychological well-being of its members, at least not like other institutions are, such as family. Surely, some argue, this young woman's suicide can be explained by unresolved problems in her psychological makeup or upbringing. Alternatively, her death can be interpreted in light of the high rate of suicide among gay and lesbian youth across the nation—possibly two to three times that of heterosexual youth (Raymond 1994, p. 127). But whatever their merits, neither psychological nor structural explanations preclude an examination of how universities, as significant life-shaping institutions, condition the ways that students resolve their personal troubles.

This chapter is about two American universities, and how students make sense of the contemporary debates about race, gender, and sexual orientation that rage around them in American society generally as well as within the walls of academe. I will show that universities are institutional settings in which specific forms of discourse about these issues develop. In the following section, I characterize the local diversity discourse that circulates at each of the universities I studied. Then I demonstrate the impact on individuals of each institution's diversity discourse by analyzing and comparing the narratives of two young women about their sexuality. I argue that a university's discourse shapes how individuals construct their selves and that that process is evident in students' personal narratives about identity dilemmas. I do not mean to say that the identities people construct are *determined* by their discursive environments; rather, their narratives reveal how they come to terms with the conditions of possibility provided by those environments (Foucault 1977). In the concluding section, I address the theoretical and practical import of my research.

Universities as Discursive Environments

I conducted my research in 1994 and 1995 at two very different universities, neither of which is my own. City University (a pseudonym) is a small, private, urban university in a politically progressive state. State University (a pseudonym) is a large, public, rural university in a politically conservative state. Both institutions have predominantly white, middle-class student bodies, although the latter has a larger proportion of students from working-class backgrounds. At each site, I began with group interviews with a broad range of campus organizations such as the student government, College Republicans, the Gay, Lesbian, Bisexual Coalition (GLBC), Women's Resource Center, Native American Student Association, and Black Collegians. I also contacted resident advisers in the residence halls who pulled together students on their floors so that I could interview groups unaffiliated with campus organizations. After the group interviews, I conducted intensive interviews with individuals I had met through the groups. On each campus, I talked with many different kinds of students, focusing on diversities of race, ethnicity, gender, sexual orientation, political perspective, and degree of campus involvement. In total, I conducted 64 interviews (18 with groups; 46 with individuals). I also visited classes, attended various public and private campus events, and read the student newspaper for several months at each site.

Although I deliberately chose dissimilar universities, I did not anticipate the significance of their differing institutional discourses. At City University (CU), a huge controversy raged on campus for several years about a diversity policy that the university adopted after concerted efforts by faculty and students. The policy affirms the university's commitment to a learning environment in which cultural differences are not simply tolerated, but celebrated. The most debated aspect of the policy concerns student groups that have been underrepresented historically or denied equal opportunity in higher education. The new policy allows them to control membership in their groups for the purposes of providing social support. The upshot is that a student organization for women, African Americans, or gays and lesbians may choose to restrict membership or limit leadership positions to persons of their gender or race or sexual orientation.

When I arrived at CU, the student government had just failed to pass amendments to its constitution that would have brought it into line with the university's new diversity policy. Student groups such as the Women's Resource Center and the Black Collegians were worried that their funding from the student government would be cut off because their practices were now in violation of the constitution. On a deeper level, they felt betrayed by their peers in the student government.

In a more general sense, I observed that issues of race, gender, and sexual orientation evoke regular discussion and a great deal of contentiousness in many contexts at CU. All first-year students attend a week-long, diversity-related orientation, while students of color arrive even earlier for specific activities organized around their needs and interests. Students participate—some willingly, some grudgingly—in occasional mandatory workshops. For example, during my visit, all 200 students in a residence hall where an incident of sexual harassment had taken place were required to attend a sexual harassment workshop facilitated by outside consultants. Public lectures, panel discussions, and theatrical performances related to diversity issues are well attended. The curriculum integrates cultural diversity as a matter of course and it is a major topic in the student newspaper. While these campus forums produce vigorous debate from all points of the political spectrum, the predominant discourse supports an open stance toward historically excluded groups, including gays and lesbians.

At State University (SU), I found that no public, collective debate about diversity takes place. The university has a typical, nondescript nondiscrimination policy, which says nothing about sexual orientation. Several years earlier, some students unsuccessfully petitioned to get sexual orientation included in the policy, but this was mentioned only by a few students, the older members of the GLBC. In any case, the diversity policy has little impact on students' everyday lives, at least in the sense that it is not now a matter of public concern. There are, however, a number of active student groups organized around race, ethnicity, gender, and sexual orientation. In addition, the professional residence hall staff train resident advisers in sensitivity to racial and ethnic differences among students, and to a lesser extent, differences in sexual orientation. Some resident advisers have taken the initiative to create a nonmandatory educational program for incoming students. In theatrical skits they enact dilemmas students are likely to encounter concerning drugs, dating, and sexual behavior. After the skits, they invite group discussion of these issues.

Nonetheless, these diversity-oriented organizations and activities have limited visibility and impact at SU. In contrast to CU, they operate within a broader institutional context that neither actively opposes nor supports them. Unlike students at CU, their counterparts at SU can easily avoid hearing or dealing with discourse about diversity. The student newspaper contains only sporadic articles about diversity issues, and students report that classes in the general curriculum rarely address such issues.

The difference between these two discursive environments shows itself most poignantly in the group interviews I did at each site, especially with students in the resident halls—those who are not necessarily involved in campus organizations. At City University, when I asked *any* group of students my opening question—how do issues of race, gender, and sexual orientation come up for you on this campus?—I encountered no hesitation. Regardless of their particular opinions, nearly every student had a lot to say and plenty of stories to tell. It didn't take long before I could just sit back and listen. The most common story I heard from white heterosexual students is that university life has produced a major transformation in their understanding of people who are different from themselves, either racially or sexually. Exposure to different people, they claim, has opened their eyes and their minds; they experience such exposure as a *self-transformation*. These students explain their transformation in terms of their move from a rural to an urban environment, their immersion in a more diverse setting than the one they grew up in, or the impact of education itself ("we're supposed to have our ideas challenged at college"). To emphasize the depth of change they have undergone, they describe their shame about earlier actions and they recount confrontations with family members about their attitudes and behavior.

Another common story, sometimes intertwined with the first, consists of complaints that diversity and "political correctness" are being shoved down their throats and that they are tired of mandatory workshops on date rape and the like. A less frequent but still poignant theme is that sexual harassment, affirmative action, and gay rights activists have gone too far and now white men and straight people are being discriminated against. Not surprisingly, students of color and gay and lesbian students told quite different stories about the trials of living in a predominantly white and straight setting.

Equally significant as the content of the stories is the form of students' talk during group interviews. Students at CU *converse* about these issues; they are practiced in speaking and hearing about them. A typical example: on one dormitory floor, a group of six students (three white men, one white woman, a Native American woman, a Filipina, all apparently heterosexual), began with a lively discussion of the student government's negative vote on the diversity policy and then gradually moved on to more personal topics. Eventually the white students asked the two women of color what it was like for them on this predominantly white campus. Although the women of color had to dispel some stereotypes about their racial groups, the white students listened carefully. The conversation was open, genuine, and clearly enjoyed by all, a perception I clarified later during the individual interviews, including those with the women of color.

Toward the end of this same interview, someone commented that they hadn't talked much about sexual orientation. The group launched into a discussion about how this is the most difficult diversity issue because it conflicts with conservative religious values. Although the students assumed they were all heterosexual, one wondered how he would feel on campus if he were gay. When another complained about GLBC members' hostility to straight people, the Native American woman explained their actions by making an analogy to her own anger about white people's racial ignorance. All discussed how a minority of any sort should present its message in order to educate others.

In short, no matter what their perspective, every group I interviewed at CU had plenty to say about issues of race, gender, and sexual orientation. The public debate about the diversity policy, along with the general focus on diversity issues at this institution, created a discursive environment in which every student was practiced in listening to and speaking about the debate and the issues. The public character of the issues gave students a common language to speak with, even if they chose to resist or reject it, as quite a few did. Members of the College Republicans, for example, were disgusted by what they perceived as the university's accommodation to gays and lesbians. Nonetheless, these conservative students were highly aware that within their discursive environment their talk would be perceived as homophobic.

By contrast, at State University, when I asked groups of students in the residence halls how issues of race, gender, and sexual orientation come up for them on their campus, many had nothing to say at first. If it weren't for the heaping piles of pizza I provided, some of the group interviews would have lasted less than five minutes. After a while I realized that my question didn't make sense to them; it didn't organize their experience like it did for their counterparts at CU (Chase 1995, p. 41; Smith 1987, p. 188). With time, the students usually raised a few incidents where race or gender or sexual orientation were salient and the discussion took off. But both the content and the form of their talk are strikingly different from what I heard at CU. The story of self-transformation, so prevalent at CU, is absent. And although the same range of attitudes—from conservative to progressive—is present, students' expressions of their attitudes are not organized around a common language, debate, or set of issues.

I'll offer a typical example. On one floor in a men's residence hall, I interviewed six white men and one African American man who was their resident adviser. In response to my opening question, the resident advisor started out by saying that sexual orientation is the most public issue debated on campus, as seen by the recent Denim Day event. (Shortly before I arrived the GLBC had chalked the sidewalks, "On Friday, wear denim if you support gay rights.") All of the young men reported that they wore denim that day, not out of support for gay rights but because they didn't want anyone telling them what to wear. They appeared indifferent and their discussion implied that the event did not influence them to think about their ideas on the matter. Individual interviews confirmed this impression.

Later during this group interview, a white student who had expressed support for gay rights earlier in the discussion, described his homophobic reaction to a friend who had come out to him a few years before. What struck me was that this young man did not seem to notice the disjunction between his ideology of gay rights and his homophobic attitude toward his friend which continued to the present. Although such a disjunction is not unusual, students at CU were more likely to be aware than students at SU of such contradictions. For example, many students at CU struggled with the clash between the values they grew up with and the values the university exposed them to. They wrestled with this clash even when they complained that the university forced its values on them through what they perceived as the barrage of diversity-related events.

Eventually, all of the groups at SU ended up having something to say about diversity issues. But even in their conversations, it seemed that the students were treading on new territory with each other; they lacked experience in talking about these issues. Of course, student groups organized specifically around diversity issues had much more to say. But in general, I was convinced after several group interviews in the residence halls that there was no public, collective discussion at SU concerning issues of race, gender, and sexual orientation. In the absence of a strong, institutionally supported public discourse about these issues, most students drew unselfconsciously on the relatively conservative ideas they absorbed earlier in life, ideas developed within their families, religious communities, and the popular media. These were exactly the same perspectives that students at CU were self-reflective about. Even students at CU who continue to believe that "homosexuality is wrong according to my religion" spoke about having learned that there are other viable perspectives.

In sum, these two institutions promote local diversity discourses that differ in both content and form. CU encourages a public, collective discourse of openness to diversity and openness to dialogue about diversity. Although conservative students reject that discourse and progressive students complain that it is lip service, this common language both incites and conditions students' talk about diversity. Specifically, they are practiced both in hearing and speaking about diversity, and no matter what their particular perspective, they speak with an awareness of others' perspectives (Chase 1995, pp. 59–60). By contrast, SU's diversity discourse can be characterized as diffuse and unorganized. The absence of public, collective discussion means that SU students have little experience listening to and talking about race, gender, or sexual orientation. As individuals, SU students express the same range of attitudes as CU students, but they exhibit little self-consciousness or self-awareness about others' perspectives on these issues and what dialogue among them would sound like.

How, then, do these two discursive environments condition individual students' stories about their lives and their identities?

Two Women's Identity Narratives

Christine is a 21-year-old white lesbian who attends State University. Jessie is a 20-year-old white bisexual at City University. In presenting excerpts from their interviews, each of which was about two hours long, I concentrate on the parts where they talk about negotiating their identities in public with people who do not know about their sexual orientation, people who are at best acquaintances.

Constructing a Closeted Sexual Identity

I met Christine during a group interview with the GLBC, a group in which she was actively involved at SU. At the time of the interview, Christine had been out as a lesbian to her friends for more than two years, and she had been living with her partner for a year and a half.

When I asked what the GLBC meant to her, Christine talked about being proud of the very existence of the group, given the conservative climate, but she also worried that the group might be ineffective because most members are either very closeted or so flamboyant about their sexuality that straight people reject them outright. She stated that heterosexuals are more accepting of gays who seem "normal." I asked how that affects her life.

> Well, a lot of times I find myself thinking a lot harder about what I'm going to wear than I should have to think about it. And when I'm in classes and we talk about topical issues like homosexuality and AIDS and abortion, I think a lot harder.

I'm more calculated about what I say than a lot of other people in my classes are because they . . . and I don't know if that has so much to do with being gay as it does being more thoughtful or more analytical than other people who just speak from their gut, you know, what they feel, and what they were raised with. But I think it's partially influenced by. . . . I don't want people to have a negative reaction to me because they think that I might be gay.

Christine attributes her careful presentation of self to her thoughtful nature and her expectation that others would respond negatively to her lesbianism. Notice that she critiques the *environment* when she states "a lot harder . . . than I should have to think about it." She implies that in a different context she might not have to think so hard about what she wears or says in public. Even her description of her thoughtful nature can be interpreted in light of the discursive environment: as a lesbian she is compelled to think about diversity issues in ways that other students do not need to because SU does not invite public discussion of them. She continues:

I think that I am influenced by that and I don't think it's *always* a negative thing. Sometimes I think that gay people *buy* into stereotypes just because it's the only thing they know. That's the only thing that they've ever known about gay people and they have the *feelings* but they don't—I think a lot of the people don't realize that they can still just *be* who they were before and happen to love somebody who's the same sex, you know, have sexual relationships and fall in love with people who are of the same sex. Other times I do think it's negative as well. I get really angry with myself when I *don't* state my opinion because I don't want people to see through what I'm saying and holler names or just, you know, *look* at me in a way that I think they're thinking, "God, she's a lesbian and she likes women."

Although it sounds like Christine is criticizing flamboyant gays, her statements can also be heard as criticizing the dominant society (and perhaps SU's discursive environment) for denying young people access to information about anything other than heterosexuality and limited stereotypes about gays and lesbians. She also rearticulates the silencing effect of the social pressure she feels to be "normal." Even though she knows that it is the discursive environment—the heterosexist atmosphere—that makes it difficult for her to come out to peers, or even to express an opinion about a topic related to sexuality, she gets angry with herself for not speaking up. She takes responsibility for her relation to the constraints embedded in her environment.

When I asked Christine whether there was a recent time when she felt that pressure to be normal, she talked about a discussion that took place during her writing class:

This girl was talking about writing a paper, sort of antihomosexual, because of what the Bible said and I didn't say anything. I thought of a lot of things that I could have said but I *didn't* because I didn't feel that I *knew* these people well enough to sort of lay my heart on the table about something that was very personal to me. And at the same time I was afraid they would say, "Oh, why are you so concerned?" and I didn't want to have to broach that issue. And I think I mentioned the other day [during the group interview] if somebody confronted me in class I don't think I would tell them *because* of that and that's kind of what I meant. I mean a lot of the people that I'm talking about, the people that *I* think would ask, are people who probably haven't had a whole lot of *dealings* with homosexuality. It's just impossible for someone to *hear* you when they just can only say one thing over and over and over again. They have *one* idea they've had for so long, it's built up so *big*, that they're just not going to listen to anything.

Because SU is in the region of the country known as the Bible Belt, it is not surprising that religion would arise in connection with heterosexist ideologies. (By contrast, Jessie's only mention of religion is her story about visiting a local church whose members are predominantly gay and lesbian.) Christine explains her silence in this class by pointing to her vulnerability and characterizing her peers as unable to listen. What's the point of talking to a brick wall? And yet, she is talking about a university classroom, one of the few contexts in our society that is supposed to be, by definition, a place where students are exposed to new ideas. Christine's narrative reflects circumstances in which students have no practice listening to others whose experiences and ideas may be different from their own.

I asked whether the teacher said anything in response to this student.

No. I don't even think that he happened to be standing with this particular group of people. He *did* though when the first girl brought up the topic about people going insane even in light of this scripture from the Bible, he told her that that was a really interesting idea. That was something she should look into. *I* took it as "It is an interesting idea, how when the Bible was written, how did people justify that?" And I think a lot of other people in the class took it as a positive reaction from *him*. You know in seeking to make a good grade and trying to *please* him, they started making ideas like that. You know "Well, the Bible does say this and you know this does happen even though it says that." And I just, I kind of, in a way I guess I think it's his fault because I think there are different things he could have said that might have better conveyed his feeling than "That's an interesting idea." (Interviewer "Yeah, it sounds pretty noncommittal.") And I *really* do just from hearing things that he's said after that and the way that he teaches I *really* honestly believe that he meant, "It's an interesting idea if it interests *you*. You should look into it for *yourself*." And I don't think that's clear to a lot of other people.

Christine faults the professor for his noncommittal response and yet she believes that he did not intend to support the student's heterosexist ideas. She works to decipher the professor's attitude from the accumulation of his statements and actions over time. Importantly, she separates herself from her peers. She presents herself as alone in this class, without allies, and as understanding better than others what is really behind the professor's statements. She describes students' talk as oriented toward pleasing the professor—not unusual by any means—rather than as organized around the ideas themselves.

In sum, Christine depicts her educational context as offering no opportunity to speak forthrightly about her sexual identity, or even about sexuality in general.

Consequently, her identity work includes sorting out how much of her silence is her own responsibility and how much is shaped by the taken-for-granted heterosexism around her (cf. Loseke, this volume). She considers what she could have said in various situations, and what others with authority—such as the English professor—could have done to make the classroom something other than stifling for her. Moreover, she portrays herself as working out these dilemmas by herself. Although she has good friends and is an active member of the GLBC, that supportive network with its alternative discourse is absent as Christine goes about her everyday public life on campus. Her narrative displays how the discursive environment discourages dialogue about sexuality and how it encourages her closeted sexual identity.

Constructing a Public Sexual Identity

I met Jessie at a dinner organized by the student-run Women's Resource Center (WRC) at City University during Women's History Month. At the time, Jessie was the program chair for the WRC. Three months before our interview, she had come out to herself and some friends as bisexual, although she had never had a sexual relationship with a woman. She was still in the process of asking herself, "Am I lesbian or bisexual?" and, "Do I even have to decide?"

In the first excerpt, Jessie is talking about a diversity workshop organized for African American Heritage Month that she attended with two close friends from the WRC just a few weeks before our conversation.

> One of the activities was we all stood in a big circle and [the workshop leader] would call out different groups of people. And *right* away when she said that I knew, "Oh boy." (Interviewer: "Oh great." [laughs]) "I'm gonna have to make a decision. Do I do this or don't I? You know, what are going to be the ramifications if I *do*? What are going to be the ramifications if I *don't*?" (Interviewer: "All in 30 seconds." [laughs]) Right [laughs]. So finally when she called out that group I just sort of went out there. It wasn't, I don't think it was really a conscious decision, I just sort of moved. And there I was. (Interviewer: "Was it 'bisexual'? Is that what she said?") Yeah, gay, lesbian, and bisexual. But that was *hard* for me. I think probably the *biggest* reason I questioned whether or not I should do it was because there were three members of the student government there and *two* of which made me very uncomfortable. And it was really hard for me just knowing that those two were there. If they hadn't been there it probably would have been very different.

The first striking feature of this story is that such a workshop was even being held. Although many universities hold diversity workshops, I doubt that very many address sexual orientation so directly. The workshop itself is a good example of the openness to diversity at CU. Second, despite the potentially negative ramifications, Jessie summons the courage to step forward when the leader calls out "gays, lesbians, and bisexuals." In response to my question asking for clarification about who was there in that circle, Jessie continues:

There were 23 people there, I think, and they were all what they considered *fu-ture* leaders of CU that were members of different student organizations on campus. So that was hard for me to *do* and the first couple of times I saw them after that it was kind of weird. I didn't know if they were thinking about that, what they were thinking about *me*, if they were thinking anything at *all*. So that was hard because *both* of them had, well they ended up voting yes for both of the amendments [for the diversity policy], but they still had a lot of reservations about the issue and I think they were voting yes for different reasons than they actually believed in what we were doing was good. So that's why it was hard for me to do that in front of them. And I also figured that, "Oh, they're just going to go back and tell the whole student government and the whole exec board and everybody and then, you know, during meetings they're all going to be staring at me." Which of course didn't happen.

After stepping forward at the workshop to identify herself, Jessie feels very self-conscious on campus. While Christine fears what others *would* think of her if she spoke out, Jessie wonders what others *do* think of her now that she has revealed herself. It's clear that her act of stepping forward challenged her: she repeats several times that it was "hard" for her to do. But notice that it is only two student government members who make Jessie's decision difficult and who are the source of her concern in the days after the workshop. This suggests that she is not terribly concerned about the remaining 20 people in the circle. She must perceive them either as supportive (like her two closest friends who were with her) or as neutral. By contrast, Christine presents herself as utterly alone among her classmates. While Jessie's internal conversation about the consequences of her action suggests a sense of aloneness, the action itself indicates that she is also a participant in a public diversity dialogue, one that provides at least a partial framework for her internal conversation (Mead 1934).

Later in the interview, Jessie talked about how difficult it is to tell people about her new sense of her sexuality, how strong the assumption of heterosexuality is, and how strange it is that she even feels she has to tell people. ("Do you just walk up to people and say, 'Hey, how are you? Oh, by the way, I'm bisexual'?") At this point, I asked how she told her close friend, Carol, the student director of the WRC. She responded by talking about a women's studies course that she and Carol were taking at a nearby university, a more conservative university than CU.

That came up because of our women's studies class and the way we kept pushing the whole homosexual issue and trying not to marginalize lesbians all the time. And one day [Carol and I] started having this conversation on our paper like we do a lot [writing notes to each other during class]. And I think in one of my reflection papers I had gotten back from the professor, [the professor] said, "I know that I can't assume that everybody is heterosexual in this class." And from that sentence I figured, "She probably thinks that I'm a lesbian and everything just because I keep pushing this issue and everything." And so I wrote that on my paper [to Carol] because I think Carol asked me, "I wonder if she thinks that we're lovers or if we're lesbians or anything?" And I'm like, "Well, I'm pretty sure she thinks that about me." And so we were having that little conversation [exchanging notes] and then after we left class I told her.

This story reveals more than how Jessie informed her friend about her bisexuality. She also presents herself as resisting what she describes as the women's studies professor's heterosexist point of view.

During my group interview with the WRC, Jessie talked about "push[ing] the homosexual issue" and "trying not to marginalize lesbians all the time" not only in her personal reflection papers but also in public statements she made in this class. Unlike Christine's mild criticism of her English professor, a criticism that she keeps to herself, Jessie directly and publicly criticizes her women's studies professor. Her assumption that she is "outing" herself by speaking up in this way does not keep her from doing so, while Christine's similar assumption keeps her quiet. Also, unlike Christine's, Jessie's story features an ally. Although Carol is heterosexual, she risks being mistaken as a lesbian, and even as Jessie's lover. Jessie includes Carol when she says "we kept pushing the whole homosexual issue." Jessie presents herself within a discursive environment in which she has a voice, even if it is a minority voice.

> Later, I asked Jessie about homophobic incidents on campus. Somebody put up on the GLBC board a sign that said, "Kill all fags. They must die." And so it was brought up at a student government meeting [by the professional staff adviser to the student government] and [she] showed us all the sign and what it said and she said, "What are you going to do about this? Something needs to be done. What are you going to do about this?" And the whole room was just completely silent. Nobody said *anything*. And *that* made me mad. I mean here we are talking about this whole diversity issue and, you know, we're *pretty* much all getting the feeling that the student government doesn't *like us* and you're just reinforcing that by just sitting there completely silent, not having anything to say. And I felt like *I* should say something or that Carol or somebody in the Black Collegians or GLBC should say something. But then I realized, "No, we're waiting for a reaction *of* a student government member because if they're supposedly the *leaders* on this campus then they need to take part in doing that." And they didn't say anything. (Interviewer: "There was nothing?") Absolutely nothing. (Interviewer: "And that was the end of it?") Yup, that was the end of it.

On Jessie's relatively progressive campus, homophobic hatred still surfaces from time to time. When the adviser to the student government asks the group to take responsibility for doing something about it, Jessie is faced with another opportunity to speak. What's significant is her reasoning about choosing not to speak. She decides that it is time for *others* to speak, for the group that represents the student population as a whole—the student government—to take action, at least by denouncing homophobia publicly. Jessie's silence here is not a matter of feeling vulnerable personally—notice the collective "we" she uses—but a matter of expecting that others should share the work of educating and disciplining their peers.

This is a very different kind of silence than Christine's. Christine does not expect peers, never mind the adults in positions of authority on her campus, to act on her behalf or to speak up for the interests of gays and lesbians. Jessie, however, does have such expectations, and they tell us something about the discursive environment at CU. Even though Jessie's point is that her peers failed to do anything about this incident, her clarity about their failure—the fact that she sees it as such—reveals her sense of the situation as one in which everyone is accountable for their actions in relation to diversity issues. This is an institutional setting that provides a young woman opportunities to risk speaking about her sexual identity and about controversial issues that concern her. This is a setting in which allies can be found and counted on in at least some public arenas. The *possibility* for open dialogue about sexuality is a fact of everyday life.

I do not want to exaggerate the progressive character of the discursive environment at CU, however. When I commented to some faculty and students about how progressive their campus seemed to me, they snorted and launched into a tirade of complaints about the administration, certain faculty and students, and how much remained to be done. But here is my point: the effort to deal with these issues in the public domain opens up conditions of possibility or opportunities for speaking—even in the form of complaints—that are hardly imaginable at SU. There, the relatively few complaints I heard from students targeted peers rather than people in positions of authority. For example, during the group interview with the GLBC at SU (where I met Christine), students focused on other students when they talked about threats to their personal safety. By contrast, during my group interview with the WRC at CU (where I met Jessie), students talked about the administration's inaction on safety issues even when students were the perpetrators.

Nor do I want to exaggerate Christine's silence at SU. She participates actively in the GLBC, she volunteers time to AIDS awareness projects on campus, and she is passionate about her plan to work professionally in an AIDS-related field. She also has friends whom she trusts and with whom she spends her free time. Yet there is a sharp disjunction within Christine's narrative between those pockets of acceptance and openness and most of the public arenas in which she finds herself on campus as she goes about her everyday student life.

While both young women struggle with questions of how and in what contexts to present their sexual identities and their ideas, they resolve their struggles in very different ways. Jessie's narrative shows that she is able, at least partially, to integrate her developing identity as a bisexual woman and her growing self-confidence as a person who can speak publicly about issues important to her. She experienced the CU student government's rejection of the diversity policy as a conservative backlash and as making life very difficult for people like herself and groups in which she was involved. Indeed, during my visit, the student-run WRC was vandalized, an incident labeled by the police as possibly politically motivated. And yet, the upheavals surrounding diversity issues, even with their negative repercussions, provided Jessie with a chance to develop her own voice. By contrast, Christine's narrative shows an uneasy separation between her public presentation of self—her closeted sexual identity—and her comfort with her sexual orientation in only a few private contexts.

For both Jessie and Christine, then, the university's discursive environment conditions the possibilities for articulating their sexual identities in public. In other words, their narratives reveal identity construction opportunities and constraints.

At the same time, their narratives show how they actively confront their respective discursive environments as they struggle with everyday dilemmas concerning their sexuality.

Theoretical and Practical Significance

I have focused on discourse at the local institutional level, yet other social factors condition the sexual identities Christine and Jessie construct. If we take a broad historical perspective, we see that their sexual identities are particular to twentieth century Western societies. The idea that a person's sexuality is an integral part of his or her identity or self first arose during the nineteenth century as scientists and medical professionals began to codify and medicalize sexual behaviors and to pathologize anything outside the male heterosexual norm. Although homosexual *behavior* has existed throughout history, the idea that sexual behavior or orientation reflects the *self* was new at that point, as was the accompanying discourse about sexual identity (Foucault 1990, pp. 42–43; 65–67; 103–5).

Similarly, the concept of and talk about a personal sexual identity is culturally specific; it is rooted in the Western conception of the individual, autonomous self. For example, because such an idea is inimical to the kin-oriented personhood characteristic of Asian societies (Kondo 1990), the concept of gay or lesbian *identity* has not taken hold there and it creates particular dilemmas for Asian Americans. In Asian societies where the cultural focus is on family relations and duties, there may be greater tolerance for homosexual *behavior* as long as it does not interfere with family responsibilities (Chan 1995).

From historical and cultural perspectives, then, Jessie's and Christine's narratives are more similar than different. Like most Americans today, they assume that their sexual orientation is an integral part of their personal identity, and that—from the point of view of the society at large—a lesbian or bisexual identity deviates from the heterosexual norm. Furthermore, their struggles to articulate their sexual identities and their confidence that those identities should be accepted as normal owe much to the gay liberation movement of the past three decades. In this sense, Christine and Jessie's narratives would have been quite different, if not impossible, even 30 years ago in the United States (D'Emilio and Freedman 1988, pp. 318–25; Plummer 1995, p. 87).

While Christine and Jessie's narratives are alike in their cultural and historical specificity, my focus on institutional discourse helps to explain the differences between them. My comparison of their narratives provides clear evidence that the two universities promote different opportunities and protocols for the contruction of sexual identities. In other words, there is plenty of evidence to reject the suggestion that Jessie is simply bolder than Christine. For example, neither has told family members about her sexual identity, indicating a shared reticence to disclose in *that* setting. The import of the idea that universities create specific discursive environments comes to the fore when we imagine the two women transferring to the other's university. My guess is that Jessie would learn quickly to silence herself and Christine would find that she can risk speaking her mind in at least some public settings.

This is not to say, however, that Christine and Jessie's narratives are simply *fixed* by their discursive environments. Each woman clearly presents herself as an active subject within her environment, as thinking about it and acting upon it. Moreover, I could present other parts of their narratives that would show how each woman brings biographical particulars to bear in her identity construction (cf. chapters by Loseke and Spencer, this volume).

In a more general sense, the import of my analysis lies in its connection to two specific sociological issues. First, many qualitative researchers are now exploring personal narratives of various sorts as rich sources of empirical data. This sociological tradition demonstrates how narratives embody the interplay between cultural and institutional constraints on the one hand, and subjects' strategies for expressing experience on the other. In other words, the stories people tell about their lives are empirical phenomena in which biography, institution, and culture intersect. Attending to those intersections within people's narratives allows us to understand more fully the constraining and enabling nature of particular social environments as well as patterns and variations in how individuals (or groups) come to terms with those environments. In theoretical terms, this leads to greater sociological understanding of the complex relationships among different levels of phenomena and analysis: macro (structural, cultural), meso (institutional, discursive) and micro (individual strategies and variation). Furthermore, the idea that personal narratives *embody* those relationships has led to methodological innovation in how researchers listen to, analyze, and present subjects' talk (Alcoff 1993; Chase 1995; Gubrium and Holstein 1997; Lempert 1994; Plummer 1995, among others).

Second, this study addresses a specific substantive question, namely, how educational institutions—through their discourse, policies, curricula, organizations, and everyday practices—frame possibilities for members' actions, speech, identities, and learning. In a nationwide study of 25,000 undergraduates, Alexander Astin found:

> Emphasizing diversity either as a matter of institutional policy or in faculty research and teaching, as well as providing students with curricular and extracurricular opportunities to confront racial and multicultural issues, are all associated with widespread beneficial effects on a student's cognitive and affective development (1993, p. 48).

Many educational researchers are particularly interested in the consequences of these social processes for women, people of color, and gays and lesbians who study or work in schools and universities (for example, Loeb 1994; McGlaughlin and Tierney 1993; Rhoads 1994; Smith 1998; Stombler and Martin 1994; Tierney 1993).

This brings practical issues into focus. My research demonstrates that a university's discourse about diversity makes a very real difference to the students who study and live within its confines. Traversing the threshold between adolescence and adulthood, university students are in the midst of major identity transformations (Karp, Holmstrom, and Gray 1998; Silver 1996). These transformations implicate not only their educational and occupational goals, but also their sexual, racial, and gender identities. This is true of all students, including those who are privileged by their heterosexuality, whiteness, or maleness. Because a university's approach to diversity shapes the kind and range of discourse that unfolds across campus, educators *should* ask themselves the questions I raised in the first paragraph of this chapter. Of course students—either as individuals or as groups—have vehicles for pursuing agendas of their own (such as the student government or newspaper). Nonetheless, administrators and faculty should take responsibility for the diversity discourse that their institutions promote.

I close with another story about a student at my own university. In a writing assignment for one of my courses, an openly gay student revealed that when he was in high school his identity as an illicit drug user was more acceptable than his identity as a gay male. Not only his peers but also his family, teachers, and school administrators communicated that drug abuse was less disgraceful than being gay. The adults around him apparently ignored the possibility that his drug habit may have been related to the shame he was taught to feel about his sexuality. Is this what we want students to learn?

REFERENCES

Alcoff, Linda, and Laura Gray. 1993. "Survivor Discourse: Transgression or Recuperation?" *Signs* 18:260–90.

Astin, Alexander W. 1993. "Diversity and Multiculturalism on the Campus: How are Students Affected?" *Change* 25:44–49.

Chan, Connie S. 1995. "Issues of Sexual Identity in an Ethnic Minority: The Case of Chinese American Lesbians, Gay Men, and Bisexual People." In *Lesbian, Gay, and Bisexual Identities Over the Life Span*, ed. A. R. D'Augelli and C. J. Patterson, 87–101. Oxford: Oxford University Press.

Chase, Susan E. 1995. *Ambiguous Empowerment: The Work Narratives of Women School Superintendents*. Amherst: University of Massachusetts Press.

D'Emilio, John, and Estelle B. Freedman. 1988. *Intimate Matters: A History of Sexuality in America*. New York: Harper & Row.

Foucault, Michel. 1977. *Discipline and Punish: The Birth of the Prison*. New York: Pantheon Books.

———. 1990. *The History of Sexuality: An Introduction*, vol. 1. New York: Vintage.

Gubrium, Jaber F., and James A. Holstein. 1997. *The New Language of Qualitative Method*. New York: Oxford University Press.

Karp, David A., Lynda Lytle Holmstrom, and Paul S. Gray. 1998. "Leaving Home for College: Expectations for Selective Reconstruction of Self." *Symbolic Interaction* 21:253–76.

Kondo, Dorinne K. 1990. *Crafting Selves: Power, Gender, and Discourses of Identity in a Japanese Workplace*. Chicago: University of Chicago Press.

Lempert, Lora Bex. 1994. "A Narrative Analysis of Abuse: Connecting the Personal, the Rhetorical, and the Structural." *Journal of Contemporary Ethnography* 22:411–41.

Loeb, Paul Rogat. 1994. *Generation at the Crossroads: Apathy and Action on the American Campus*. New Brunswick, N.J.: Rutgers University Press.

McLaughlin, Daniel, and William G. Tierney. 1993. *Naming Silenced Lives: Personal Narratives and Processes of Educational Change*. New York: Routledge.

Mead, George Herbert. 1934. *Mind, Self, and Society.* Edited by C. W. Morris. Chicago: University of Chicago Press.

Plummer, Ken. 1995. *Telling Sexual Stories: Power, Change and Social Worlds.* New York: Routledge.

Raymond, Diane. 1994. "Homophobia, Identity, and the Meanings of Desire: Reflections on the Cultural Construction of Gay and Lesbian Adolescent Sexuality." In *Sexual Cultures and the Construction of Adolescent Identities*, ed. J. M. Irvine, 115–50. Philadelphia: Temple University Press.

Rhoads, Robert A. 1994. *Coming Out in College: The Struggle for a Queer Identity.* Westport, Conn.: Bergin and Garvey.

Silver, Ira. 1996. "Role Transitions, Objects, and Identity." *Symbolic Interaction* 19:1–20.

Smith, Dorothy E. 1987. *The Everyday World as Problematic: A Feminist Sociology.* Boston: Northeastern University Press.

Smith, George W. 1998. "The Ideology of 'Fag': The School Experience of Gay Students." *The Sociological Quarterly* 39:309–35.

Stombler, Mindy, and Patricia Yancey Martin. 1994. "Bringing Women In, Keeping Women Down: Fraternity 'Little Sister' Organizations." *Journal of Contemporary Ethnography* 23:150–84.

Tierney, William G. 1993. "Academic Freedom and the Parameters of Knowledge." *Harvard Educational Review* 63:143–60.

J. WILLIAM (JACK) SPENCER

Self-Presentation and Organizational Processing in a Human Service Agency

In dealing with the myriad troubles that plague clients of human service agencies, staff members and clients alike find themselves assembling the biographical particulars of clients' selves in order to dispense the agency's services. Institutional selves are needed to conduct institutional business. Indeed, constructing clients' selves is an integral aspect of the "social problems work" (Holstein and Miller 1993) that is the stock in trade of the human services.

A social constructionist perspective on the seemingly familiar activities of human service work draws our attention to the discursive practices of everyday life (see Gubrium and Holstein 1997), highlighting the way service workers and their clients actually produce selves as they accomplish routine bureaucratic tasks. Donileen Loseke (1992), for example, shows us the interpretive work engaged in by staff members of a battered women's shelter as they select clients for admission to the shelter. In the process, they articulate the prevailing understanding of just what locally constitutes "the battered woman," elaborating the particulars of a troubled self that accords with the shelter's notion of the type of woman the shelter is designed to serve (also see Loseke, this volume). This discourse portrays "the battered woman" as having experienced severe, frequent, and unrelenting violence. The discourse's informing identity is of women who want to leave their partners but, for lack of various resources, cannot get away. Loseke shows how shelter workers use the discourse to frame their ongoing understandings of clients' experience, backgrounds, and motives, and to decide which women, among all those seeking help, are "appropriate" clients.

In human service encounters, clients typically must describe themselves and their troubles in order to establish their eligibility for services. Conceptualizing service encounters as discursive practice emphasizes the socially constructive features of talk and interaction, suggesting that it is only by way of language use that clients' troubles, their needs, and appropriate interventions are established for the purposes at hand. William Darrough (1990), for example, shows how a probation officer arranges for the placement for a troubled and troublesome teenager by rhetorically casting the boy, his problems, and the remedial options in terms that will be acceptable to the boy's skeptical parents. Likewise, James Holstein (1993) illustrates how public defenders and district attorneys construct person-descriptions in involuntary mental commitment hearings in order to establish the relevant dimensions of personal competence and incompetence that account for their particular stances and interests in the cases in question. Interactional studies of human service encounters are replete with descriptions of how client selves are assembled so that human service workers can do their work (see Holstein 1992; Loseke 1993; Miller 1991a; Spencer 1983).

The construction of clients' troubled selves and human service remedies draws upon institutional discourses, which range from the religious and medical to the social and psychiatric. As a locally recognized, standardized framework for anticipating, acting, and understanding, an institutional discourse provides the conditions of possibility for constructing persons and their troubles (Miller 1994). Each institutional context commonly privileges a particular way of constructing persons and their troubles. Dominant institutional discourses not only serve to articulate the prevailing set of accounts for constructing troubles, but provide staff members with related orienting questions, ways of issuing directives, and the means for challenging resistance from clients.

Some institutional settings are characterized by multiple and competing discourses. Physicians may differ from nurses in the way they speak of patients and problems in the same physical setting (see Anspach 1987). Legal environments may abound in alternate discourses of justice and fairness (see Conley and O'Barr 1990), which provide divergent assessments and outcomes in legal proceedings. Multiple discourses may address different audiences in the same setting (see Gubrium and Buckholdt 1982). The interplay of available discourses and discursive practices produces the social organization of the settings—both its patterns and its tensions.

The notion of multiple institutional discourses and the possibility of discursive conflicts are the focal points of this chapter on the organizational fate of client self-presentations in a human service agency. The chapter shows how clients' self-presentations of service worthiness, which are informed by a discourse of morality, engage the organizational processing that transforms this into a discourse of institutional rules and resources, constructing associated client identities.

The Service Agency

The analysis is based on transcripts of intake interviews conducted by social workers at an agency I call "Homeless Assistance" (HA), which is located in a midsized southeastern city (here called "River City"). While the formal mandate of the agency extended its services to all who were traveling and found themselves stranded and without resources in River City, in practice HA functioned as a multiservice referral agency for homeless persons who had been in River City less than six months.

At the time of the study, HA staff included an executive director, two casework supervisors, a volunteer coordinator, eight direct service workers, an administrative assistant, and a receptionist. Each administrative and direct service staff member possessed, or was working toward, the master of social work (MSW) degree. While social workers provided some material services to clients, such as tokens for local bus travel, most of the service work at HA centered on network referrals (Spencer 1993), such as offering information about other agencies where clients might find help in obtaining clothing, employment, vouchers for food, and shelter. The human service network used by the homeless in River City comprised numerous organizations, mostly private and nonprofit, that followed diverse service ideologies and provided a broad range of assistance governed by different eligibility rules. Since HA occupied a key position in this network, most clients were referred from or to these other organizations. All of these organizations, including HA, operated on scarce resources.

In the institutional philosophy of HA, human service work with the homeless was a combination of crisis-intervention and social casework approaches. The crisis-intervention perspective is short-term and practical, emphasizing the nature of clients' current troubles, the immediate causes of those troubles and potential remedies. The social casework perspective, in contrast, focuses on clients' long-term stability and self-sufficiency. From the social casework perspective, services are seen as "resources" provided, in part, as a remedy for clients' immediate troubles but also as a means to achieve stability and self-sufficiency. From this perspective, short-term remedies to immediate troubles are deemed unproductive, and shortchange attempts to establish clients' long-term stability and self-sufficiency. Together, the perspectives were a tense combination.

From the social workers' perspective, doing social work with the homeless was different from, and more difficult than, doing social work with other types of clients. The homeless were seen as beset by numerous problems that required multiple remedies. Equally difficult, successful social casework with the homeless required the ability to assess these various troubles and multiple service needs as well as the skills to "work" informal organizational networks to provide referrals. Social workers viewed themselves, and believed that others viewed them, as possessing a special sensitivity to the problems and needs of their clients. This sensitivity, coupled with skills developed through years of experience working with the homeless, fostered successful service delivery.

Social workers spent much of their work day conducting intake interviews with clients. These encounters typically represented the clients' first contact with the agency. Social workers undertook two major tasks in these interviews: assessment and planning. In doing assessments, social workers and clients jointly constructed working pictures of clients' troubled lives and formulated their service requests through a series of solicitation-response sequences. In some instances, solicitations focused on specific pieces of biographical information as illustrated in the following extract from an interview between a social worker and a client:

SOCIAL WORKER: Okay, you're from Illinois.
CLIENT: Umhm.
SOCIAL WORKER: How long you lived there?
CLIENT: Well, I was lived off and on the past two years.
SOCIAL WORKER: Umhm. So, it's kind of your home.
CLIENT: Yeah.

In other instances, solicitations were more open-ended, allowing clients to construct their troubled lives through longer narratives as illustrated by the following: "[Social worker:] Okay, let's see. How can we help you today?" And,

SOCIAL WORKER:	Okay, Mr. Smith. How are you today?
CLIENT:	Uh, could be better.
SOCIAL WORKER:	What's goin' on?

Planning focused around social workers' and clients' attempts to construct a service plan, or set of remedies, that could accountably address clients' troubled lives. The social workers' goal was to establish a working consensus in which clients acceded to social workers' preferred plans irrespective of their own preferences. In some instances, this consensus was easily established, as seen in the following extracts:

SOCIAL WORKER:	Are you hungry? Do you want to have lunch?
CLIENT:	No, I haven't had anything.
SOCIAL WORKER:	Okay, what about tunafish? You like tunafish?
CLIENT:	Tunafish is fine.

SOCIAL WORKER:	You haven't acquired any new clothes?
CLIENT:	Right.
SOCIAL WORKER:	Well, there are a few clothing resources in River City. Sometimes they have some, sometimes they don't. But I'll see what I can do.

In other instances, establishing this working consensus was more problematic. In the following case, the client came to HA seeking money for a bus ticket to another city. In this extract, the social worker responds:

SOCIAL WORKER:	Okay, I'm going to give you information about where you can spend the night. You have to think about some other type of way so you can get the money.
CLIENT:	[loudly, angrily] In other words, I can't get the money.
SOCIAL WORKER:	We can't give you the money.

Instead of honoring the client's request, the social worker makes an alternative service offer of information about temporary shelter and help finding a way the client could earn the money for the bus ticket. In this kind of disagreement, participants used aspects of clients' troubled lives as well as agency rules as rhetorical devices to account for their preferred service plan. For example, a social worker might tell a client, "We don't pay for bus tickets, but we can help you find work," invoking the agency's case-management mandate as a reason for not providing concrete resources (see Spencer and McKinney 1997).

Client Self-Presentation

In intake interviews at HA, clients and social workers constructed the biographical particulars of clients' selves for organizational processing. They would consider things like clients' current situation, where they used to live and why they left, how and why they came to River City, and friends or relatives they might be able to ask for assistance. Clients would formulate their self-presentations in relation to their claimed needs. For the social workers, these particulars were important for assessing clients' eligibility for specific services in addition to providing rhetorical resources they used to persuade clients to accept their preferred service plan. From the social worker's perspective, clients' self-presentations also were meaningful in relation to a service plan.

First, we consider client self-presentations. Clients attempted to account for being homeless in River City, the biographical particulars of which were assumed to accord with their service requests. They presented institutional selves which they viewed as worthy or deserving of the services they requested. Clients emphasized three basic qualities of the deserving self: *"the troubled self," "the stranded self,"* and *"the tryin' self."* Each of these aspects of the deserving or service-worthy self was organized around specific features of *clients'* biographies, with little or no reference to agency rules and regulations.

The Troubled Self

The troubled self was one that claimed to be hungry, didn't have a place to sleep, or was broke and out of work. This self had arrived in these circumstances because of problematic events or conditions involving family, jobs or money, health or illness, and criminal victimization.

In *job or money troubles*, clients claimed to have arrived in River City because they had either lost their previous jobs or were searching for better employment. Once in River City, they discovered that jobs were hard to come by and soon found themselves broke and lacking in such basic needs as clean clothing and a place to stay. Consider the following two extracts, which begin with the social worker soliciting the reasons for clients' moves to River City:

SOCIAL WORKER: Okay, my name is Jennie. What I want you to do is tell me a little about your situation and what brought you to River City.

CLIENT: I come to River City to see if I can find me a job and a different start. I got down here, I been to the unemployment office and they didn't have anything. They tell me to keep checkin' back and I don't have anywhere to live.

SOCIAL WORKER: What brings you to our area?

CLIENT: I wasn't able to find any work in Houston and by the time I got here I was broke and run down and all my clothes are dirty and jus' need some help. Those people over at those centers said I might come over here and talk to you guys.

In the first example, the client's response of "find me a job" and "different start" can be read as meaning that before he came to River City, he was unemployed and quite likely experiencing other troubles as well. This lack of work, and subsequent lack of money, accounts for his lack of "anywhere to live," which in turn, accounts for his request for help in finding temporary shelter. In the second extract, the client was unsuccessful in finding work in another city, and found himself in River City looking for work, broke, tired and without clean clothes to wear. It is worth noting that clients often coupled claims of lack of work with lack of clothing as an accountable reason for coming to HA. In particular, clean clothes were portrayed as necessary for finding work, but more importantly portrayed the clients as *serious* in their desire for employment.

In *family troubles*, clients expressed a variety of problems with family members, typically involving relationships and illness. The following illustration is from an interview in which the client had asked for help finding work and shelter.

CLIENT:	Because when I left home [my mother] was trying to get me away from home. I was having problems.
SOCIAL WORKER:	Bad relationship?
CLIENT:	Bad relationship with my mom and my girlfriend. She didn't like my girlfriend and they were just driving me nutty so I had to get out of there.

In this extract, the client begins by describing "problems" with his mother. Following up on the social worker's formulation these problems are redefined as a "bad relationship." The client then uses this definition to depict problems with his girlfriend, which seem to be created by his mother's dislike for her. All of this results in his need "to get out of there." The client thus presents a deeply troubled relational self, one worthy of HA's assistance because of domestic turmoil. The client appropriates select biographical and interpersonal particulars into his service request in terms that the social worker intimates are relevant in the local social service scheme of things.

In other interviews, family troubles involved illness or death, as shown in the following extract.

SOCIAL WORKER:	What brought you to our area?
CLIENT:	I had a death in the family
SOCIAL WORKER:	You came down for the funeral?
CLIENT:	I didn't know she was gonna pass. My grandma was very sick and she had amputations on her legs and she just passed away a couple of days after I got here. I've been pretty much tryin' to keep myself alive. Stayin' Salvation [army shelter] and meetin' people and jus' tryin' to stay alive.
SOCIAL WORKER:	You came down here and were living with whom?
CLIENT:	I was livin' with my sister.
SOCIAL WORKER:	And she said it was okay for you to come here and stay with her.

CLIENT: Through the time when she wanted me to stay. She demanded
                   a lot of me. She wanted me to be her housekeeper and baby-
                   sitter and she promised me a ticket [back home]. It got to be too
                   much for her. The kids are unruly and she's got a terrible atti-
                   tude and I guess she's under a lot of pressure. I just couldn't
                   deal with it and we had a few words. So I had to leave.

Here, the client describes how she came to River City to visit her ill grandmother,
who died shortly after the client arrived. The client's sister invited her to stay at
her house and promised to buy her a bus ticket back home. However, that relationship soured after the two "had a few words," and the client soon found herself without shelter, money, food, or clothes. In this extract, both aspects of family
troubles account for the client's current predicament as well as her service request.

Troubles also involved *criminal victimization*, as in the following extract:

CLIENT: Since I been here, I got my credentials and everything taken from me.
          My wallet. My clothes. The only thing I have left is some clothes at
          the bus station. I don't have enough [money] to get them out [of the
          locker].

In this extract, the client is robbed of his wallet and most of his clothes. The social worker and the client both understand that without money and identification, the client won't be able to stay at any of the local overnight shelters or apply
for work. As he presents himself, the client rhetorically accounts for his request
for help in obtaining a replacement for his social security card, finding a job, and
locating temporary shelter.

Finally, there were *health troubles*, which sometimes prevented clients from
getting around town to find work or find a place to stay. For example:

CLIENT: I came down here with a friend and I got like robbed and I was
                   severely hurt. Just got out of the hospital Thursday. The prog-
                   nosis is that I am paralyzed. Believe me there's no . . . It's not
                   easy getting around. My foot has gotten swollen from walking
                   around.

SOCIAL WORKER: How long you been separated from your husband?

CLIENT: [Inaudible]

SOCIAL WORKER: Uh huh, and what'cha been doin'?

CLIENT: I was in the hospital for two months.

SOCIAL WORKER: What was that for?

CLIENT: Depression. From the divorce. And then I got out of the hospi-
                   tal and didn't have nowhere to go so I stayed on the streets.

SOCIAL WORKER: Then you started hitchhiking and ended up here.

CLIENT: Just ended up here.

In these extracts, the clients are beset by health problems that help account for
their predicaments. In the second extract, family problems account for the client's

health problems which, in turn, account for her being on the streets and, ultimately, hitchhiking to River City, where she fnds herself without money and shelter. In the first extract, criminal victimization accounts for health problems, which then explain why the client has trouble getting around to look for work.

In the following case, the client had requested money for a bus ticket to another city where he sought work. Instead, the social worker responds:

SOCIAL WORKER: Okay, can you work like [temporary] labor pool for a couple of days?

CLIENT: I don't think my body can take it. I'm not all that well. I've been sick. I threw up yesterday morning and the day before.

While health troubles sometimes accounted for clients' current homeless situation, in this extract they account for the client's refusal of the worker's alternative service offer of temporary work that would provide the money necessary for the bus ticket.

The Stranded Self

While the "troubled self" highlights the problems that lead to a client's current situation, presenting a "stranded self" focuses more on the results, such as being geographically stranded in River City and unable to get home. For example:

CLIENT: Me and [my wife] came down [for a vacation]. We stayed for about a week and we had a fight and she left me. I haven't seen her since. Or heard from her. I been walking around, I don't have no money.

In this extract, the client describes how he and his wife came to River City for a vacation. He then explains how family troubles resulted in his being broke and unable to get home. In other instances, self presentations attribute being stranded to being robbed or illness, as illustrated in the extracts in the previous section.

Clients also portray themselves as being *socially* stranded, that is, as now unable to rely on family or friends for assistance. For example:

SOCIAL WORKER: Do you have any family, any relatives, somebody you can call and maybe send some money?

CLIENT: No, none of my people on my mother's side. She died and they won't help me.

SOCIAL WORKER: They won't help.

CLIENT: No, ma'am. I even tried to move in and they said; they refused me. They won't help at all and on my father's side, they said I'm old enough to take care of myself. When I had hepatitis none of my kin people would help me and that's the truth.

SOCIAL WORKER: Have you been in contact with your family since Friday?

CLIENT: Well, I called my sister and let her know what happened. So she said [she'd help] if I need her but she don't have no money so

> I guess I got only moral support if I need her I could call her
> and talk to her.

As illustrated in these extracts, clients cast themselves as alone because of
their troubles, unable to rely on family or friends for assistance. Sometimes this
meant family and friends were financially unable to provide help, as in the second extract. Other times, as in the first extract, help was not forthcoming because
family and friends had actually abandoned them.

The Tryin' Self

A "tryin' self" was presented as attempting to resolve or overcome the predicaments that beset the troubled self and the stranded self. While not completely
helpless, some clients present themselves as in need of some assistance since prior
attempts at self-help were never totally successful. This presentation is typically
polite and grateful; as illustrated in the following extract, a client who is "tryin'"
may even decline some services.

> CLIENT: I came down here to see if someone can help me find a job. Unless it's
> exactly necessary, I prefer not to stay anywhere. I'm not asking for no
> assistance for a place to sleep. I just prefer to try and find a job and pay
> my own way. I figured I needed to find a job and start making some
> money. I figured as long as I got a job I'm sure I can pay my own way
> and get me a place of my own.

In this extract, after the client requests help finding work he tells the social worker
he does not need any help with shelter, preferring to "pay [his] own way." The
client goes on to describe how, for the past three weeks, he had been able to stay
with a series of strangers who would take him into their houses for a day or two
at a time, always being careful never to overstay his welcome. For example:

> CLIENT: I hooked up with this guy here about a week ago. He took me in for a
> couple of nights and let me sleep on the couch but his old lady didn't
> want me stayin' there long. I could see she was getting perturbed about
> an extra mouth to feed. He let me work with him, ya know, kinda tried
> to pay my my own way a little bit.

In the following extract, the client was traveling by bus back home to California after a trip to bury his father who recently died. During a stop in River
City, he was robbed, leaving him no money to buy food for the two-day trip.

> CLIENT: I need some type of assistance to California. I have my bus ticket already
> [but] I'm quite sure I'll find two days on the bus fasting is not going to
> get it.

After offering the client some canned food for the trip and a sandwich while he
was at HA, the social worker makes another service offer:

SOCIAL WORKER: I'm going to give you a few dollars for your drinks.

CLIENT: Well, I don't even need to worry about getting a drink 'cause there's water, but I'll probably need the few dollars for when I get there so I can make a phone call and let them know I'm there. I can catch the bus to where I got to go.

In this extract, the client could have merely accepted the offer of cash and used it for any purpose. Instead, this client prefers to make it clear that he can drink water and use the money for making phone calls and to "catch the bus" once he arrives back home. He presents himself as one who wants to make good and not be a burden.

Presentations of the tryin' self often play off features of the troubled self, as illustrated in the following extract:

SOCIAL WORKER: How are you doin'?

CLIENT: That's why I stopped here. I've been running the streets trying to find work and nothin's come about. I've been trying to keep as clean as I can. I went to the thrift shop and buy me this shirt and a pair of pants. I still been tryin' to find somethin', tryin' to just hook onto somethin' so I wouldn't be on the streets.

This client had come to HA requesting help finding clean clothing and a place to wash up. In this extract, the client describes how he is trying to "keep clean," has tried to find clothing, and "tryin' to find somethin'." These aspects of the tryin' self are based on his troubled self: being "on the streets" and being out of work. That these attempts have been unsuccessful accounts for his presence at HA requesting help.

Presentations of the tryin' self also made use of the stranded self. In the following case, the client had requested help getting back home to Arkansas where she would live with her mother. During the interview, the client described how, during their time in River City, she and her two children had been staying with a friend while she looked for work. However, her friend's husband had demanded they leave, prompting the client to come to HA for help. In this extract, the social worker responds:

SOCIAL WORKER: Do you have any other resources in Arkansas besides your mother?

CLIENT: All my relatives are there, but like at this time when I call everybody, it's like "I ain't got no money," "I got this deal." It's like ain't nobody care. They got their own problems.

Competing Discourses of Service-Worthiness

As clients applied for assistance at HA, their self-presentations were crafted from a distinctive discourse of "service worthiness." Presenting themselves as having troubles, being stranded, and tryin' required clients to engage in a broader rhetoric of personal responsibility and fundamental valuation of the selves as stake; they manifested the sort of morally deserving character that would justify service provision. This competed with staff members' emphasis on organizational rules and resources. For example, in the case of requests for tickets for bus travel to another state, organizational rules prevented social workers from simply buying a ticket. Instead, social workers worked with clients to find alternative ways for the client to obtain money for the ticket such as temporary work or locating a friend or relative who could send the money. As such, client self-presentations were not just situationally attended, as Goffman (1959) might have viewed them, but engaged the competing discourses that were organizationally in place.

In most matters, staff's discourse linked service-worthiness with the formal details of institutional processing. What staff members could and couldn't do "because of the rules" and what they could or couldn't provide because of short supply and high demand, say, often served as warrant for whatever action staff members decided to take. This bureaucratic discourse competed with, and sometimes overshadowed, the morally oriented claims of clients' self presentations. (See chapters by Hopper and Weinberg in this volume for parallel discussions of discourse variation.)

The Discourse of Morality

For clients, the troubled self, the stranded self, and the tryin' self provided the discursive foundation for service requests. These character types were constructed from a *discourse of morality* that rhetorically framed the relationship between clients' fundamental selves and their service requests in moral terms, emphasizing personal responsibility and obligation. For example, in this discourse, a client who was in River City and needed help because of family problems viewed himself as worthy of assistance because the client had responsibly dealt with family obligations such as attending a funeral or coming to care for a sick relative. Alternatively a stranded client deserved help because relatives had abrogated *their* family responsibilities or obligations for providing help.

Emotions were a salient element of these moral claims to self-worth, as the following extract shows. In this instance, the client made an impassioned plea that he not be turned away by HA:

> CLIENT: The minute you might walk out of this block here [at HA], somebody stab a knife in your back thinkin' you got a quarter or a dollar. You got killings here in River City every day. Excuse me, but you know it's the truth, man. I'm not ready to die.

Here, the dangers of River City were emotionally cited as the warrant for granting services. The client uses his fear of crime as a rhetorical device to provide a reasonable account for his need to get out of River City.

This emotionally suffused discourse of morality, and the clients' self-presentations that it shaped, drew on a number of broader cultural images and expectations. Clients' troubled selves, beset as they were by problems for which they were not responsible, appropriated resonating images of the victim (Holstein and Miller 1990; see chapters by Lowney and Holstein, and Loseke in this volume). Accordingly, clients deserved help because they did not bring their current predicament on themselves. These self-presentations also appropriated the family as a rhetorical device (Holstein and Gubrium 1994; Miller 1991b). In this case, the troubled self was on the streets because, say, he had met his family obligations by coming to River City to help care for family members. Or stranded selves might deserve assistance because family members had failed to meet *their* obligations. This discourse of moral responsibility also drew on images of the "new homeless" (Spencer 1996) that, in turn, appropriated long-standing images of the deserving poor (Katz 1989, Stern 1986) and the morally worthy needy (Loseke and Fawcett 1995). Both the new homeless and the morally worthy needy refer to those who were not responsible for their poverty, have tried to make it on their own, who avoided assistance whenever possible yet were grateful for assistance when it became necessary.

Clients' self-presentations were also shaped by another cultural image of the homeless (Snow and Anderson 1987). By requesting services from HA, clients were making at least an implicit claim to a status that in contemporary American society is devalued because its incumbents lack even the most basic resources. Of course, in constructing the troubled self, clients made these claims explicit. Such face-threatening acts (Brown and Levinson 1978; Goffman 1959) could be partially mitigated through self-presentations in which clients took some responsibility for resolving their current situation, were not responsible for that situation, or in which they limited their service requests. For example, in some presentations of "tryin'," clients often appeared to express pride in their attempts to "make it" on their own. In this regard, while troubled and stranded, clients were not totally helpless, not totally bereft of resources.

The Discourse of Rules and Resources

If clients presented worthy selves out of a discourse of morality, social workers approached service-worthiness in relation to formal standards of service provision. As discussed above, staff discourse at HA emphasized agency rules and the scarcity of agency resources as well as clients' immediate situation and their long-term stability. I call this a *discourse of rules and resources*. Within this discourse, clients' selves provided a rough predictor of their use of agency resources. In part, because HA resources were scarce, social workers typically saw agency services as properly used by clients who could establish long-term stability. In this discourse, scarcity of resources was related to a preference to avoid the duplication of services across agencies. Also, within this discourse, clients who had a "plan" (that is, who had thought about effective use of their own resources, how they would obtain work, shelter, food, and other basic necessities) were seen as likely to make effective use of HA's resources. Alternatively, clients who evidenced a "pattern of flight" (or simply a "pattern") or who did not plan their moves and seemed to always be going "where the grass was greener," were seen as likely to "waste" these scarce agency resources. The scarcity of agency resources and emphasis on long-term stability also accounted for the agency preference for clients to obtain resources from friends or relatives before using agency resources as well as the preference for clients to take permanent jobs rather than relying consistently on temporary labor.

This discourse of rules and resources shaped the ways that social workers asked questions, solicited biographical particulars, elaborated on clients' claims, and made alternative service offers. In their fashion, social workers helped assemble a portrait of clients whose three qualities became salient for this alternative institutional discourse. For example, social workers' interest in clients' troubled selves was shaped, in part, by their concern with assessing their service needs. Social workers' interest in clients' tryin' selves was important in their search for evidence that clients had a "plan," that is, had planned their moves and assumed some responsibility for their long-term stability. Clients' stranded selves were salient to social worker's concerns with clients' social networks and their preference for helping clients find their own resources before dispensing the agency's.

In many ways, clients' discourse of morality was at odds with the discourse of rules and resources at HA. While both discourses focused on the "deserving or worthy client," they established different bases or criteria for just what made clients deserving or worthy. In the discourse of morality, deservedness was based on cultural notions of sympathy that obligated the social worker to provide services. In contrast, in the discourse of rules and resources deservedness was based on meeting formal agency rules regarding eligibility and more informal expectations regarding long-term responsibility and stability. However, since both discourses shaped interpretations of clients' selves around notions of deservedness or worthiness, points of divergence between the two discourses were subtle. For example, from the perspective of a client asking for a bus ticket out of town, to present herself as *stranded* meant that she deserved assistance because she needed help; she was stuck in River City and had no one to ask for help. From the perspective of the workers' discourse of rules and resources, being stranded meant that clients had no one who could guarantee a place to stay once they arrived in the new town. From this perspective, workers assumed that the client would end up in the same situation in the new city; that is, providing scarce services would not result in an improvement in the client's long-term stability.

It wasn't until social workers denied clients' service requests or made alternative service offers that the participants typically attended to these divergent discursive themes. The following extract comes from a case in which the client requested a bus ticket back home. The extract begins with the client's description of his being stranded:

CLIENT: I don't have nobody to help me or anything.

SOCIAL WORKER: Okay. Let me explain to you what HA is about. You see in the brochure, the front will explain that we're a counseling and planning agency. What we do is crisis intervention. Basic counseling for those who are new to the area and who are interested in either relocating to River City or in one area or another.

CLIENT:	I can't get home.
SOCIAL WORKER:	I didn't say that. There are certain requirements and certain ways that we can help you in getting home.

The social worker couches her response to the client's self-presentation in terms of what HA does, the kinds of services offered there. The client's response again invokes a stranded self while, at the same time, seemingly characterizing the social worker's account as a denial of his request, which is he "can't get home." However, the social worker challenges that interpretation and replies that it isn't that HA doesn't help people get home, but that there are "certain requirements" that need to be met and "certain ways" that this help can be provided.

In this case, the client claims to have come to HA because he is stranded, and because he is stranded there is no one else to turn for help. By definition, being stranded and beset by troubles renders the client worthy or deserving of help. The discourse of morality presents him as worthy of the help he is seeking and the social worker is morally obligated to provide that help. However, from the perspective of rules and resources, the client's constructed self does not provide an adequate account for his service request. What would render the client worthy of help would be his ability to meet agency rules regarding eligibility for other kinds of services.

This last extract also illustrates how social workers used elements of the discourse of rules and resources as rhetorical devices. Note how the social worker discursively constructs HA as a "counseling and planning agency" that offers "crisis intervention" and "basic counseling." Constructing HA in this fashion provides a way of accountably making alternative service offers while at the same time not openly challenging the moral claims to service-worthiness that are part of this client's self-presentation. Within the discourse of morality, there appears to be a "working consensus" (Goffman 1959) that obligates social workers to accept the truth value of clients' presented selves, against which a counter-discourse requires counter-legitimation.

Although the two discourses shaped different interpretations of the relationship between clients' selves and their service requests, this does not necessarily mean that social workers are oblivious to the moral or emotional implications of client self-presentation. Consider the following extract in which a social worker is talking to a casework supervisor:

CASEWORK SUPERVISOR:	What are we going to do? It's so difficult. Gosh. It's like [they] just want to get their money and go about their business. They expect that. They expect you to just give them their money. They really thought that's what HA was.
SOCIAL WORKER:	Uh huh.
CASEWORK SUPERVISOR:	I have a bleeding heart.
SOCIAL WORKER:	I know. I mean I wanna get this family home. Another thing to consider here is there does not appear to be a pattern. And if there was a pattern I would want them to

learn to be a little more independent. Put a little more responsibility on the situation.

In this case, the client had requested money for a bus ticket home to her
mother. According to her claim, the client is stranded in River City without money,
has no place to stay, and her children are preventing her from looking for work.
While the social worker and supervisor both express sympathy for the client's
plight, her request will be a difficult one to meet. They can understand the client's
self-presentation within the discourse of morality and want to "get this family
home." However, from the perspective of rules and resources, just "giving them
the money" is not a preferred remedy since it would not teach the client "a little
more responsibility" about making it on her own. As such, the assistance would
be a bad investment of resources since it would not enhance her long-term
stability.

Discursive Options

The differences between the discourses that mediated client worthiness in HA
was often obscured because the two perspectives tend to be *sequentially* relevant
or salient to the participants. In the early stages of intakes, the discourses were
primarily important as interpretive resources for producing and interpreting initial self-presentations and service requests. In the latter stages of intakes, when
disagreements arose and participants produced accounts for their divergent
stances regarding service plans, each discourse was mobilized as an explicit rhetorical device. Thus, social workers accounted for their service preferences in terms
of agency rules and resources while clients accounted for their preference in terms
of moral expectations and obligations. At each stage of intakes, each discourse
was relevant and salient, but unfolded in different ways or for different purposes.
It was only when they became relevant as rhetorical resources, in contested matters of service provision, that they become obvious.

Of course in the latter stages of intakes, clients were left in a vulnerable position. Since they had presented selves in ways that accounted for their service
requests, they had already gone "on record" with a service request, painting themselves into a rhetorical corner. When social workers did not honor their initial request, clients were left with few options. One option was for clients to reformulate
their self-presentations. Consider in that regard the example of a client who presented a troubled (he is ill) and stranded self (he has no family to help him) to
account for a request for a bus ticket. In this case, an accountable denial of such
a request in terms of agency rules would have required the client to provide ver-
ification that he had a job and a place to stay in the new city. The social worker
also would have offered temporary labor and shelter until he had made enough
money to purchase his own ticket. This client could have claimed that he was, after all, well enough to accept an offer of temporary work or that there was someone staff members could call. However, clients typically did not choose this option
and there appear to be at least two good reasons for shunning this kind of refor-

mulation. First, this reconstruction would have rendered the client less worthy of services from the client's perspective by revising the very qualities of the troubled self and the stranded self that rendered him worthy in the first place. Second, this reconstruction would seem to run afoul of the assumption of the working consensus that obligated participants to accept at face value the truth value of clients' pitiful self-presentations.

As a second option, clients might also negotiate services with social workers within the discourse of rules and resources. Indeed, the reconstructed self outlined above would have rendered the client more deserving of help from this perspective. However, most clients did not avail themselves of this option either, probably because they were unfamiliar with the specifics of organizational processing and its discourse. Being new to River City, they were likely not to be as familiar with this perspective as the social workers. One way to acquire this knowledge would have been recurrent contact with HA. The catch here would be that such repeated contact would probably take several weeks, after which the client would have technically become a River City resident and no longer be eligible for service.

What clients typically *did* do when confronted with social workers' denials and alternative service offers was extend or elaborate on their previous self-presentations from within the discourse of moral responsibility, which served to extend the discursive contest that shaped their institutional identities in the first place. Consider the following extract in which the social worker begins by responding to a client's request for a bus ticket:

SOCIAL WORKER: We don't automatically buy bus tickets or plane tickets or things like that because we're a small agency. We could not afford to do that, but we could assist you in contacting your family and your friends who are in Chicago.

CLIENT: If I coulda did that I coulda called someone for a ticket. I'm just stranded. I'm tired and I'm hungry.

Here the social worker makes an alternative offer: she will help the client find family or friends who can provide help. She accounts for this alternative offer by portraying HA as a "small agency" that "could not afford to" buy tickets for everyone making such a request. In his reply, the client notes the irony of this alternative offer, and a major point of divergence between the two discourses, arguing that if there were someone else who could offer him help he wouldn't be in HA asking for a bus ticket. The client offers up his stranded self and elaborates by displaying his troubled self: he is tired and hungry. After several more interchanges, the client finally declares:

CLIENT: I thought y'all help people who are stranded.

Here, the client constructs a moral imperative that provides a basis for his appeal: the social worker is *supposed* to help clients who are stranded. This moral entreaty is also illustrated in the following extract:

CLIENT: I don't drink. I don't use dope. I need help. I'm not fussy or nothin' I just need help.

This client is "not fussy or nothin'"; he doesn't drink or use drugs. This self is morally pure, clearly deserving of help.

Finally, and oddly enough, the discourse of morality also might itself set limits on service-worthiness. In this discourse, provision of services is based, in part, on meeting cultural expectations of sympathy worthiness, some of which have been elaborated by Candace Clark (1987) in her work on sympathy rules. According to Clark, these rules include: not accepting sympathy too readily, expressing gratitude, and not claiming too much sympathy. As appropriated to the discourse of morality, these rules would appear to translate into: don't accept or request too many services too readily, express gratitude for the services that are offered, and don't portray yourself as too troubled or too helpless. Such rules may also shape the ways in which clients present their service-worthiness, culturally percolating around service encounters.

BIBLIOGRAPHY

Anspach, Rene R. 1987. Prognostic Conflict in Life-and-Death Decisions. *Journal of Health and Social Behavior* 28:215–31.

Brown, Penelope and Stephen Levinson. 1978. "Universals in Language Use: Politeness Phenomena." In *Questions and Politeness: Strategies in Social Interaction*, ed. E. Goody, 56–289. Cambridge: Cambridge University Press.

Clark, Candace. 1987. "Sympathy Biography and Sympathy Margin." *American Journal of Sociology* 93:290–321.

Conley, John M., and William M. O'Barr. 1990. *Rules vs. Relationships*. Chicago: University of Chicago Press.

Darrough, William. 1990. "Neutralizing Resistance: Probation Work as Rhetoric." In *Perspectives on Social Problems*, vol. 1, ed. J. Holstein and G. Miller, 163–88. Greenwich, Conn.: JAI Press.

Goffman, Erving. 1959. *Presentation of Self in Everyday Life*. New York: Doubleday.

Gubrium, Jaber F., and David R. Buckholdt. 1982. *Describing Care: Image and Practice in Rehabilitation*. Boston: Oelgeschlager, Gunn and Hain.

Gubrium, Jaber F., and James A. Holstein. 1997. *The New Language of Qualitative Method*. New York: Oxford University Press.

Holstein, James A. 1992. "Producing People: Descriptive Practice in Human Service Work." *Current Research in Occupations and Professions*. 6:23–39. Greenwich, Conn.: JAI Press.

———. 1993. *Court Ordered Insanity: Interpretive Practice and Involuntary Commitment*. Hawthorne, N.Y.: Aldine de Gruyter.

Holstein, James A., and Jaber Gubrium. 1994. "Constructing Family: Descriptive Practice and Domestic Order." In *Constructing the Social*, ed. T. Sarbin and J. Kitsuse, 232–50. London: Sage.

Holstein, James A., and Gale Miller. 1990. "Rethinking Victimization: An Interactional Approach to Victimology." *Symbolic Interaction* 13: 103–22.

———. 1993. "Social Constructionism and Social Problems Work." In *Reconsidering Social Constuctionism*, ed. J. Holstein and G. Miller, 151–72. Hawthorne, N.Y.: Aldine de Gruyter.

Katz, Michael B. 1989. *The Undeserving Poor*. New York: Pantheon.

Loseke, Donileen. 1992. *The Battered Woman and Shelters*. Albany, N.Y.: State University of New York Press.

———. 1993. "Constructing Conditions, People, Morality and Emotion: Expanding the Agenda of Constructionism." In *Constructionist Controversies: Issues in Social Problems Theory*, ed. Gale Miller and James A. Holstein, 207–16. Hawthorne, New York: Aldine de Gruyter.

Loseke, Donileen, and Kirsten Fawcett. 1995. "Appealing Appeals: Constructing Moral Worthiness, 1912-1917." *The Sociological Quarterly* 36:61–78.

Miller, Gale. 1991a. *Enforcing the Work Ethic: Rhetoric and Everyday Life in a Work Incentive Program*. Albany, N.Y.: State University of New York Press.

———. 1991b. "Family as Excuse and Extenuating Circumstance: Social Organization and use of Family Rhetoric in a Work Incentive Program." *Journal of Marriage and the Family* 53: 609–24.

———. 1994. "Toward Ethnographies of Institutional Discourse." *Journal of Contemporary Ethnography*. 23:280–306.

Snow, David, and Leon Anderson. 1987. "Identity Work Among the Homeless: The Verbal Construction and Avowal of Personal Identities." *American Journal of Sociology* 92:1,336–371.

Spencer, Jack W. 1983. "Accounts, Attitudes and Solutions: Probation Officer-Defendant Negotiation of Subjective Orientations." *Social Problems* 30:570–81.

Spencer, J. William. 1993. "Making 'Suitable Referrals': Social Workers' Construction and Use of Informal Referral Networks." *Sociological Perspectives*. 36:271–85.

———. 1996. "From Bums to the Homeless: Media Constructions of Persons Without Homes From 1980-1984." In *Perspectives on Social Problems*, ed. J. Holstein and G. Miller, 39–58. Greenwich, Conn.: JAI Press.

Spencer, J. William, and Jennifer L. McKinney. 1997. " 'We Don't Pay for Bus Tickets, But We Can Help You Find Work': The Micropolitics of Trouble in Human Service Encounters." *The Sociological Quarterly* 38:185–203.

Stern, Michael J. 1986. "The Emergence of Homelessness as a Social Problem." In *Housing the Homeless*, ed. J. Erickson and C. Wilhelm, 113–23. New Brunswick, N.J.: JAI Press.

KATHRYN J. FOX

Self-Change and Resistance in Prison

Institutions play vital roles in defining the boundaries within which troubled individuals can be reformed. According to Erving Goffman (1961), total institutions such as prisons strip away the self through a process of coercive "degradation" or "mortification," dismantling the signifying aspects of one's previous life. In total institutions, the erosion of liberty and privacy contribute dramatically to the reconstruction of identity. Relatedly, coercive programmatic practices, such as sentence-contingent therapies and rehabilitation, can virtually "bribe" new selves into being.

This chapter explores the process of self-construction in a "Cognitive Self-Change" (CSC) treatment program for violent offenders in prison. The concept of "self-change" implies a regimen wherein inmates cooperate in their reform. But, although the program emphasizes self-knowledge and -regulation, the conditions of possibility for self-knowledge are set by the institution. In CSC, prison treatment facilitators insist that violent offenders suffer from "cognitive distortions"— so-called thinking errors associated with a criminal personality. The construction of these thinking errors reflects the interpretive work participating inmates must engage in order to produce locally viable identities. Concurrently, successful participation in the program affects the length of one's prison sentence. The chapter will focus on the ways in which the institutional discourse of CSC coercively constructs new selves for inmates and the inmates' responses to these constructions.

The Cognitive Self-Change Program

I began observing CSC group meetings in the summer of 1997 with the permission and full cooperation of the Vermont Department of Corrections, as well as the group facilitators and members. My role has been that of a passive observer. Although I interact with other participants, most of the time I take notes quietly (for a more complete explanation of my methodology, see Fox 1999a, 1999b).

The groups take place in a regional correctional facility that houses both men and women of all levels of security. There are introductory groups and a second phase for those returned to prison. All participants have been classified as violent offenders. Each group consists of between six to eight inmates and two co-facilitators, most of whom are correctional case workers or probation officers. Each group meets twice a week for an hour and a half. Members are required to begin each session with a "check-in" relating recent situations that had put them "at risk" for violent behavior. In addition, inmates identify the thoughts, feelings, and attitudes that accompanied the incidents and describe the interventions, or "new ways of thinking," they used to defuse them. Check-ins are viewed as practice in the art of self-reflection and reformation.

The rest of the sessions consist of discussions of inmates' criminal histories (called a "Fearless Criminal Inventory"), their patterns of cognitive distortions, and the analysis of homework assignments. Much session time is filled with facilitators and inmates arguing over the criteria for prison release, about the conditions in prison, and the legitimacy and effectiveness of the CSC program. Inmates are required to complete the program satisfactorily in order to be eligible for early release. Thus, a fair amount of time and energy is spent debating the finer points of matters related to "choice" and "force." The Department of Corrections and CSC facilitators view the program as voluntary, while inmates insist it is not. Facilitators repeat that there is no "passing and failing" and that they are not "grading" the thoughts that inmates report. Yet inmates must demonstrate competency in self-reflection in order to be recommended for release.

A body of knowledge about the nature of the criminal self is essential to support correctional rehabilitation and discipline. Individual pathology must be assumed in order to justify incarceration; it is taken for granted that the inmates' personal selves are pathologically violent. Inmates' situations, the contexts for their violent acts, and the nature of their true "selves" are interpreted in a way that supports this assumption and its related institutional practices. Not only have such professional understandings slipped into the public mind and persuaded citizens of the need for self-reflection and rehabilitation (Margolin 1997; Rose 1996a, 1996b), but correctional personnel wield the cultural authority of psychological concepts like a nightstick, reinforcing the power to say who stays inside the prison and who is freed.

The group process of CSC is an effort to instill in inmates a sense of their own responsibility and criminality. The program is based upon the work of Samuel Yochelson and Stanton Samenow (1976) and their assessment of the "criminal personality." In their psychologistic model, criminal violence is the result of poor choices stemming from "cognitive distortions." Rose (1996b, p. 33) has documented the prevalence of such constructions of the self in disciplinary programs that rely upon notions of "selves with autonomy, choice, and self-responsibility." CSC relies on the same "intellectual machinery" (Rose and Miller 1992, p. 182) to drive home its emphasis on self-regulation, the outcome being the integral construction of criminal selves.

The program represents an interesting mix of formulations: a self that is at the same time rational, capable of change, and yet one that is essentially cognitively distorted and in some ways innately criminal (cf. Weinberg, this volume). Within this discourse, confession is essential as it shows self-reflection and, hence, rational thought. In CSC, inmates are required to ". . . accept responsibility for crimes for which they have been convicted" and demonstrate a "willingness to report one's [risky] thinking." This reinforces the institution's disciplinary regimes. Selves that are enmeshed in criminal thoughts can easily be regarded as

criminal; they are at risk of recidivating. As such, the institution not only specifies the nature and presence of "risky" thoughts, but simultaneously differentiates these criminal selves from their healthier counterparts.

Although participation in CSC is technically voluntary, inmates in the program are eligible for early release whereas those who opt not to participate serve
their maximum sentence. In this way, coercion is evident; as a program designer
said "authority is the keystone piece." The paradoxical position of being coerced
to volunteer generates anger and resentment among inmates, many of whom refer to the program as "jumping through hoops." Nonetheless, most violent offenders choose to participate.

In each meeting, inmates are asked to report their recent "risky" situations
"objectively." For example, an inmate phrased her situation as "not getting my
mail on time" and was informed that her phrasing was not objective: "late for
you maybe, but not for them." Once inmates have mastered the objective phrasing of situations, they are required to list the thoughts, feeling, attitudes, and
beliefs that accompanied the situation. When inmates assert that they just "re-
acted" in a situation and that there were no thoughts involved, the facilitators
insist that they are simply unaware of their underlying thoughts. In this respect, CSC discourse dissects the self as one that has hidden thoughts and feelings—and there are particular ones that motivate violence. Once inmates have
properly dissected the thoughts in their heads, they can actively construct new
selves.

Inmates are generally adept at describing the feelings they experienced in
these risky situations, although they are given a list to consult. Often inmates enu-
merate dozens of feelings, such as being angry, frustrated, irritated, or disrespected. "Good" check-ins identify the risk for violence or anger, and associate
thoughts with feelings. They implicate erroneous thoughts as the culprit for es-
calating anger and "intervention" thoughts as the reason for de-escalation. Acknowledging the role of these thoughts and choices leads to positive evaluation
by facilitators.

According to CSC program literature, fundamental change in inmates is unnecessary; rather inmates are required to demonstrate that they know *how* to
change. This means that they must use the discourse of the program effectively.
Inmates need to reconstruct their crimes—their lives—within the approved interpretive and linguistic framework (Pollner and Stein 1994). For example, inmates
must identify their own criminal patterns from a list of "thinking errors characteristic of the criminal." Among the most popular are "victim stance" (an erroneous perception of victimization), "justification," "anger," and "failure to
consider others." Intervention plans for averting future crimes are based upon an
understanding of one's own cognitive patterns.

CSC facilitators enforce standards for measuring program competency in inmates by assessing inmates' responses. While facilitators note repeatedly that they
do not "judge" or "grade" inmates' thoughts and beliefs, they acknowledge that
inmates have to change their beliefs—their selves—at least superficially to meet
competency requirements. In this respect, the program establishes the conditions
of possibility within which inmates can reconstruct themselves.

Competency is evaluated on the basis of performance in the group, written journal assignments, and relapse prevention plans. Each offers opportunities to demonstrate an ability to curb risky thoughts and attitudes. While behavior in prison matters insofar as assaults would count as evidence of incompetence, language is more essential. Competency is gauged by the use of appropriate concepts and terminology. An inmate who refuses to accept that his thoughts are errors is suspended from the group indefinitely for "not buying it," according to the facilitators. A facilitator explained, "There are no wrong beliefs—there are wrong ones for making it through the program." Acceptance of a criminal identity is essential for success in CSC. Notions of pathological selves are reproduced discursively by recontextualizing inmates' acts and motivations, and reconfiguring their true selves, a language game that inmates must play to reduce their sentences, but one which they ultimately cannot win (Fox 1999a).

The persuasive talk of CSC functions to impose particular kinds of criminal selves on inmates. These selves are reproduced by the institution in order to effectively carry out its work. Prison rehabilitation cannot begin until a criminal subject is created. Likewise, incarceration cannot end until inmates' identity work has reconstituted a pathological self. In effect, inmates must first construct criminal selves, which are then reconfigured into reformed identities (Gubrium and Holstein 1995).

Producing Criminal Selves

Because CSC draws heavily from research on criminal personalities, the program relies upon ideal-typical characterizations of criminal thought patterns. In practice, facilitators interpret inmates' actions and thoughts according to a discourse of criminality. Inmates are asked to construct a biography consistent with this discourse (Gubrium, Holstein, and Buckholdt 1994). This sets the parameters for the potential meanings of criminal acts. Inmates reflect upon their "core patterns" of thinking that preceded violent actions, and are instructed to devise "new thinking." In effect, inmates are persuaded that their thought processes were fundamentally inferior. This construction of the criminal mind is the foundation of CSC and offers a basis for possible self-reconstruction in the group meetings.

Inmates' reports on recent risky situations focus on the "mindsets" that fuel violence. The self viewed by facilitators as underlying violence is one that is in the habit of seeing the world incorrectly. In opposition to this, inmates can convey thoughts about how deserving their victims were or about how vindictive and mean correctional personnel are. The purpose of the groups is not to solve problems associated with living in prison, although facilitators occasionally acknowledge that overcrowding, say, is a problem. Rather, facilitators use inmates' complaints about the conditions in prison or their treatment by the guards as evidence of their "mindsets" in connection with violent conduct. For example, in one session, inmates complained about harassment by prison guards and the facilitator suggested this was an example of a "mindset." One inmate asked how it could be a mindset when so many inmates experienced the same phenomenon.

He was told that criminals share similar mindsets, implying that it was no coincidence that they all ended up in prison. The inmate joked, "I guess the mind is a terrible thing," playing on the television advertisement that "a mind is a terrible thing to waste."

On another occasion, an inmate was told he needed to reflect on his past behavior to discover what patterns of thought he exhibited. He denied there was any pattern because his few acts of violence were situational. He and the facilitators argued for a long time about this, which at one point prompted the following exchange:

FACILITATOR: We're just going through a loop. Unless we're going forward [trails off] . . .

TODD: Forward? Forward to what? What do you want from me? It was bad judgment. It [his story] ain't never gonna change.

FACILITATOR: We'll keep trying to break you down.

Todd refused to grant that his thought patterns were responsible for his actions. Although his claim to poor judgment could be construed as an admission of poor thoughts, it is interesting to note that he was required to construct his biography according to a specific vocabulary. The vocabulary was expected to reflect an institutionally sanctioned view of the criminal mind. Todd needed to accept the global identity of a criminal self, not just admit that he used poor judgment in one instance. Todd would not or could not frame his thoughts as those typical of *criminal thinking* and was eventually given a negative evaluation for program performance, which resulted in suspension. In general, counterclaims deemed illegitimate by facilitators were regarded as "distorted concrete thinking." In the struggle to construct criminally violent selves, conflicting biographies could not be entertained.

Group work functions to detach inmates' actions from biographical particulars and to re-contextualize them in a framework of essential criminality (Fox 1999b). Yet as one facilitator bemoaned: "[CSC] doesn't consider the forces outside the person; it assumes that thinking alone causes behavior. There's more to it than that!" Nonetheless, reducing explanations of inmates' biographies to the connection between thoughts and risk for violence has programmatically useful consequences. The simple "underlying pathology" argument actively disables other explanations for inmates' criminal behavior, sustaining criminal selves and advancing program goals.

Merging Criminal Acts Into Criminal Selves

Inmate explanations that provide a mediating context for their violence sound like "justification" to facilitators. As an administrator explained: "There's a difference between the *reason* for what they did and what they did." CSC is only interested in what the inmates did; their reasons are simply thinking errors that explain poor choices. Reasons offered by inmates that try to place the act within a situational context are considered illegitimate. Such accounts are reminiscent of

Gresham Sykes and David Matza's (1957) "techniques of neutralization" that juvenile delinquents use to rationalize deviant activities. Inmates' claims that they fought, say, because someone "disrespected" them are examples of the "denial of responsibility"; claims that their victims deserved abuse represent the "denial of the victim." Such socially contextual claims clash with the construct of the criminal mind.

In order for CSC rhetoric to function as intended, criminal acts have to be viewed in a social vacuum. A facilitator once confided that "when he told me about what happened, I thought his actions were understandable but I couldn't tell him that. I gotta be careful not to feed into that." Thus, an important function of the group process is to decontextualize inmates' behaviors. This has the effect of making their actions seem irrational and unregulated. When, on one occasion, an inmate described his part in a situation as, "I was provoked and hit someone with a baseball bat," a facilitator told him to remove the part about being provoked. This brings the inmate's violent act into focus, telegraphing his motives as problematic.

A more extended example comes from another group meeting. Here, an inmate (Alice) suggested that she was justified in defending herself by cutting someone with a broken bottle. This is eventually transformed into the actions of a violent offender:

FACILITATOR:	But the fact is that you cut this girl.
COFACILITATOR:	You kinda minimize by saying you didn't cut him: "I didn't do it" because you didn't mean for it to happen. But you're responsible because you had the bottle.
ALICE:	But if he hadn't come after me . . .
FACILITATOR:	That's justification.
ALICE:	But it was justified!
FACILITATOR:	You're saying "it wasn't my fault."
ALICE:	But I think I got screwed. The charges are wrong because they say I went in with intent to do bodily harm.
SECOND INMATE:	You're still justifying what you did. You're still saying it wasn't wrong.
FACILITATOR:	It doesn't matter what the charge is; it's taking responsibility for what you did.

In this instance, the inmate's attempts to justify or minimize her violence are thwarted. Alice is supposed to describe the situation "objectively," which means she is expected to decontextualize it, to exclude from her narrative all causal references to anything but herself. Alice is reluctant to omit information about the context in which her violence erupted because, the facilitators imply, she is making a subtle attempt to "minimize" her violence (see Potter 1996, p. 187). Such a contextual explanation would undermine the program's effort to make offenders individually accountable for their crimes.

Alice was asked to simply refer to her own actions, not those of others. In this sense, the only aspect of the situation of interest in the group process is the act, in and of itself, of cutting someone with a bottle. Insofar as the act is discussed and analyzed out of context, the actor figures as the sole agent of violence. Out of context, it appears that Alice cut someone with a bottle for no apparent reason—other than that she is a violent person.

Inmates contextualize their violent acts in various ways, from talking about individuals who provoked them to stating that poverty causes violent outbursts. This constructs social accounts of their actions. Interestingly, this very discourse is a target for treatment in CSC and serves as proof of extreme criminal thinking. The very reasoning that inmates use to justify their actions is taken to be a part of their problem by the program. The institutional setting for CSC relies upon a construction of inmates as individually pathological; incarceration could not be justified and rehabilitation would make no sense without such a construction. The program enforces a discourse of criminality that validates itself and is impervious to challenge (Fox 1999a).

Manufacturing Thinking Errors

Criminals are deemed to be suffering from thinking errors; indeed, such faulty thinking constitutes the criminal mind. Errors in thinking are the cornerstone of interpretations of inmates' actions. Consistent with correctional rhetoric and ideology, cognitive distortions are tied to notions of free will and autonomy. CSC discourse regards as distortions inmates' claims that other people compelled their actions. As a facilitator explained, "Bare bones, you gotta take responsibility for [your] offense." In addition, regardless of others' conduct, inmates need to fit their own actions and thoughts into a pattern suggestive of individual pathology. For example, an inmate named Alicia described a situation in which she was "wrongly accused of stealing" cigarettes. When the facilitator tried to identify Alicia's typical violent pattern, the following exchange developed:

FACILITATOR: What about victim stance?

ALICIA: Is that where someone wrongly accuses you?

FACILITATOR: It's where you *feel* like a victim.

ALICIA: Yeah then.

In the discussion that ensued, the facilitator explained to Alicia that these feelings were evidence of a criminal way of thinking. In general, interactions between facilitators and inmates are designed to reorient inmates' interpretations to focus the blame on themselves.

Inmates' counterclaims are regarded as indicative of how entrenched violent thought patterns can be. CSC presumes that criminal thinking determines the full range of inmates' actions, from extreme resistance to ready capitulation. Indeed, claiming to be a "changed" or renewed person often reinforces facilitators' views. Because distorted thinking is the subject for intervention, some resistance is expected, and this is targeted as well. This is illustrated by an exchange between inmate Todd and two facilitators:

TODD:	I have a dilemma because my way[s] of thinking's changed and I know I gotta show you that but I don't get into beefs any-more—I'm above all that.
FACILITATOR:	Don't show us that you've changed your thinking, show us that you have interventions.
COFACILITATOR:	[incredulously] Yeah, how did you change your thinking?
TODD:	You're saying someone can't change their thinking?
COFACILITATOR:	Well, we think you may *respond* differently now.

If the essence of a criminal self is distorted thinking, then new and different thinking patterns should reflect a self-transformation. Clearly the object of reha-bilitation in CSC is thought processes, yet in the preceding extract, Todd's sug-gestion that he thinks "differently" than he did before was greeted with skepticism. The suspicion is that Todd may not have changed his real self at all. Thus, the program's discourse reifies the deeply criminal self.

In manufacturing thinking errors, even signs of right thinking may be dis-missed. In another exchange, inmates were discussing various intervention thoughts that might prevent violence or anger when an inmate had been waiting for two weeks to be seen in the prison medical facility. One inmate, Lee, spoke to another, Alice, and the following exchange unfolded:

LEE:	Two wrongs don't make a right—that's one I use. [And] no matter what someone else does, they don't deserve to be hit.
FACILITATOR:	Doesn't that justify why she's mad? They *made* her mad? How did you justify?
ALICE:	My being mad? That I've got a right to be mad because of the way they're [correctional personnel] horsing me around. I'm waiting for two weeks!

This answer was met by a sort of knowing smile by the facilitator. Even inter-vention thoughts that ostensibly help to prevent violent behavior can serve as ev-idence of justification. Implicit in this exchange is the presumption that when inmates believe they are devising "real" interventions—and even when the in-tervention "works" in averting violence—their intervening behaviors emanate from the criminal thought patterns that are so much a part of them.

In another instance, an inmate was upset over a meeting with his caseworker and he intervened in his anger by working on his relapse plan, to which the fa-cilitators responded:

FACILITATOR:	Intervention should be working on the angry part. It's supposed to help you deal with the anger, not the caseworker. It's about *you*.
COFACILITATOR:	"Cognitive" means thinking, changing your thinking so you're less risky. It's not a problem-solving course, it's about how can you change your thinking.

Regardless of others' actions toward participants, the "problem" and target of intervention is their angry thoughts. Anger is never justified for inmates because it emerges from a set of faulty thought patterns. In the interpretive schema of CSC, inmate anger is evidence of faulty, pathological thinking rather than legitimate complaints. This, of course, sustains and reproduces angry criminal selves.

Constructing Angry Criminals

In CSC rhetoric, individuals are constructed globally as either victims or victimizers (Best 1997; Young 1996; see also Loseke and Lowney and Holstein, this volume). In the cultural imagination, as well as in social scientific research on criminal minds, criminal selves are deemed essentially distinct from those of law-abiders. CSC was adapted from research and public understandings that erect and sustain the dichotomies of normal thinking/criminal thinking and rationality/anger. As these dichotomies are put into practice, they become part of the disciplining repertoire of social control (Foucault 1977; Rose 1988), serving to clearly distinguish those incarcerated and in treatment from those who are not.

Let us briefly examine the use of anger in constructing the violent offender. In a group meeting, a recently returned inmate, Doug, complained about being forced to complete CSC again even though his recent offense was nonviolent. In an exchange with a facilitator, Doug was reminded that CSC was designed to treat rule-breaking behavior generally:

DOUG: But if it's all that, why would I have to take a separate drug and alcohol program?

FACILITATOR: Did you recently get some bad news?

DOUG: No, it's just that . . .

FACILITATOR: Did you recently get some bad news?

DOUG: [Angrily] No! I see what you're getting at!

In this exchange, Doug's complaints are interpreted as evidence of his anger. As he becomes angry at the suggestion that his resistance was "about" something else, he is characterized as an angry person by the facilitators. In this example, the self-reproductive capabilities of CSC are clear: based upon assumptions of violent offenders as essentially angry, any angry resistance simply reinforces the case for what the inmate is "deep down."

Changing Criminal Selves

Ironically, rehabilitation calls on "essentially" pathological selves to do the work of self-recovery. The goal of producing nonviolent individuals seems to clash with the vital premise that inmates' deeply personal selves are criminal and violent. The resolution of this contradiction unfolds in the interactional practice of reconstructing inmate selves. When facilitators and inmates are dealing in criminal identities, the self that is talked into being is essentially violent and criminal. When the same people engage in transforming these criminal selves, however, their identity work focuses on producing selves capable of rehabilitation and change. The contradiction is kept under control because the discursive acts of constructing troubled selves and reformed selves are managed separately. In effect, different selves are "done with words" when criminals are produced than when these selves are rehabilitated.

While CSC attempts to change criminal selves by insisting on self-reflection and reform, with captive audiences like incarcerated inmates, institutional rhetoric also draws significantly from an outside world brought into relief. Release from prison is dangled like a carrot and is forceful in additionally fashioning the new selves that, if successful, will see the outside world sooner than expected.

Coercing Changed Selves

Facilitators coerce changed selves by subtly demanding that inmates embrace the representation of themselves as angry; in other words, inmates have to confess to their sub-rosa anger. In an exchange with a facilitator, for example, Alice explained her thoughts about a situation in which a prison official reneged on a promise to let her daughter visit her in prison:

ALICE: I did my end of the bargain; [she's] not doing hers.

FACILITATOR: Something else is going on in that head of yours—those are awfully tame [thoughts].

When Alice then confessed that she was thinking more angry thoughts, the facilitator seemed satisfied. Alice was concerned that feeling angry would be counted against her in the program, but she was assured that it was "normal" for them to have "risk." In this instance, the facilitator rewarded the inmate for having risky thoughts, because anger in inmates is normalized and expected, yet reducing them or intervening in them is also required. Inmates are coerced into "being" angry selves in the context of self-construction. Subsequently, in the context of change, they are coerced into trying to change that aspect of their nature.

Facilitators often asked inmates to find themselves in a "thinking errors list." The list includes various distortions considered typical of criminals, such as "victim stance" and "justification" for criminal acts. Insistence that they had "no patterns" was sanctioned negatively. To complete the program, inmates were required to identify patterns of criminal thought that applied to their ways of thinking. In one instance, when a facilitator persuaded an inmate, Todd, to see himself in the thinking errors list, Todd identified the thinking error that states "the criminal believes that he is a good and decent person. He rejects the thought that he is a criminal." He said that a criminal is "a thief who steals for drugs." He was then told that he misunderstood the point of the assignment; that he should have reflected upon "hurtful, destructive" things he'd done. Todd became frustrated because he was trying to do what he understood to be the assignment, as the following exchange indicated:

TODD:	What do you want me to put here?
FACILITATOR:	Whatever you want.
TODD:	Obviously not. [They discussed the crime for which he was convicted.]
FACILITATOR:	Do you think that's criminal?
TODD:	Yeah, I guess. But what do you want [for the assignment]?
FACILITATOR:	"A thief" is someone else, it's not you. It's supposed to be about you.
COFACILITATOR:	How are *you* criminal?
TODD:	I reject the thought of being a criminal. That's what it says [on the thinking errors list]. That's what I do.

In this instance, the inmate thought he was supposed to write down the patterns that apply to his thoughts—he believes he is a good person. However, he did not perceive this to be an error. Later, when he reiterated that he was not a criminal because he had only one conviction, a facilitator replied, "It does make it difficult when your view is that you're innocent." In effect, he is asked to internalize a "criminal" identity, to accept that his thoughts are merely "typical" criminal ones, thereby adopting his essential criminality as a "master status" (Becker 1963). Acknowledging the criminality of his act is the first step in the process of talking him into being a criminal *person*—a criminal self. Clinging to the belief that he is essentially a decent person is deemed erroneous and further evidence of how deeply ingrained his criminal thinking is.

Although the target of intervention is the inmate's "mind," the only resources available for making change in group sessions are interactional devices such as writing and speaking (Young 1995). As one facilitator said, "You gotta fake it till you make it," meaning that inmates have to use discursive techniques to demonstrate that they "know *how* to change." Because this interpretive lens shapes the interactions between facilitators and inmates and is built into the rhetoric of "thinking errors," resistance is regarded as extreme criminal thinking. An exchange in a group meeting demonstrates this point:

FACILITATOR:	You gotta get past this, "This isn't gonna work" stuff.
LEE:	So what you're saying is that I shouldn't be honest. I should tell you what you wanna hear?
FACILITATOR:	Well, by telling us what we want to hear, you're gonna *know* what we want. . . .
LEE:	I don't have a clue what you want!

In this example, the facilitator suggests that giving the facilitators "what they want to hear" would show competency in understanding the program. Resistance, or a reluctance to "try," is perceived as extreme willfulness, a typical criminal pattern. "Trying" is measured by attempts to use the appropriate vocabulary and complete the assignments properly. Whenever inmates would ask about the possibility of failing the program, they were told that "it's not like school, no pass or fail." As one inmate responded: "You say it's not like school, but why does our RP [relapse prevention plan] have to be accepted by you, by whoever? What standard do you use? If it's our thinking, there's no way you can grade it." At times like these, when arguments between inmates and facilitators became circular, facilitators would refer to "the program" and its requirements. Occasionally when inmates objected to the language of "thinking errors" or "criminal personalities," a facilitator would say something like "it's from a book by some psychologists!" in order to reify the program's stance.

Becoming Disciplined

Rose (1996a, p. 46) suggests that decisions about self-conduct and self-presentation are often institutionally embedded in "a web of vocabularies, injunctions, promises, dire warnings, and threats of intervention." In CSC, some inmates adopt the language of the facilitators and even interject programmatic thinking in exchanges with other inmates. For example, a group member named Doug did a thinking report on his frustration over the fact that he was not being released. The thoughts he mentioned evinced the theme of "why in the hell are they fucking with me?" Another inmate responded that Doug put himself in this predicament by disobeying the stipulations of his release in the first place, thus being returned to jail, after which the following exchange unfolded:

DOUG: . . . I can relate because Department of Corrections didn't put me here. I put myself here.

FACILITATOR: Then how did you get to these thoughts?

SECOND INMATE: If you knew you were out of place, then are they really fucking with you? . . . If you did all this to get back inside, how can you maintain the belief that they want to keep you in here?

This example illustrates how CSC enforces a discourse of personal responsibility. Denying responsibility for one's criminal actions is the subtext of several of the "thinking errors."

Inmate Resistance

Resistance among inmates is part of the process expected by CSC, but it is assumed also to be worn down with time, persistence, and threats. Inmates resist in a variety of ways. Some may oppose the characterizations of their violence entirely and may suffer the consequences, such as suspension from the group and a stalled release date. Others may confess as required, adopt the rhetoric of CSC, and manifest changed selves. Inmates joke among themselves about how simple it is to perform for the facilitators, to become "expedient confessors" (Scott 1969). This is not to suggest that inmates never change through the group process or that all evidence of reform is false, but that many inmates do resist the power of correctional personnel by "faking" their transformation.

Resisting Victimizing Narratives

In meetings, inmates are asked to reconstruct the narratives of their criminal impulses and narratives of victimization. They are asked to forsake being victims and to take responsibility as agents of their own criminal actions. As inmates persist in their claims, attempting to excuse their criminal behavior as mitigated, such language is stifled. For example, in the retread group, in the following exchange, Pete explained how he ended up back in jail.

PETE: I had three domestic assault priors . . . and she stuck me with a fourth one.

FACILITATOR: She stuck you with it?

PETE: Yeah, she did.

FACILITATOR: What was the charge for?

PETE: She said I had her on the ground by the throat.

FACILITATOR: And it didn't happen?

PETE: Yeah, I had her on the ground by the throat . . .

Note that the facilitator continued to push Pete to accept that his ex-wife did not "do" anything to him, but Pete vehemently disagreed. Subsequently, the other alumni in the group laughed and shook their heads, acknowledging that Pete's story of his own victimization would not succeed by the program facilitators' standards. Claims to victimization are subject to interpretation and negotiation, and are thus "interactionally constituted" (Holstein and Miller 1990, p. 103). Again, though, the dichotomy of victimizer/victimized is not challenged, and in this sense, the larger discourse shapes the context of resistance.

CSC's emphasis on self-regulation is evident in group meetings. For instance, a facilitator reported an inmate saying: " What you're asking me to do is be my own [parole officer]!" The facilitator responded, "Exactly! You want me [to be]?" Facilitators stress that one can only control one's own behavior, not the actions of others. For example, when an inmate said his wife "made" him feel guilty, he was told that no one could make him feel anything. Similarly, once in the introductory group, an inmate was complaining about harassment by other inmates, saying:

They've agitated and provoked me all week, man . . . Let me tell you something. It's kinda hard to deal with this shit . . . On the street, you can get away from that situation, but in here, you only have three choices: get off the unit, grab the mop wringer and smash his head, or endure that stuff.

The facilitator told the inmate that the group's function is not to solve the problems of life inside prison; rather it is to focus on "what am I thinking and feeling?" and "how can I think and feel a little differently?" The inmate responded angrily that he could write "five or six thinking reports a day on this one issue!" indicating that thinking reports would not make the trouble disappear. Then he added, "You want us to allow ourselves to be victimized by this guy for months on end . . . I am *not* a victim!" In this interesting twist on the meaning of victimization, the inmate suggested that the program's insistence on nonviolence sabotaged inmates' survival.

In this regard, the inmate complained that the program asked him to place himself at risk for victimization in prison. As a guard told me, the program asks inmates to change "all their beliefs, their associations, everything they've developed to feel safe on this planet." Therefore, a clash between inmate discourse and CSC discourse seems inevitable. As another facilitator despaired: "We're saying 'we want you to live the way we think you should, like our lives.' " In other words, simply typifying people as good or criminal is perhaps an inadequate interpretation of the complexity of inmates' situations.

Sometimes, the categories of deviant and victim are challenged as acts of resistance. For example, an inmate claimed that he "got shafted" by the juvenile justice system. In another example, he explained that a charge he received for domestic assault was his girlfriend's fault:

> . . . I pushed my girlfriend. She deserved it; she should have gotten more, but I'm a nice guy. If someone is touching me, I'm gonna defend myself. I don't care what society says about it . . . I don't see why you can't understand where I'm coming from.

He continued that he felt "justified" when his safety was threatened:

ANGEL:	She was hitting me.
FACILITATOR:	How did it get to that point?
ANGEL:	Oh I see, so it's my fault.
FACILITATOR:	It might be—who knows?
ANGEL:	No, it wasn't.
FACILITATOR:	So victim stance?
ANGEL:	Yeah, most definitely. I don't think that's a thinking error. I mean look at the situation. I shoulda fucking smashed her head in. . . .

Here, the inmate is using the concept of "victim stance" quite differently than the program intended. Angel's explanation of the situation rests on understanding his position as a victim; he thoroughly rejects the assertion that this stance represents an erroneous assumption. Thus, he takes the program's language and subverts it to reinforce his construction of events. In this way, then, the process of shaping subjectivity may not always work as planned; CSC concepts can be coopted, if not overtly rejected.

Resisting Willful Selves

CSC's rhetoric casts individuals as autonomous actors making willful decisions about what they do and how they behave. It stresses that adopting a victim stance allows offenders to choose anti-social behavior. The inmates, however, argue that certain behaviors are not the result of choice. Insofar as inmates maintain a "victimized" self-image, they portray their choices as constrained. By contrast, if actions are the result of individual agency and personal choice, as the program insists, then violence is never justified.

Inmates reported experiencing violence not by choice, but as either a response to victimization, an outgrowth of masculine values, or simply as a matter of pleasure. For example, in an exchange with a facilitator, two inmates, Jan and Angel, argued that sometimes people (in this case, a female offender) react after "putting up with abuse":

ANGEL: . . . After a while, it pushes you mentally over the edge.

FACILITATOR: Well, maybe she can't do anything about how people treat her, but she has a choice in how she reacts to it.

JAN: But they can aggravate and provoke you to do it [to commit violence].

FACILITATOR: But that's a choice.

JAN: [Angrily] No, it's not a choice. I'd fucking kick all their asses.

Although the inmates believe that their aggression is a response to being victimized by others, in another sense, they refuse to be victimized. Thus, violence is in order to avert victimization.

As John Irwin (1987) points out, hypermasculinity and aggression are features of prison culture, in part, because of identification with subcultures outside prison, but also as adaptations to prison life. It makes sense, then, that male inmates' resistance to the CSC program emerges from their values associated with masculinity. Some of this stems from their socialization (mainly by their fathers) that taught them that aggression was indicated in certain situations. Indeed, some women reported that their fathers encouraged them to fight as well. Several times, inmates countered the program leaders by saying that "I was brought up to defend myself," and many had difficulty believing that they should respond otherwise. As Matt explained, "It makes me feel weak." Inmates saw some violence as wholly consistent with their subcultural and/or familial value system.

When I suggested to a facilitator that the program might be stripping inmates of their sense of identity without offering an alternative means of achieving status within the prison (or their family) context, he responded: "We aren't trying to take anything away from them. They can keep their values; we are just asking them to modify them." Yet it was clear at times that the goal of value-modification was difficult to reconcile with the life experiences and sanctions of significant others in inmates' lives. A facilitator told me that offenders have said to her: "If I give up these things you say are risky, then who am I? What do I stand for?" From the inmates' points of view, the models proposed in prison treatment programs "are undignified and at times unfeasible" (Irwin 1987, p. 37).

CSC privileges a particular brand of reasoning in its suggestion that conflicts should be resolved nonviolently. On the one hand, the program claims to want only to modify values, yet as correctional personnel, the CSC program leaders and facilitators convey an absolutist ideology—backed by psychological expertise—of right versus wrong, good thinking versus bad thinking, and acceptable behavior versus unacceptable behavior. And all of these aspects—morals, thoughts, and actions—are bound together through the rhetoric of cognitive self-change. In this sense, CSC extends correctional power beyond the discipline of the body that restricts inmates' physical freedom. Inmates' selves—their sensibilities, actions, feelings, and values—are targets for evaluation, intervention, confession, and reconstruction. But, at the same time, by fighting back against institutional power, inmates rhetorically resist institutional "rehabilitation" in an attempt to preserve the very selves the institution tries to mortify.

The Complexities of Self-Construction

Overt social control, such as incarceration and physical discipline, is relatively straightforward in its application. In contrast, cognitive social control, as exercised by CSC, is more subtle, yet pervasive, addressing inmates' minds, choices, talk, and identity. On the dynamic terrain of everyday talk and interaction, selves are contested and reconstructed as the prison asserts its institutional will in intricate and penetrating ways.

As Michel Foucault (1983) pointed out, power dynamics are characterized by the coercion that prompts resistance. Prison inmates resist, in part, because they are constantly confronted by institutional force. They steal bits of freedom by flouting rules and defying definitions. In the process, they bring coercion into relief. In CSC, the interplay between institutional efforts at rehabilitation and inmates' resistance to personal change creates a constantly shifting landscape of self-construction. Some selves are constructed to suit the institutional preference for right-thinking, nonviolent individuals. Some resist to the point of becoming more angry and violent. And some—the "expedient confessors," for example—may superficially comply, while trying to sustain their sense of an unchanged, inner self that they have lived by all along.

In each scenario, the institution sets the parameters for interactions and conditions of possibility for accountable self-construction. But, as imposing as these conditions may be, selves cannot be institutionally dictated or determined. While the prison prescribes formal procedures for rehabilitation and reform, it can't specify the final product because its control of the discursive environment of self-construction is far from complete. CSC certainly operates from a position of discursive advantage; it stipulates the rules and motivations for engaging in the discourse of cognitive self-change. But inmates are neither institutional puppets nor discursive dopes. Institutional discourses can be appropriated for unsanctioned claims. Rules can be bent, interpreted to account for unanticipated acts of resistance. Such resistance embodies more than simply the repudiation of institutional will. It also involves the creation of alternate possibilities for self preservation. The feigning of self-reform is but one manifestation of these possibilities. The prison may strive for self-mortification, but it can never fully determine the selves that will be produced to fill that vacant space of identity.

REFERENCES

Becker, Howard. 1963. *Outsiders: Studies in the Sociology of Deviance.* New York: Free Press.

Best, Joel. 1997. "Victimization and the Victim Industry." *Society* 34:9–17.

Foucault, Michel. 1977. *Discipline and Punish: The Birth of the Prison.* New York: Vintage.

———. 1983. "The Subject and Power." In *Michel Foucault,* 2nd ed., ed. Hubert L. Dreyfus and Paul Rabinow, 208–26. Chicago: University of Chicago Press.

Fox, Kathryn J. 1999a. "Changing Violent Minds: Discursive Correction and Resistance in the Cognitive Treatment of Violent Offenders in Prison." *Social Problems* 46:88–103.

———. 1999b. "Reproducing Criminal Types: Cognitive Treatment for Violent Offenders in Prison." *The Sociological Quarterly,* 40: 435–53.

Goffman, Erving. 1961. *Asylums.* Garden City, N.Y.: Anchor Books.

Gubrium, Jaber F., and James A. Holstein. 1995. "Life Course Malleability: Biographical Work and Deprivatization." *Sociological Inquiry* 65:207–23.

Gubrium, Jaber F., James A. Holstein, and David R. Buckholdt. 1994. *Constructing the Life Course.* Dix Hills, N.Y.: General Hall.

Holstein, James A., and Gale Miller. 1990. Rethinking Victimization: An Interactional Approach to Victimology." *Symbolic Interaction* 13:103–22.

Irwin, John. 1987. *The Felon.* Berkeley: University of California Press.

Margolin, Leslie. 1997. *Under the Cover of Kindness: The Invention of Social Work.* Charlottesville: University Press of Virginia.

Pollner, Melvin, and Jill Stein. 1994. "Narrative Maps of Social Worlds: The Voice of Experience in Alcoholics Anonymous." *Symbolic Interaction* 19:203–23.

Potter, Jonathan. 1996. *Representing Reality: Discourse, Rhetoric and Social Construction.* London: Sage.

Rose, Nikolas. 1988. "Calculable Minds and Manageable Individuals." *History of the Human Sciences* 1:179–200.

———. 1996a. "Governing 'Advanced' Liberal Democracies." In *Foucault and Political Reason,* ed. Andrew Barry, Thomas Osborne, and Nikolas Rose, 37–64. Chicago: University of Chicago Press.

———. 1996b. *Inventing Our Selves: Psychology, Power, and Personhood.* Cambridge: Cambridge University Press.

Rose, Nikolas, and Peter Miller. 1992. "Political Power Beyond the State: Problematics of Government." *British Journal of Sociology* 43:173–205.

Scott, Robert A. 1969. *The Making of Blind Men: A Study of Adult Socialization.* New York: Russell Sage Foundation.

Sykes, Gresham M., and David Matza. 1957. "Techniques of Neutralization: A Theory of Delinquency." *American Sociological Review* 22:664–70.

Yochelson, Samuel, and Stanton E. Samenow. 1976. *The Criminal Personality.* New York: J. Aronson.

Young, Alison. 1996. *Imagining Crime: Textual Outlaws and Criminal Conversations.* London: Sage.

Young, Allan. 1995. *The Harmony of Illusions: Inventing Post-Traumatic Stress Disorder.* Princeton, NJ: Princeton University Press.

Author Index

Subject Index